Can We Trust
the New Testament?

Books by G.A. Wells

Herder and After (1959)
The Plays of Grillparzer (1969)
The Jesus of the Early Christians (1971)
Did Jesus Exist? (1975; second edition, 1986)
Goethe and the Development of Science (1978)
The Historical Evidence for Jesus (1982)
*The Origin of Language: Aspects of the Discussion from Condillac
     to Wundt* (1987)
*Religious Postures: Essays on Modern Christian Apologists and
     Religious Problems* (1988)
Who Was Jesus? A Critique of the New Testament Record (1989)
*Belief and Make-Believe: Critical Reflections on the Sources of
     Credulity* (1991)
What's in a Name? Reflections on Language, Magic, and Religion
     (1993)
The Jesus Legend (1996)
The Jesus Myth (1999)
The Origin of Language (1999)
Can We Trust the New Testament? (2004)

Edited Works

Language: Its Origin and Relation to Thought (co-edited with D.R.
     Oppenheimer), by F.R.H. Englefield (1977)
The Mind at Work and Play (co-edited with D.R. Oppenheimer), by
     F.R.H. Englefield (1985)
J.M. Robertson: Liberal, Rationalist, and Scholar (1987)
*Critique of Pure Verbiage: Essays on Abuses of Language in Literary,
     Religious, and Philosophical Writings* (co-edited with D.R.
     Oppenheimer), by F.R.H. Englefield (1990)
The Old Faith and the New, by David Friedrich Strauss (1997)

Can We Trust the New Testament?

Thoughts on the Reliability of Early Christian Testimony

G.A. WELLS

OPEN COURT
Chicago and La Salle, Illinois

To order books from Open Court, call toll-free 1-800-815-2280, or visit our website at www.opencourtbooks.com.

Open Court Publishing Company is a division of Carus Publishing Company.

Printed and bound in the United States of America

Library of Congress Cataloging-in-Publication Data

Wells, George Albert, 1926–
    Can we trust the New Testament? : thoughts on the reliability of early Christian testimony / G.A. Wells.
          p.   cm.
Includes bibliographical references and indexes.
      ISBN 0-8126-9567-4 (trade pbk. : alk. paper)
    1. Bible. N.T.—Evidences, authority, etc.   I. Title.
      BS2332 .W42 2003
      225.1—dc21

                                                            2003010939

Contents

Preface

There is much disagreement in early Christian literature. The New Testament (NT) authors and their second-century successors take issue, often acrimoniously, with persons and groups (many of them within Christianity) whom they dislike. In this book I am more concerned with the way in which a tradition in the earlier of these writings is, in the later ones, transmuted into something very different. This is sometimes done deliberately, so as to make the older material more acceptable to the later writer's beliefs and situation. But it can equally well result from very imperfect knowledge of the earlier state of affairs, and from the feeling that this 'must' have accorded with what the later writer found acceptable. Fraud or deliberate misrepresentation is not involved.

Chapter 1 traces the changes in Christology (the conception of who and what Jesus Christ was) as between the earlier and the later books of the New Testament—changes which well exemplify the mythological process whereby earlier ideas become, over time, changed into very different ones. The four gospels are not the earliest of the twenty-seven books of the NT, and their trustworthiness is very much impaired by the failure of its earlier books to confirm what they say. This discrepancy is fatal to the claims of the Christian churches, yet few theologians have properly faced it.

Chapter 2 shows how the real situation in the early churches was given very ideal shape in Acts. The 'Peter at Rome' material of Chapter 3 is an equally good example of the mythological development of earlier ideas. In Chapter 4 we see Christians of today subjecting—quite openly and deliberately—both the earlier and the later Christian traditions of the first two centuries to radical reinterpretation so as to make them more acceptable. Such attempts are, of course, strongly, even fiercely opposed by the powerful Christian groups which see change as a threat.

The title of the present book, suggested by Open Court, may put readers in mind of the 1977 *Can We Trust the New Testament?* by the Cambridge scholar and sometime bishop J.A.T. Robinson. Two books on the same subject which are more different from each other than his and mine could hardly be imagined. I have criticized Robinson's views at some length in my books of 1982, 1986, 1991, and 1998, and see no need to repeat any of that here.

Disagreement between persons of good will is ineradicable. The lesson tends to be impressed on us as we age and our expectations become restricted, long experience of mankind inducing resignation in the place of youthful reforming zeal. There is however some satisfaction in trying to understand the causes of discord and controversy, even if one accepts that one cannot remove them. It at least occupies the mind agreeably, and enables curiosity to replace less pleasant emotions.

Fortunately disagreement does not always entail unpleasantness, as we can learn from Darwin's relation with his local vicar. Gavin de Beer records in his 1963 biography of Darwin that the vicar told him: "You are one of those rare mortals from whom one can differ and yet feel no shade of animosity, and that is a thing of which I should feel very proud if someone said it of me." Darwin, for his part, described their relationship equally positively, saying: "He and I have been fast friends for thirty years, and we never thoroughly agreed on any subject but once, and then we stared hard at each other, and thought one of us must be very ill."

Here, then, there was real disagreement without conflict. But a recent way of avoiding conflict, or of at any rate trying to mitigate it, has been to attenuate the ideas propounded so that they have become too vague to clash with anything. That this can be charged against much that passes for religion today is indicated in my fourth chapter.

Acknowledgements, Abbreviations, and Conventions

Each of my four chapters is written so that it can be read independently of the others. This has entailed a few small overlaps where material from one chapter occurs also in another.

Earlier versions of Sections iii and iv of Chapter 1 and of some parts of Chapter 4 have previously appeared as articles of mine in Volumes 6 and 8 of *The Journal of Higher Criticism* and Volume 114 of *New Humanist*. I thank the editors of both journals for permission to rework this material here.

The original version of Chapter 2 was given as a lecture to the South Place Ethical Society of London in April 2000. It was rewritten and expanded for publication by the Society as a booklet in December 2000. I gratefully acknowledge the Society's permission to republish it here.

I have at times, particularly in Chapter 1, indicated that further or more detailed discussion of certain issues is given in earlier books of mine, notably those of 1996 and 1999a. I have nevertheless tried to give readers here what they need to assess the case I am making.

Works mentioned or quoted (listed under their authors' names at the end of this book) are referenced in my text and notes simply by the relevant page numbers, prefaced by a date of publication when it is necessary to distinguish between different publications by the same author.

Books of the Bible are quoted from the Revised Version (RV), published 1881–85, of the Authorized or King James Bible (AV) of 1611. On some few occasions I refer to more recent translations—the Revised Standard Version (RSV) or the New English Bible (NEB)—or have rendered the Greek text literally or adapted it to the syntax of my sentences.

OT and NT designate the Old and New Testaments.

The terms Mark, Matthew, Luke, and John sometimes designate the author of the relevant gospel, and sometimes that gospel itself. Which meaning is intended will be clear from the context. 'Luke' also designates the author of the Acts of the Apostles. Quotations from a number of NT books are referenced with abbreviations. These, in the order in which the relevant books are printed in modern Bibles, are:

Mt., Mk., Lk., Jn. (for the four gospels).

Acts (for the Acts of the Apostles).

Rom., 1 Cor., 2 Cor., Gal., Ephes., Phil., Coloss., 1 and 2 Thess., 1 and 2 Tim. (for epistles ascribed to Paul).

Rev. (for the NT apocalypse or book of Revelation).

I thank my wife Elisabeth not only for unselfishly keeping things going in the household, and so enabling me to devote my energies to study, but also for helpful comments on my manuscript.

I thank Mrs Elke Wagstaff for her careful typing of a very tatty original.

Actual Historical Order of Writing of New Testament Books

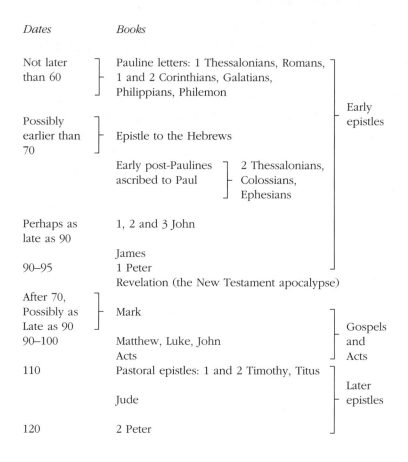

Dates	*Books*		
Not later than 60	Pauline letters: 1 Thessalonians, Romans, 1 and 2 Corinthians, Galatians, Philippians, Philemon		
			Early epistles
Possibly earlier than 70	Epistle to the Hebrews		
	Early post-Paulines ascribed to Paul	2 Thessalonians, Colossians, Ephesians	
Perhaps as late as 90	1, 2 and 3 John		
	James		
90–95	1 Peter		
	Revelation (the New Testament apocalypse)		
After 70, Possibly as Late as 90	Mark		
			Gospels and Acts
90–100	Matthew, Luke, John		
	Acts		
110	Pastoral epistles: 1 and 2 Timothy, Titus		
			Later epistles
	Jude		
120	2 Peter		

These dates are not controversial, and hardly anyone disputes that Paul's epistles antedate the gospels. Paul must have converted to Christianity before A.D. 40, for he tells that King Aretas of the Nabateans, who is known to have died in that year, had at one time sought to have him arrested because of his Christian activities (2 Cor. 11:32). He probably wrote his letters up to twenty years later, for Gal. 2:1 was written when he had been a Christian for at least fourteen years, and Rom. 15:19 when he had already completed a very substantial missionary program. Yet he wrote before Jerusalem had begun to suffer during the war with Rome which began in A.D. 66 and culminated in Jerusalem's capture and destruction in A.D. 70; for he mentions current dealings he is having with a Christian community there, which was obviously still untroubled by any such upheavals. In some of the gospels, however, there are clear indications that this war was already a thing of the past at their time of writing. Evidence for this and for other reasons for dating the gospels post-A.D. 70 is given in Wells 1998, pp. 14–49, where I also give (pp. 78–94) the very widely agreed reasons for the late dating of the Pastoral epistles. Some of the reasons for the generally accepted late date of 2 Peter are given in Chapter 3 below.

The epistles I have bracketed together as 'early' are not all of earlier date than the first of the gospels; but they all belong together because the novel way in which Jesus came to be portrayed in the gospels (and which is to some extent reflected in the epistles I have grouped as 'later') is alien to them all. This suggests that there was an interval before the novelties introduced by the gospels became generally known and widely accepted (cf. below, p. 44). That older Christologies should have persisted in some quarters while newer ones were emerging in others is hardly a matter for surprise, especially as we cannot assume perfect communication between different Christian centres.

1

A Revolution in Christology

i. The Earliest Evidence

a. JESUS ON EARTH

The gospels included in the New Testament (NT) are widely agreed to have been written between A.D. 70 and 100. In these four gospels, it is claimed that Jesus taught in Galilee in the opening decades of the first century, worked miracles there, or what at any rate were taken for miracles, and died in Jerusalem at the behest of the Roman governor Pontius Pilate. And yet, as I have reiterated in *The Jesus Legend* (1996) and *The Jesus Myth* (1999), none of these things are claimed, or even mentioned, in the earliest surviving Christian documents. In other words, none of these supposed historical events are touched upon in extant Christian documents which are either earlier than the gospels or early enough to have been written independently of them (that is, before those gospels or the traditions underlying them had become generally known in Christian circles).

This discrepancy is particularly striking when behaviour or teaching recorded in the gospels has obvious relevance to the concerns being pursued by the earlier Christian authors. The NT scholar Graham Stanton frankly calls it "baffling" that Paul, writing in the 50s, fails to "refer more frequently and at greater

length to the actions and teaching of Jesus," particularly at
points where "he might well have clinched his argument by
doing so." And Stanton is aware that epistles by other NT
authors present us with "similar problems" (p. 131). The
German NT scholar Walter Schmithals likewise notes that, "for
his central soteriological message," Paul "never appeals to the
appropriate Jesus tradition," as represented in the gospels, and
never refers to their "narrative material" (p. 312). He adds that,
in order to extract at any rate one such reference from the
Pauline letters, scholars have relied on Luther's inaccurate rendering (perpetuated in many modern translations) of 1 Cor.
11:23 as "in the night when he was betrayed"; whereas in fact
the Greek does not posit a betrayal (let alone a betrayal by
Judas, whom Paul never mentions). It says only that Jesus was
"given over" or "was delivered" to martyrdom—by God, as was
the servant of Yahweh in the Greek of Isaiah 53:6, 12: "the Lord
gave him up for our sins" and "his soul was delivered to death."
(The passive voice, as in Paul's "was delivered," was often used
in the OT and in early Christian literature as a *passivum div-
inum*, viz. to indicate that God was the agent, while avoiding
having to use the divine name.) Other Pauline passages, such as
Rom. 4:24f., likewise show that it was the Lord who both "delivered him up for our trespasses" and then "raised him for our justification." He "spared not his own Son," but "delivered him up
for us all" (Rom. 8:32). Jesus "gave himself up" voluntarily to
God's will for our redemption (Gal. 2:20). There is no suggestion that he was compromised by a third party.

My critics will seize on a few further statements in Paul's letters which, if read from prior knowledge of the gospels, might
likewise be taken to imply that he knew of Jesus's ministry, as
depicted there. I shall discuss them below (pp. 35 ff.), and what
I say there can be supplemented with the more extended discussion of them in my 1996 and 1999a books.

Schmithals stresses (p. 314) that, apart from the gospels
themselves, most other books of the NT show as little concern
with the historical Jesus as does Paul. This is certainly true of
those NT books which, although later than the Pauline letters,
are still relatively early. This group includes three post-Paulines

inaccurately ascribed to Paul by church tradition (2 Thessalonians, Colossians, and Ephesians) and also the letter to the Hebrews, the epistle of James, the first epistle of Peter, the three epistles of John, and the book of Revelation. If Paul alone had written as he did, one might just possibly be able to attribute this to some personal idiosyncrasy; but a consistent silence by numerous independent authors about matters which, had they known of them, they could not but have regarded as important and relevant, cannot be so explained. It is perverse when many scholars reduce the whole problem—if indeed they acknowledge it at all—to the discrepancy between Paul's writings and the gospels. There is a disparity between the earliest documents generally and later ones that should not be brushed aside.

The most striking feature of the early documents is that they do not set Jesus's life in a specific historical situation. There is no Galilean ministry, and there are no parables, no miracles, no Passion in Jerusalem, no indication of time, place or attendant circumstances at all. The words Calvary, Bethlehem, Nazareth, and Galilee never appear in the early epistles, and the word Jerusalem is never used there in connection with Jesus (Doherty, pp. 68, 73). Instead, Jesus figures as a basically supernatural personage who took the "likeness" of man, "emptied" then of his supernatural powers (Phil. 2:7)—certainly not the gospel figure who worked wonders which made him famous throughout "all Syria" (Mt. 4:24). He was indeed crucified for our redemption, yet the Passion is not as in the gospels. In Paul, for instance, as the NT scholar V.P. Furnish points out, there is "no cleansing of the Temple" (which according to Mark and Luke was what it was that made the chief priests and scribes decide to kill Jesus), "no conflict with the authorities, no Gethsemane scene, no trial, no thieves crucified with Jesus, no weeping women, no word about the place or the time, and no mention of . . . Judas or Pilate" (p. 42). Paul's colourless references to the crucifixion might be accepted as unproblematic if it were unimportant for him compared with, say, the resurrection. But he himself declares it to be the substance of his preaching (1 Cor. 1:23 and 2:2). He spent three years of his Christian life before

even briefly visiting Jerusalem (Gal. 1:17f.), and says nothing
that would indicate any awareness of or interest in holy places
there. I do not expect him to document the crucifixion as a historian would; but I do expect him, in his extensive writings and
repeated references to this important event, to have betrayed
some knowledge of the circumstances in which it had occurred,
if he had known of them.

Some recent scholars (such as Freke and Gandy in their 1999
book, and Earl Doherty, whose book was also published in
1999) hold that the earliest Christian writers did not believe
Jesus to have come to Earth as a man at all. I have never maintained this view, although it has often been imputed to me by
critics who have been anxious to dispose of my arguments without troubling to see wherein they consist.[1] Doherty's view is
that the vagueness of Paul and others about the salvific crucifixion, and their failure to specify biographical happenings that
preceded it, are much more readily understandable if we suppose them to have regarded Jesus as "an entirely spiritual figure
who operated only in the supernatural/mythical part of the universe." To view him otherwise would be to put him out of line
with all other saviour gods of the day (to whom he is in many
respects akin); for "the saving deities of the Greco-Roman mystery religions were regarded as entirely mythical." I question
this, and Doherty himself allows (pp. 104, 122) that "some of the
average devotees" may well have regarded the gods of the mysteries as having lived on Earth in a primordial past. His evidence
establishes that pagan *philosophers* did allegorize these deities
and their activities. Allegorical exegesis normally occurs as a
secondary and sophisticated interpretation of stories originally
understood as literally true, when defence of their literal truth
has become difficult. Admittedly, there remains a disparity
between Jesus and the deities of the mysteries, in that the lives
of the latter were not assigned to historical times. But the pagan
mysteries of the Roman Empire were adaptations of very ancient
cults; and if a god is worshipped by a primitive society before it
acquires written records, there is no historical framework in
which to fit him. Jesus, however, was from the first regarded as
the Messiah descended from David—"born of the seed of David

according to the flesh" (Rom. 1:3)—and so had to be placed somewhere in a known chronology. Sooner or later, in order to answer critical questions, his worshippers would have to be explicit about the where and the when.

Of course Doherty does not ignore the small number of references in the early epistles which do seem to establish Jesus's humanity; and he and I agree that these are not to be set aside as interpolations. (Interpolators, aiming to bring these letters into line with the gospels, would have done the job much more thoroughly.) Gal. 4:4, for instance, states that "God sent forth his Son, born of a woman, born under the law." Commentators regard 'born of a woman' as an idiomatic way of saying 'human being'; and to be born under the (Jewish) law is surely to live the life of a Jew, to be "a servant to the circumcision" (Rom. 15:8). Doherty observes that Paul "would hardly have to inform his readers that a human Jesus was born of a woman." But if Paul is here insisting, as I believe to be the case, that this supernatural personage did become human, then the statement is to the point. (Cf. 1 Jn. 4:9, "God sent forth his only begotten Son into the world.") Doherty interprets Gal. 4:4–6 to mean that God sent only the "Spirit" of his Son. But Paul's statement is: God sent forth his Son to liberate Jews (and Judaizers like the Galatians) from the restrictions of the Jewish law, so that, in consequence, "we might receive the adoption of sons." Now that this status has been achieved ("because ye are sons"), he sent forth the Spirit of his—presumably by this stage risen—Son into our hearts (verse 6), into the hearts of those who have been liberated from the law by Jesus's sacrificial death.

That Jesus was crucified is certainly repeatedly mentioned in the early letters. Doherty and I agree that, if he was to suffer on our behalf, he had to descend from on high to a sphere where he could be clothed with flesh. Doherty argues that "the sphere of flesh" (an acceptable translation of *kata sarka* in Rom. 1:3) can include the firmament, the lowest celestial sphere, where the demon spirits reside and operate, but which is still higher than the Earth. In this sphere Jesus could take on some semblance of humanity, and in Doherty's view he was not believed to have descended still lower, to Earth itself. Certainly, it is the demon spirits, the *archontes* who, according to I Cor. 2:8, crucified him, with no explicit statement (see, however, below, pp. 36f.) that they employed human agents. (The article *archōn* [ruler] in Kittel's standard *Theological Dictionary of the New Testament* observes that Paul is not here referring to earthly rulers—and so certainly not to Caiaphas and Pilate—and that arguments to the contrary are "not convincing." The article also gives Old Testament (OT) and other parallels to the use of the term 'rulers' to denote celestial beings.) Coloss. 2:15 likewise seems to place the event in a supernatural milieu. Whether or not this suffices to establish Doherty's interpretation, he is certainly right to note how remarkable it is that, if not some truly historical, then at least some legendary details about a life on Earth, do not appear in epistles before the time of the gospels. Nevertheless, to my mind "born under the law" as a "servant to the circumcision" gives Jesus more than just a semblance of humanity.

Jesus's resurrection was as important as his crucifixion. Paul describes himself as "called to be an apostle" (Rom. 1:1), since he had seen the risen Jesus and on this basis had been called to his service (1 Cor. 9:1). No one in these early documents is called a 'disciple' (a personal companion of the earthly Jesus). The word used is 'apostle', and it here means no more than Christian missionary. It does not have the meaning which Luke gave it: "Luke sees in the apostles the witnesses of the *historia Jesu*, whilst Paul sees in them the messengers of the gospel" (gospel in the sense of Christian tidings, Hennecke, 1965, p. 30). And the post-resurrection appearances of Jesus which Paul and other 'apostles' witnessed are not as in the gospels. In Paul's thinking Jesus at his resurrection was exalted immediately to heaven: he died, and God exalted him (Phil. 2:8f.), with no suggestion of discontinuity between the two events. And he rose from death not in his earthly, physical body, but in a body of heavenly radiance. For Paul, "flesh and blood cannot inherit the kingdom of God"; and so the dead are raised "in glory," in a body that is "spiritual" (1 Cor. 15:43f., 50). At Phil. 3:21 he argues directly from the resurrection body of Christ to the future resurrection body of believers: Christ will change our lowly bodies to be like his glorious body.

It follows from all this that, for Paul, the post-resurrection appearances to himself, and to some believers contemporary with him, were made from heaven, or by the glorified Jesus descending from heaven—as is implied even in Acts' version of the appearance to Paul, who there is said to have "seen a light out of heaven" (9:3ff.). In a recent study, A.W. Zwiep has spelled out these points very clearly, saying that in earliest Christianity—in the epistle to the Hebrews as well as in the Pauline letters—Jesus's resurrection meant "resurrection to heaven," "from grave to glory"; and his journey from the grave to the right hand of God was "not interrupted by interim appearances" (pp. 129f., 143). Hence "the appearances were *ipso facto* manifestations of the already exalted Lord, appearances from heaven."

It is in the gospels, not in the early epistles, that the risen Jesus tarries on Earth in physical body; for the evangelists were anxious to establish the reality of his resurrection by representing him as returning—even if, in some cases, only briefly—to the company of disciples who had known him before his death. This gave the evangelists the possibility of terminating his post-resurrection appearances with a distinct act of ascension—a possibility not taken up by Mark and Matthew, but fully exploited by Luke.

Paul does not even commit himself to designating Jesus's death, burial and resurrection as recent events. In the well-known passage 1 Cor. 15:3–8, he specifies eyewitnesses (including himself) of the appearances, stresses that most of these persons are still alive, thus stamping the appearances as recent, but not the death, burial, and prompt resurrection (three days after the death), which he merely says occurred "in accordance with the scriptures." "The scriptures" does not, of course, mean the gospels, which did not then exist, but the sacred books of the Jews. The significance of the recent appearances will have been to convince him that the general resurrection of the dead, and the final judgment of both living and dead, already heralded by Christ's (not so recent) resurrection, were now very near indeed. Christ raised from the dead was, then, the first indication that this general resurrection was forthcoming; it was "the first fruits of those who have fallen asleep" (1 Cor. 15:20). But now that he was not only risen, but had also begun to manifest himself from heaven, the final events which would bring the world to an end cannot be long delayed. Earliest Christianity was certainly a charismatic movement where ecstatic experiences were, as the Finnish NT scholar Heikki Räisänen has said, "daily bread" (1987, p. 233). "In the spirit," says Paul, a man can "speak mysteries" (1 Cor. 14:2). It was in such a milieu that the apostles had their visions of the risen Jesus. This is surely the answer to the objection that it is absurd to think that they could have known only very little of Jesus's life, since this supposition would impute to them worship of some Mr.-We-Don't-Quite-Know-Whom. In fact they worshipped the personage who had appeared to them in resurrected form, "in power" (Rom. 1:4), completely transformed from what he had been on Earth.

If, then, Paul did not regard the earthly Jesus as recently deceased, Alvar Ellegård may be right in suggesting, in his 1999 book, that the earliest Christian ideas about him were to some extent shaped by imprecise knowledge about the Teacher of Righteousness who figures in Dead Sea Scrolls written around 100 B.C. as a revered leader (not the Messiah and not a supernatural personage) to whom God had made known all the mysteries of the prophets, and who had been severely persecuted. Whether he was an actual historical figure or largely a construction to give substance to his followers' conception of the founder of their movement cannot now be determined. In any case, the Scrolls show that his memory was still treasured a century or more after his presumed death. What his followers thought they knew about him was that he had lived long ago and had been maltreated and persecuted, probably dying as a martyr. It would be natural for those who knew, even indirectly, of what is said of him in, for instance, the Qumran Habakkuk commentary to assume that the persecution eventually led to his martyrdom. The Scrolls do not name him—they avoid actually naming the sectarian personages (including the Teacher's chief enemies) whom they mention—but 'Jesus', which means 'Yahweh saves', and hence has connotations of 'salvation', would be an appropriate name to have been given at some stage to someone of such religious importance. Eisenman and Wise observe that at Qumran the use of the noun 'Salvation' or the verbal noun 'His Salvation' is both "fairly widespread and much underrated." They instance a phrase such as "the children of Salvation" (pp. 243f.).

Ellegård points out that the Essenes, whose ideas about the Teacher are reflected in the Scrolls, were established not only in Palestine, but also in the Diaspora, where Jews were numerous and where some of them developed religious ideas which were quite accommodating to their gentile environment. Certainly, the description of the Essenes given by Philo Judaeus of Alexandria around A.D. 20 and by Josephus around A.D. 80 portray a much more open community than that of the Qumran Scrolls. The Jewish Diaspora also housed some important Christian communities, and the notable similarity between Christianity and Diaspora Judaism is exemplified by Philo, the Jewish sage of Alexandria. Ellegård instances the Therapeutae—Philo said they existed "in many parts" of the Empire—as a special contemplative section of the Essenes who were so close to Christian ideas that Eusebius and other Christian writers could regard them as Christians. Philo tells that they studied "the writings of the founders of their way of thinking," so they will surely have known of the Teacher of Righteousness.

It has also been shown (by De Jonge, pp. 179–184, and others) that the idea of a martyr's death functioning as an atoning sacrifice, to be followed by his immortality, was not unfamiliar in Paul's Hellenistic environment. I give relevant details in my 1999a book (pp. 98f.), where I also note that Paul must have known of crucifixions in bygone days of holy Jews (while they were still alive and not, as was usually the case, as a supplement to execution by other means). These were incidents which had made a strong impression on the Jewish world. Musing on the OT will also have contributed to ideas about the earthly Jesus. Paul declares that the "mystery" is made known through the prophetic writings (Rom. 16:25f.). He could well have had in mind passages such as Zechariah 12:10 (about "one whom they had pierced"), Psalm 22:16 ("they pierced my hands and my feet") and of course the servant of Yahweh of Isaiah 53 ("wounded for our transgressions" and "by whose stripes we are healed").

Christian scholars point out that Paul's account makes it clear that the apostles understood their visions of the risen one to be manifestations of a particular person whom they could name as 'Jesus', and who therefore must have been in some way already known to them (just as those who had visions of Jupiter or Isis experienced a figure known from their traditions); and it is the gospels which supply what does seem to be the obvious basis for their knowledge of this Jesus, namely that they recognized him as a resurrected form of the person in whose ministry some of them had so recently participated. Thus even so critical a theologian as Räisänen can insist that, while Jewish apocalyptic eschatology provided ideas of resurrection which enabled the apostles to interpret their visions as evidencing the resurrection of someone, it was their recent (first-hand or reported) experience of the pre-crucifixion Jesus which enabled them to understand that these visions confronted them with a person whose company at any rate some of them had recently kept: "Whatever it was that they 'saw', they interpreted it in the framework of resurrection faith as it was known to them, but also in the light of their recent experience of life with Jesus of Nazareth" (2000, p. 196).

However, 'Jesus' implies, as we saw, 'salvation', and would have been an appropriate name for the earliest Christians to give to anyone regarded as ensuring their salvation, whether or not he was a recently deceased familiar. Even the relatively late gospel of Matthew betrays, at 1:21, that he shall be called Jesus "because he will save his people."

Another factor which may well have contributed to the naming of Jesus is that, in Greek, 'Joshua' is rendered as 'Jesus', and Joshua had not been lost from sight in the religious thinking of the time. He was the model for some who, between A.D. 40 and the outbreak of the Jewish war with Rome in A.D. 66, claimed (or were expected to come and claim) supernatural powers. Josephus tells of a fanatic named Theudas who promised to lead a multitude dryshod over the Jordan (*Ant.* 20:97), thus duplicating the achievement of Joshua before Jericho. Another fanatic, an Egyptian Jew, posed as a new Joshua when he proposed to command the walls of Jerusalem to fall down so that his followers could participate in God's overthrow of the Roman-dominated authorities there (*Ant.* 20:169f.; *War* 2:261f.). These so-called 'sign prophets' thought of themselves as something like *Joshua redivivus* (Krieger, p. 185). They believed that, "if only a 'sign' of the Exodus-Conquest could be performed," it would "force the hand of God to speedily bring his 'Salvation'" (Barnett, p. 688). Josephus makes it clear that they had a large following.

The Messiah or Ta'eb ('he who returns') expected by the Samaritans was also thought of as a returning Joshua (Merx, pp. 42f.; Colpe, column 1354); and the Christian epistle of Barnabas, of the early second century, links Joshua with Jesus (12:8). Earl Doherty has pointed out that the Greek for 'Joshua Messiah' is 'Jesus Christ'; and if 'sign prophets' were trying to substantiate messianic claims (or something like them) by imitating Joshua, would this not mean, as R.M. Price appositely asks, that "there was some currently available category like a 'Joshua Messiah', a 'Jesus Christ'?" (p. 247).

Phil. 2:5–11—a pre-Pauline hymn which Paul has incorporated into his epistle—is of interest here; for the hymn states that it was God who bestowed the name Jesus on the supernatural personage who had submitted to taking human form, and that God bestowed this name only after having exalted him (following his death), and as a reward for having obediently "humbled himself" (verse 8) to death on the cross:

> (9) Wherefore God highly exalted him and gave him the name which is above every name;
> (10) That at the name of Jesus every knee should bow, in heaven, on Earth and under the Earth,
> (11) And that every tongue should confess that Jesus Christ is Lord.

The name above all names (verse 9) to which all bow (verse 10) is clearly Jesus, not Lord (verse 11), which in any case is a title, not a name. R.M. Price comments, taking up a hitherto overlooked 1938 observation by P.L. Couchoud:

> For the heavenly Christ subsequently to receive the name Jesus
> implies . . . that the form of the salvation myth presupposed in the
> Philippians hymn fragment did not feature an earthly figure named
> Jesus. Rather, this name was a subsequent honor. Here is a fossil
> of an early belief according to which a heavenly entity . . . subse-
> quently received the cult name Jesus. In all this there is no histor-
> ical Jesus the Nazorean. (p. 85)

The name of Jesus was believed to have magical efficacy
(Acts 3:16; 4:7 etc.), especially as a purifying and sanctifying
agent (1 Cor. 6:11), very much in the manner of ancient beliefs,
both Jewish and pagan, in the power of holy names. Speaking
the name of a god summons him (as it would a man) and so
elicits his protection. Ephes. 1:21 assures us that the risen Christ
sits "far above every name that is named," i.e. his name is more
powerful than that of any rival deity. Such ideas concerning the
Jesus-name surely did not derive from knowledge of a
Palestinian preacher so named.

b. THE EPISTLE TO THE HEBREWS

The canonical letter to the Hebrews is regarded as the early
epistle that has most to say about the historical Jesus; so let us
see what overlap it has with material represented in the
gospels. Attridge's detailed commentary dates it, uncontrover-
sially, at some time between the years 60 and 100 (p. 9). It is
not, and does not purport to be, by Paul. The title in the RV
"The Epistle of Paul the Apostle to the Hebrews" is corrected
in the New English Bible to "A Letter to Hebrews"; and even
this is no more than an ancient conjecture as to who were the
addressees—assumed to be Jewish Christians because the letter refers repeatedly to Jewish cultic traditions and includes
much sophisticated exegesis of the OT. These features do not,
however, necessarily indicate a Jewish audience, for "other
Jewish-Christian authors such as Paul write to what are exclusively or predominantly Gentile communities, such as Galatia
or Corinth, and argue with Jewish techniques and themes"
(Attridge, p. 12).

The epistle was not ascribed to Paul until late in the second century, when Clement of Alexandria said it was his, and this attribution was then "promoted to gain acceptance of it in the canon of the New Testament at a time when there was much dispute about which books should be included" (Lindars 1991, p. 16). The style of the letter is un-Pauline, and at 2:3 the author declares himself to be at best a second-hand recipient of tradition: salvation is here said to have begun when it was spoken by the Lord (whether by the historical or by the risen Jesus is not indicated), whereupon "those who heard him" attested it "to us"—meaning either to Christians generally, or to the Christian community of the author. Attridge is surely right to say (p. 2) that Paul, who so emphatically affirms his status as an apostle and eyewitness of the risen Christ, could not have put himself in such a subordinate position.

What the epistle tells of the historical Jesus has been carefully documented by the NT scholar Erich Grässer, who admits that the letter exemplifies the "thoroughly enigmatic fact" that earliest Christianity as a whole seems to have no real hold of the Jesus of history (p. 89)—a state of affairs which "remains an unsolved riddle to this day" (pp. 63f.n3). The epistle, he says (p. 68), nowhere quotes or even alludes to any sayings of the earthly Jesus. The words which, in two passages (2:12f. and 10:5–10), are put into his mouth are from the OT (from the Psalms and Isaiah). Nor, Grässer adds, does the epistle have any of the gospels' narrative material. The faith of a whole list of OT characters—seventeen of them are named—is praised, but nothing is said of the numerous gospel personages whose faith impressed Jesus. Nor is there mention of his baptism, his cleansing of the Temple, or his miracles. (The latter is a particularly striking omission, as at 2:3–4 the missionary importance of miracles is stressed.) We are told that he was tempted (2:18)—not, however, on a specific occasion in the wilderness, but "in every way" (or "at all points"), *kata panta* (4:15). The idea is that this supernatural personage (1:2f.), if he was to help mankind, and thus "succour them that are tempted," must have lowered himself so as to become completely human, and in no way above the weaknesses of the flesh. The tempting and the "suffering" which went with it (2:18) are soteriological requirements, necessitated by his function as saviour, not reflections of the historical experiences recorded in the gospels.

Jesus's sufferings also included endurance of "hostility from sinners" (12:3)—stated only in these general terms, with no mention of altercations with scribes and Pharisees or of accusers at a trial. The author seems not to have known the passion story of the gospels. Had he known of Judas and the betrayal, he would have found him a better example than Esau of someone "falling short of the grace of God," causing "trouble" whereby "the many be defiled" (12:14–17). Had he known of Peter's denial, he surely would not have declared that no second repentance is allowable, that apostates can never be forgiven (6:4–6).

The author's reliance on the OT appears again at 2:6, where the phrase 'Son of man' is quoted from Psalm 8, where it means simply 'a human being'. In the following verses of the epistle, he quotes the very next words in the Psalm to establish the exalted status of Jesus, yet he values the phrase 'Son of man' solely as indicating solidarity with the human race. There is no awareness that the phrase could be used—as repeatedly in the gospels (for instance at Mk. 14:62)—to indicate precisely the exalted status for which the epistle is here pleading. Attridge allows that "it is quite possible that the author simply did not know the Son of man tradition" (p. 74). Lindars says, bluntly drawing the obvious conclusion: there was no 'Son of man' title in the Christology of early Christianity, and the use of the phrase in this way is "a development within the sayings tradition of the Gospels" (1991, p. 4n.).

The portrait of Jesus at 5:7 is what Attridge calls "vaguely reminiscent" of the Gethsemane scene in the gospel passion narrative, and has often been taken as an allusion to it, although "there are problems with this assumption" (p. 148). The statement in the epistle is that Jesus, "in the days of his flesh, offered up prayers and supplications, with loud cries and tears, to him who was able to save him from death, and he was heard for his godly fear." None of the gospel accounts of the agony in Gethsemane reports 'loud cries and tears'. Many commentators have ascribed these, and the granting of the prayers, to general reminiscences of the Psalms. Nor is it true that Jesus's prayer in Gethsemane to be spared death ("remove this cup from me," Mk. 14:36) was 'heard'. Deliverance from death (*ek thanatou*) in the epistle can mean either 'from (impending) death', or 'out of (the realm or state of) death' (a return, after death, to life). Attridge finds this latter meaning consonant with the most common use of the phrase 'to save from' (*sōzein ek*), so that Jesus can be understood as requesting resurrection and exaltation to God, which was duly granted (his prayer was "heard"). Commentators who suppose the passage to allude to the Gethsemane scene argue that saving from impending death is meant. But "it is difficult to see how such a prayer could be said to have been heard," since the epistle does not deny the reality of Christ's death (Attridge, p. 150).

Attridge concludes that, while the epistle's picture of Jesus at prayer cannot be derived from any known tradition about him on the subject, it does on the other hand "correspond quite closely to a traditional Jewish ideal of a righteous person's prayer, an ideal based on language in the Psalms and developed explicitly in Hellenistic Jewish sources" (pp. 148f.). The tearful prayers, like the all manner of temptations, also go to show that "in the days of his flesh" Jesus was not immune to human weaknesses.

The two further references to the earthly Jesus in the epistle are that he was descended from David ("of the tribe of Judah," 7:14) and was crucified for our salvation—both firm elements in the Christianity of the earliest documents, and the Davidic descent a common theological postulate for the Jewish Messiah. The crucifixion is not given a historical setting, but is said to have occurred "outside the gate" (13:12). The author will have known that it was universal practice to carry out executions outside the town to avoid pollution; and he specifies this detail, first in order to show that Jesus fulfilled the Tora's stipulations concerning the sin offering (verse 11), and second as a moral model, an encouragement to us to share his humility and lowliness: "Let us therefore go forth to him outside the camp, bearing his reproach, for we have not here an abiding city, but we seek the city which is to come" (verses 13f.).

Of Jesus's subsequent fate we are told that God raised him from the dead (13:20), that he is now "seated at the right hand of the throne of majesty" (8:1), and that he "will appear a second time," not to deal with sin, but to save those who eagerly await him (9:28).

In sum, all that is predicated of the earthly Jesus—his Davidic descent, his suffering and his pious prayers—are soteriological requirements, and do not have the appearance of reminiscences of a man who died in known circumstances a generation ago. Attridge calls the epistle's Christology a "mythic scheme" widespread in early Christianity, "a product of the syncretistic environment of the first century" wherein "ancient mythological patterns were appropriated and reinterpreted in various religious traditions" (p. 79), the "most blatant" mythical element being "the defeat of death's master" (p. 81). He has in mind 2:14, where we learn that Jesus "partook of flesh and blood so that through his death he might bring to nought him that had the power of death, that is, the devil."

How Jesus's death broke the devil's power is not explained; and whether the power of evil has really been broken at all has been a continuing question since earliest Christian times. On the one hand it is proclaimed that, in some unclarified sense, his death and resurrection has freed those who believe in him from evil—in the words of our epistle, "we have been sanctified through the offering of the body of Jesus Christ once for all" (10:10). On the other hand it has to be admitted that evil is still very much a present reality, and is perpetrated even by those whom, by dying, he has saved from it. The contradiction is illustrated very clearly in the first of the three epistles ascribed to John, which operates what Judith Lieu calls a "sharply dualistic scheme" (1991, p. 108): 3:4–10 declares that the coming of Jesus has destroyed the power of evil and enables believers to live free from it. Again, 5:18f. states that "we are of God," and "whosoever is begotten of God sinneth not." Yet Christians do notoriously sin (1:9f.), and we may well see a "brother" doing so (5:16). The writer is trying to argue that one either belongs to God or to the devil, and that there is no middle ground: he that sins is "of the devil" (3:8). But the letter itself shows that there is in fact a good deal of middle ground.

All this talk in these early Christian documents of cosmic salvation by a basically supernatural figure has very little, if anything at all, that links it with the recent career of a Palestinian preacher.

c. JESUS AS A HEAVENLY FIGURE

Belief in immortality was gaining ground at the beginning of the Christian era. Long absent from the Jewish world, the hope of resurrection is quite clearly evidenced there in the second century B.C., when it helped to sustain the Maccabean martyrs. And the Pharisees taught the doctrine in the first century A.D. In the Greek world of the time, the popular pagan mystery religions assured devotees of their immortality.

The idea of a general resurrection of the dead at some future time had, then, become firmly embedded in some of the Jewish religious groups. But that the resurrection of a particular person, Jesus, was a significant prelude to and foretaste of this general event was a specifically Christian doctrine. In time, as the world went on unchanged, the feverish expectation that a general resurrection would follow that of Jesus receded; and the more this eschatological hope, in which his resurrection had originally been envisaged, waned, the more similar did he become to such pagan figures as Herakles, Asclepius, and Dionysos (cf. D. Zeller, p. 90). Thus Justin Martyr could declare in the mid-second century, as part of his attempt to make Christianity acceptable and credible to pagans, that the Christian doctrine of a son of God who died, rose and went to heaven, was nothing new, but well represented in pagan thinking about Herakles, Dionysos, and others (*Apol.* I, 21).

Christian scholars accept, from such evidence, that pagan ideas about dying and rising gods help to explain Christianity's appeal once it had been launched; but there is considerable reluctance to allow such ideas any influence in moulding the earliest Christian thinking about Jesus. This is partly a reaction against exaggerated claims of this kind that were widely made in the first half of the twentieth century.

Nevertheless, it is not easy entirely to discount the importance of some pagan ideas even in oldest Christianity. They are evident in Paul, and D.G. Bostock—a clergyman writing in a theological journal—has recently argued strongly for his indebtedness to Egyptian religion, a faith which had then spread "all over the classical world." Paul, he says, justifies belief in the resurrection of the dead "on the basis of what the Egyptians believed to be the central principle involved, namely that a person is able to germinate in the manner of a plant from its seed." Paul's example of a grain of wheat (1 Cor. 15:37) "recalls the Egyptian image of the corn growing out of the mummified body of Osiris as a sign of the germination of the spirit-body." Moreover, Christ has put all his enemies under his feet (1 Cor. 15:25); and this, although a natural image, and one used at Psalm 110:1, was also "a marked feature of Egyptian theology in that Osiris is reported to have sat on his enemies in triumph over them." But "by far the most important parallel between Christ and Osiris is the way that Paul depicts Christ as the archetype of a universal resurrection" (1 Cor. 15:22–23). I would add, as a further parallel, that according to Plutarch (see Griffiths, pp. 85, 181) the festival of Osiris was spread over three days, his death being mourned on the first and his resurrection celebrated on the night of the third with the joyful shout "Osiris has been found."

Dr. Bostock does not mean to deny the reality of Paul's experience of the risen Jesus, but is concerned only to argue that Egyptian ideas provided him with a "resurrection theory" that would more readily account for this experience than anything then available from Judaism or Hellenism—although here, as we shall see, he underestimates what Paul could relevantly have drawn (and did in fact draw) from those quarters. However, remaining for the moment with what could have come to him from his pagan environment,we may note his belief that mystical assimilation, achieved through baptism, makes the believer a participant in Christ's destiny, and opens eternal life to him. Such ideas, says the ecclesiastical historian W.H.C. Frend, "approximate to the beliefs instilled in converts to the mysteries" (1986, p. 104). Paul writes:

For as many of you as were baptized into Christ did put on Christ (Gal. 3:27).

Having been buried with him in baptism, wherein you were also raised with him (Coloss. 2:12).

The argument here is that the three constituents of baptism are symbolical: going into the water stands for death, submergence under it means burial, and emergence from it denotes a new— and sinless—life, and a promise of eternal life. These ideas are spelled out in Chapter 6 of Romans:

We who were baptized into Christ Jesus were baptized into his death. We were buried therefore with him through baptism into death; that like as Christ was raised from the dead through the glory of the Father, so we also might walk in newness of life. For if we have become united with him by the likeness of his death, we shall be also by the likeness of his resurrection. (Rom. 6:3–5)

Paul adds that our old selves have in this way been crucified with Jesus, so as to liberate us from "the bondage of sin"; and "if we died with Christ, we believe that we shall also live with him"—eternally, for in his risen state "death no more hath dominion over him." Hence we should reckon ourselves "to be dead to sin, but alive unto God in Christ Jesus." As in the epistle to the Hebrews, Jesus's death has vanquished sin—yet, as Paul is all too well aware, sin somehow still exists, even among believers.

Marcel Simon finds "some rather striking analogies" (p. 139) between all this and initiation in the religion of Isis, which was, in the description given by Apuleius, "like a voluntary death and a gracious recovery," a god-granted 'salvation' in this world and the next ("ad instar voluntariae mortis et precariae salutis," *Metamorphoses* [better known as 'The Golden Ass'], 11:21).[2] Simon adds that, although baptism was known in pre-Christian Judaism, Jewish baptism cannot account for "the idea of a salvation mystically achieved through the baptismal rite by appropriation of, or identification with, the fate of a Saviour who died and rose again"—an idea "fundamental in Paul's conception of

baptism" (p. 143). And he finds that it was "good missionary tac-
tics" for Paul to express his message in terms which a pagan
audience would understand (p. 139). But surely not just tactical
missionizing was involved. The new religion will naturally have
attracted to itself ideas and practices well represented in its
Hellenistic environment.

The other most prominent early Christian rite was the
eucharist, styled by Ignatius of Antioch "the medicine of [that is,
the means of attaining] immortality" (Ephesians 20). Although
there are no exact pagan or Jewish parallels, both Justin Martyr
and Tertullian felt it necessary to explain away the resemblances
of this Christian rite to the Mithraic sacred meal.

The religion of one day is largely a reshuffling of ideas of a
yesterday, and so we shall not expect Christian thinking to have
exactly paralleled what in the world surrounded it or preceded
it. The gods of the mystery religions are indeed "saviour gods,
since they liberate the initiate from the tyranny of evil." Yet none
of them is a redeemer: "Their passion is not intended to atone
for the sins of men and to restore the original order of a universe that went astray. It is not deliberate, and has no vicarious
efficacy" (Simon, p. 138). Above all, "Christianity is a product of
Judaism" (p. 137), and it is there that one must look for its most
significant antecedents.

Jewish Wisdom traditions are here relevant. Wisdom is a primordial being who, in the Wisdom of Solomon from the OT
apocrypha, sits beside God's throne as his consort (9:4) and par-
ticipates with him in the creation of the world (Proverbs
8:22–31). When she sought an abode on Earth, mankind refused
to accept her, whereupon she returned in despair to heaven (1
Enoch 42:1f.). Ultra-conservative Christian apologists today dismiss with scorn any suggestion that this feminine figure could
have had any influence on Christian thinking about Jesus. They
find here a fine opportunity to demonstrate to their audiences
that a sceptic can oppose Christian orthodoxy only by resort to
blatant absurdities. In response I need only point to the article
'Jesus Christ' (by R.H. Fuller) in Metzger and Coogan's 1993
Oxford Companion to the Bible, where it is stated that the
"Christology of pre-existence and incarnation" (according to

which Christ existed in heaven before his birth on Earth) is "generally agreed" to have "developed from the identification of Jesus with the wisdom of God" (p. 362). Fuller adds that this Jewish Wisdom notion had originally been no more than "the personification of a divine attribute," but later it "developed in the direction of hypostatization" and so "became something like a person in the sense in which that term was later used in the Christian dogma of the Trinity."

The gender question was raised at an early stage. For Philo, the Jewish sage of Alexandria who died around A.D. 50, although Wisdom's Greek name is feminine, her nature is masculine, and she is called feminine only to indicate her inferiority to the masculine maker of the universe (cf. Grant 1990, pp. 32f., quoting Philo). Philo made her almost synonymous with the 'Word', the masculine Logos, the highest of God's 'powers' which functioned now as aspects of him and now as independent of him. "Philo's Logos," says C.D. Dodd, "is in many places almost a doublet of Wisdom" (pp. 66, 276); and Hamerton-Kelly calls the Logos "a Hellenistic Jewish term for pre-existent Wisdom" (p. 241). In Chapter 24 of Ecclesiasticus (the 'Wisdom of Jesus son of Sirach' from the OT apocrypha), Wisdom comes forth from the mouth of God, and is in this way identified with the 'Word'. That the divine word should be hypostatized may have resulted from the fact that it goes forth in physical form as a breath from the mouth of the deity. A word of blessing or malediction thus becomes an independent power that cannot be hindered in its course of action (Ringgren, p. 191).

Philo called the Logos "a son of God," even a "second God" (Hayman, p. 14). By the time we reach the prologue of the fourth gospel, the masculine Logos had come to be established as a designation of the supernatural figure so close to God. Nevertheless, "virtually everything" said of the Logos in this prologue had "already been predicated of wisdom in Judaism" (Moody Smith, p. 29). The Jesus of the fourth gospel, says Martin Scott, is "none other than Jesus Sophia incarnate" (p. 170).

The influence of Jewish Wisdom ideas on Paul is undeniable, for Jewish statements about Wisdom are made about Jesus in the Pauline letters. Paul calls Christ "the power of God and the Wisdom of God" (1 Cor. 1:24). In him "are hid all the treasures of Wisdom and knowledge" (Coloss. 2:3). Like Wisdom, he assisted God in the creation of all things (1 Cor. 8:6)—an idea spelled out in the Christological hymn of Coloss. 1:15–20. It was, then, "the Wisdom/logos archetype" that was used to give Christ "his role in creation" (Hayman, p. 14). And like the Jewish Wisdom figure, he sought acceptance on Earth, but was rejected and returned to heaven.

These features are present also in other early Christian texts. In the epistle to the Hebrews the description of the Son is based on Jewish ideas of Wisdom. The obvious parallels are given in Montefiore's commentary (p. 36). Thus the Son existed before the world, which God "created through him" (1:2); and he "reflects the glory of God," and so forth (1:3). Lindars (1991, p. 34) thinks this is probably directly indebted to 7:26 of the Wisdom of Solomon, which reads: "for she is a reflection of eternal light, a spotless mirror of the working of God, and an image of his goodness."

Admittedly, the Jewish Wisdom literature does not state that Wisdom lived on Earth as a historical personage and assumed human flesh in order to do so. The statement is that she was available as man's counsellor, but was rejected, even humiliated, and then returned to heaven. However, commentators have shown how easy it would be for readers to suppose that, when the texts spoke of Wisdom "setting up its tent" on Earth, the meaning was that Wisdom assumed human flesh, since "house of the tent" or simply "tent" is used (even by Paul, 2 Cor. 5:1 and 4) in the sense of man's earthly existence (Cf. Haenchen 1980, p. 129). We may recall 2 Peter 1:14 where Peter is represented as foretelling his own martyrdom with the words: "I know that the striking of my tent will come soon" (see below, p. 122). From the tradition that Wisdom was active in creation and sought a dwelling-place with humanity, it is, as Martin Scott observes, "only one final logical step" to 'Wisdom became flesh'—a natural drawing out of the process of Wisdom's "development as an active force involved in the affairs of the world" (pp. 105, 243).

Additionally to Wisdom traditions, Jewish conceptions of the Messiah also played a part in the earliest thinking about Jesus.

William Horbury has shown that, although often understood as thoroughly human, the Messiah could alternatively be envisaged as "the embodiment of an angel-like spirit," and not just in texts such as 2 Esdras, which are regarded as exceptional, but more generally in Jewish writings. There is thus "a considerable extent of common ground . . . between ancient Jewish conceptions of a pre-existent Messiah, among other pre-existent entities, and . . . Christian conceptions of the pre-existent Christ reigning over the church or creation"; so that it is necessary to "modify the sharp contrasts often drawn between a 'human' Jewish Messiah and a 'divine' Christian figure" (pp. 86–88, 151). There is, then, a strong Jewish background, additional to statements in the Wisdom literature, to Paul's idea of a supernatural personage embodied in human form. Horbury is quite orthodox in accepting that Jesus ministered in Galilee, as depicted in the gospels. He is concerned only to explain how the cult or worship of him originated, and supposes that it probably developed from praise offered by his followers during the ministry (p. 111). But his book does show how extensive were the Jewish traditions on which Paul and other early Christians could draw for their portraits of Jesus.

It is sometimes argued that, because of the monotheism of the Jews, statements in their literature about Wisdom or Logos as a divine agent distinct from God must be understood as no more than poetic personifications. Lindars (1991, pp. 33f.) speaks of "a widely ranging and fluctuating use of metaphors" in this regard. In fact, however, Jewish theology was much less uniformly monotheistic than is commonly supposed. Its "emanations, hypostatizations, and various heavenly and angelic beings constantly threatened the stricter boundaries of monotheism" (Wilson 1995, p. 269). Hayman even finds 'monotheism' a "misused word in Jewish studies" (p. 1). "It is clear," he says, "from both the Hebrew Bible itself and from extra-biblical literary, inscriptional and archaeological evidence that many, perhaps the majority, of ancient Israelites worshipped Yahweh alongside his female consort, his *asherah*. Biblical and post-biblical wisdom literature preserves some of the language of this earlier time in the way in which it speaks about personified Wisdom"

(p. 14). Jewish monotheism did not inhibit such speculations any more than Christian monotheism prevented Christians from seeing Jesus as God.

In this connection it is relevant to keep in mind what may be called the degradation of ideas, something very often significant in religious history. Statements which may perhaps in some authors have originated as poetic hyperbole can readily be taken more literally in the course of their transmission. The classical scholar Gilbert Murray gave as examples the way in which, in some late pagan documents, "'the providence (*Pronoia*) of God' becomes a separate power; 'the wisdom of God' (*Sophia*) becomes 'the divine Sophia' or 'Sophia the daughter of God', and even in one case gets identified with Helen of Troy." He adds that "the doctrinal history of the conception 'Logos', the 'word' or 'speech' of God, shows similar developments" (p. 34). It is easy to see why. Religion comprises beliefs and practices, and while a practice can be imitated without reference to any underlying belief—it is common for even educated persons to conform to rites the precise purpose of which they cannot explain—a belief cannot be imitated in the same way; for, unless arising spontaneously out of common experience—and with religious beliefs this can seldom be the case—it must be conveyed from one mind to another by some kind of language. The essential ambiguities of language, combined with different capacities for abstraction in the persons who use it, are bound to lead to different interpretations of the same formulae; and this distinction will result in religious change, or at least affect the uniformity of belief even in a small community. In this way, complicated and sophisticated ideas become degraded into more tangible concretes.

d. MAN'S REDEMPTION AND JUSTIFICATION: THE RELIGION OF PAUL

Paul's letters are the earliest extant witnesses to Christianity and also form the most substantial body of early Christian doctrine. Hence it is appropriate to conclude this section on the earliest

Christologies with a summary of the principal elements in his religious ideas. It will show how influential they have been, and yet how different they are from much that is in the gospels.

As the basis of this summary I have taken the exposition of Paul's thinking given by the German NT scholar William Wrede in his book on Paul of 1904. It reached a second edition in 1907, and an English translation (from which my quotations derive) appeared in that same year. Wrede is better known for his epoch-making book *The Messianic Secret in the Gospels* of 1901, which underlies Heikki Räisänen's equally important *The Messianic Secret in Mark* of 1990, on both of which I have written in Chapter 5 of *The Jesus Legend*. Although Wrede's publications are now some 100 years old, what he has to say, both on the gospels and on Paul, is still very much to the point.

We have seen already that, for Paul, Christ is the Son of God, older than created things, and even took part in their creation; that in order to redeem us he left heaven and "emptied himself" of his divinity so as to live on Earth as a man, accepting even the restrictions of the Jewish law as part of this abasement, before returning to heaven into his former glory. Human form was, says Wrede (1907a, p. 90), "something strange to him, a beggar's garment which the heavenly prince assumed for a while, to lay aside again." Hence the statement that God sent him to Earth in the "likeness" of "sinful flesh" (Rom. 8:3), "in fashion as a man" (Phil. 2:8). For our sake God "made him to be sin who knew no sin, so that in him we might become the righteousness of God" (2 Cor. 5:21). Not that he actually sinned. Paul is thinking of the sinfulness which he believed goes with human nature—a sinfulness which "exists before it reaches the point of actual transgression" (p. 98. This and further page numbers are references to Wrede). Man is "carnal, sold under sin. . . . I know that in my flesh dwelleth no good thing" (Rom. 7:14, 18). In an earlier chapter Paul explains that sin became part of man's essence historically, as a result of Adam's transgression: "Through one man sin entered the world, and death through sin, and so death passed unto all men" (Rom. 5:12).

Assuming human form brought Christ into the domain of the *archontes*, rulers of this world, the evil angelical powers vari-

ously designated by Paul as authorities, powers, thrones, dominions, principalities (1 Cor. 15:24; Coloss. 1:16; 2:10, 15), and also
as the elements of the world (Gal. 4:3, 9; Coloss. 2:8, 20). Wrede
rightly stresses that these "rulers" are supernatural powers, and
that the reference is not to Pilate and his like (p. 98n. Cf. above,
p. 6 and the detailed discussion in my 1991 book, pp. 96–106).
It was the *archontes* who really crucified Jesus, but they would
not have done so if they had known the wisdom of God (1 Cor.
2:6–8), if, that is, they had suspected that the cross of Christ
would bring salvation to the world and make an end of them;
for through death he passed out of their sphere. Stripped of his
flesh, he has nothing more in common with sin, and death is no
longer lord over him in his risen state (Rom. 6:9f.). Moreover,
what happened to him happened to all who have faith in him:
from the moment of his death they are "redeemed, as fully as
himself, from the hostile powers," and with his resurrection they
are "transferred into indestructible life" (p. 100). Hence neither
"angels" nor "powers" are able to separate the redeemed from
the love of God (Rom. 8:38f.). The clear implication is that, prior
to this redemption, they were able to do so: "Paul believes that
mankind without Christ is under the sway of mighty spirits,
demons and angelic powers" (p. 95).

In the previous chapter of Romans, Paul puts this whole
argument as follows. To escape from the demon powers, man
had to be freed from the bonds of the body and the earthly
world: "Wretched man that I am, who will deliver me from this
body of death?" (Rom. 7:24). It is not difficult to anticipate that
the answer to this question is: Jesus Christ. To escape from his
body of death, man had to die, and Christ has done this for him,
and so liberated him: "One died for all, therefore all died" (2
Cor. 5:14). Hence "reckon yourselves to be dead unto sin but
alive unto God in Christ Jesus" (Rom. 6:11). Paul is thinking of
a mystic participation in Christ's death and resurrection, not of
a successful ethical struggle to overcome sin (pp. 102f.). For
him, no human excellence can confer worth on someone who
does not believe in the crucified and risen Son of God (pp. 164f.
Cf. Rom. 7:14–25). Purely human standards of morality have
ceased to count. What is vitally important is baptism, which vis-

ibly announces acceptance of the faith. It is "baptism into the death of Christ" (Rom. 6:3. Cf. above, p. 19). Eucharist too enables believers to participate in Christ's sacrifice (1 Cor. 10:16), just as those who partake of a pagan sacrificial meal enter thereby into communion with the demon gods of paganism (verse 21).

Yet the redeemed, although "dead unto sin," continue to sin, and so Paul finds it necessary to exhort them not to do so (Rom. 6:12f.). This contradiction—that sin has been conquered but is nevertheless still there—is, as we saw (above, pp. 16f.), widespread in early Christian literature. It appears again when Paul declares that the faithful are already God's adopted sons, not slaves (Rom. 8:2, 14), yet are still awaiting their adoption (verse 23). Similarly, the demon spirits are already overcome by the cross (Coloss. 2:15), yet in the last times, about to come, they must be fought and conquered by Christ (1 Cor. 15:24ff.). One must not, says Wrede, look for consistency in Paul (p. 77).

Wrede observes (p. 81) that a great role is played in Paul's theology "by the thought that what happens to the first of a historical series happens in consequence to the whole series." Thus, Wrede continues:

> Adam is the headspring of humanity. He represents the whole race of mankind. What is true of him is therefore true of all that are connected with him. Since he dies, all who belong to his race also die. Christ is again the first of a series. Therefore, since he arises from the dead, all rise with him—simply on this account. (Rom. 5:12ff.; 1 Cor. 15:22, etc.)

At 1 Cor. 15:47–50, Adam figures as the first or earthly man, and Christ as the second or heavenly one. Paul continues:

> As is the earthly, such are they also that are earthly, and as is the heavenly, such are they also that are heavenly. And as we have borne the image of the earthly, we shall also bear the image of the heavenly.

In sum, Paul's Jesus lived on Earth in abasement. His Messianic glory was looked for in the future, at his second coming. But as Christian tradition developed, his earthly life came to be understood as already a manifestation of his glory, not a concealment of it. He became "not only the Messiah that should come, but the Messiah that had come" (p. 172). As early as the fourth gospel, the whole of his life on Earth is a continual radiance of divine glory which shines through the veil of flesh (p. 91).

Wrede concludes that Paul's conception of Christ did not originate from an impression made on him by the personality of the historical Jesus (p. 147), but from his Jewish background. "Jewish apocalyptic books are . . . cognizant of a Messiah who, before his appearance, lives in heaven and is more exalted than the angels" (p. 152). What was most important to Paul in the humanity of Jesus was not any ethical or other human behaviour, but the abnegation of his divine existence. He can call Christ obedient not because his life on Earth was characterized by this moral quality, but because he did not oppose the divine decision to send him for the salvation of the world, even though "it cost him his divine nature and brought him to the cross" (p. 149). He can call Christ meek because he humbled himself to the lowliness of the Earth. These predicates are not based on "an impression of the moral character of Jesus," but "originate in the apostle's own doctrine of redemption" (p. 150). Apart from Christ's assumption of human form and his resurrection, only one event in his earthly life is important to Paul, "namely the destruction of that life, Jesus's death"; and this is "no historical fact at all; it transcends history; it is an occurrence in a world above that of sense, for, without its redeeming power, it is nothing" (p. 148).

It is obvious from all this that the "wisdom" Paul preached is quite different from human wisdom: it is "not of this world" (1 Cor. 2:6) and unintelligible to the "natural man" who "receiveth not the things of the Spirit of God" (verse 14). It is wisdom imparted by the Spirit, which knows and reveals things which are far beyond the intellect. The believer is no longer "in the flesh" but "in the Spirit" (Rom. 8:9).

If Paul's doctrine of redemption derives from his pre-Christian religious background, his doctrine that justification comes from faith alone, and not from keeping the Jewish law, has a quite different origin, namely the missionary experience that Gentiles would accept Christianity only if it did not obligate them to the burdensome requirements of this law. So much, says Wrede (p. 123), is clear from the fact that this doctrine of *sola fides* surfaces only when Paul is dealing with conflict with Judaism (Romans, Galatians, and Phil. 3:6–9). It is, then, a polemical doctrine: Paul did not want Jewish customs to be made a condition of Christianity for the Gentiles. But if not, if these customs were not necessary for salvation, then they were unnecessary even for Jews. Hence Paul needed a doctrine which would make them dispensable for both parties, and so came up with the proposition that faith in Christ—simply an obedient acceptance of and assent to the preaching of redemption—is all that man needs for his justification. Christ's death "is taken to be the death of a sacrifice; it has therefore the same virtue as the sacrifice, namely the expiation or remission of sins; that is, it confers righteousness on man" (p. 133). Justification is at bottom nothing else than Christ's act of redemption, namely his death. "By this act God has declared for all men that grace and faith, not works and law, are really important" (p. 132). Paul's argument involves something of a caricature of Judaism, which "was not ignorant of grace but stressed it" (p. 127). It suits his polemical purpose to suggest that the Jews thought they could earn salvation by obeying their law, while the Christian's relation to God does not depend on performance and merit, since God justifies man "freely," "of grace" (Rom. 3:24 and 4:4). Wrede notes incidentally (p. 160) that, in his polemic against the law, Paul never suggests that the historical Jesus did anything to infringe or abrogate it. On the contrary, as we saw, he believed that Jesus accepted it as part of his earthly abasement.

In the period immediately following Paul, his doctrine of justification "practically disappeared" (p. 173)—because the situation for which it was devised had disappeared. How one stands in relation to the Jewish law had ceased to be a question of any importance once Christianity had broken with Judaism and become a predominantly gentile religion. It is certainly noteworthy that the Jesus of Mk. 10:17–22 makes salvation dependent on keeping the law (the commandments) and giving all one has to the poor, completely contradicting the idea of justification by faith and not by good works.

Wrede sums up: "Paul's whole innovation is comprised in this, that he laid the foundation of religion in acts of salvation, in the incarnation, death and resurrection of Christ." And "if we are to designate the character of this conception, we cannot avoid the word 'myth'" (pp. 178f.). Angelic powers, good or evil, did not impress Wrede: "Angels, in our time, belong to children and to poets" (p. 95). Moreover, Paul's Christ "must needs for the most part crush out the man Jesus" (p. 182). Yet major theologians over centuries have followed Paul even more than they have the gospels. Tertullian, Origen, Athanasius, Augustine, Anselm of Canterbury, Luther, Calvin, Zinzendorf—"not one of these great teachers can be understood on the ground of the preaching and historic personality of Jesus" (p. 180). Rather is their Christianity a remodelling of Paul's. To this we may add, a century after Wrede, that it is likewise from Paul that fundamentalist teachers of today derive their doctrine that, at a time known only to God, true believers will be 'raptured' out of the world and "caught up in the clouds to meet the Lord in the air" as he "descends with a shout" at his second coming (1 Thess. 4:17). The rest of us will, it is believed, perish miserably.

Wrede has not endeared himself to the traditionally minded among the theological fraternity: "Indistinguishable from the shallowest of freethinkers" was the verdict of one of them in 1939 (quoted by Strecker in a 1960 article which effectively brings out Wrede's true worth). Wrede would have had no sympathy at all with present-day efforts to salvage unacceptable scriptural doctrines by turning them into vague and barely intelligible philosophemes. On the contrary, he suggested (1907b, p. 25) what is surely an apposite supplement to the beatitudes: "Blessed are the unpretentious in speech, for they shall be understood" (Selig aber sind, die keine Phrasen machen, denn sie werden verstanden werden). Räisänen finds Wrede an outstanding representative of the "tradition of calling a spade a spade" that has survived all too rarely in Pauline studies (1987, p. 11).

In his important 1987 and 1992 books, Räisänen supports many of Wrede's positions. He agrees that Paul's complex and often fiercely hostile attitude to the Jewish law—an attitude unique in its hostile elements in early Christianity—developed only from his missionary experiences, and was not an integral part of his Christianity at the time of his conversion, even though his conversion experience called him to preach to Gentiles (Gal. 1:15f.; 2:2). For some time he preached at Antioch, where, as we shall see in Chapter 2 (p. 98), a mixed Jewish-Gentile church had been founded by 'Hellenists'— Greek-speaking Jews who had developed a somewhat relaxed attitude to some of the central requirements of the law (such as circumcision and the food rules). We know from Philo that Jews living in gentile environments were tempted to content themselves with a symbolical rather than a literal understanding of the law's prescriptions, and so it is not surprising that some of the new Christian communities should have a liberal, though not hostile attitude towards it. It was such Christians that Paul, while still a zealous Pharisee, had persecuted, and it was presumably to their views that he was converted (cf. below, pp. 95f.). But later he found that Christian congregations were being pressurized by 'Judaizers'—Jewish Christians who were insisting on full literal acceptance of all the law's requirements, including in particular circumcision (Gal. 2:12ff.; Phil. 3:1ff.). It was in opposition to these 'theological restorers' that he felt driven to make harshly critical assessments of the law, so much so that in Philippians he says nothing positive about it, and calls the restorers "dogs" who "insist on mutilation." In Galatians he even declares that these agitators may as well go the whole way and castrate themselves (5:12). Yet it is clear from other passages that he still felt obliged to respect the law, as it was instituted by God (although at Gal. 3:19–20 he seems to question even that). Thus in Galatians he follows his polemic against it by grounding the necessity of love on this same law that he has been disparaging (5:14; cf. Rom. 13:8–10). He even claims that it is his teaching that has really fulfilled or "upheld" the law (Rom. 3:31). In sum, as Räisänen shows, he asserts both its abolition through what God has done in Christ—"if righteousness comes through the law, then Christ died for nothing" (Gal. 2:21)—and its permanent and normative character. This is a contradiction which even the resources of modern 'dialectical theology' have not resolved.

In the course of his polemic, Paul suggests that, according to Judaism, salvation can be earned by human efforts, by performing the works which the law enjoins. His talk of "works," "wages" and payment of "what is due" in Chapter 4 of Romans certainly gives the impression that he views Judaism in this way, which, as already Wrede saw, does actual Judaism less than justice. The Jewish doctrine was that God's covenant with Israel, to which observance of the Mosaic law belonged, was an act of grace, while man's obedience to the law expressed his gratitude for the promises included in this covenant and his willingness to stay within it. Such obedience was not a means by which man entered into the covenant and reaped its benefits. Yet it is understandable that Paul should speak as he does about the Jewish position; for it could easily seem to those outside Judaism—and much of Paul's work was with Gentiles—that submission to circumcision and other Jewish observances were not (what they were to observant Jews) efforts to take God's promises seriously, but 'works' which aimed at eliciting his favour. This, Räisänen notes, "opened the way for contrasting Judaism (including observant Jewish Christianity) with law-free Christianity in such a manner that the former appears—whether or not that was Paul's intention—as a religion of works and the latter a religion of grace" (1992, p. 35). He notes too (p. 33) that Paul was surely not deliberately distorting the true nature of the religion he had formerly so zealously practised and had now abandoned, but was speaking in heated dispute with Christians who were still beholden to its central doctrines; and if in such a situation he had done full justice to their standpoint, he would have been a most unusual figure in religious history. It must, then, be admitted, as this scholar sadly allows (1987, p. 268), that Paul "conveys a distorted picture of the Jewish religion which has, contrary to Paul's intentions to be sure, had a share in the tragic history of the Jews at the mercy of Christians."

That Paul can refer both positively and negatively to Judaism and its law shows his concern to satisfy a deep need which so often plagues a new development in religious thinking and practice—the need to show that this novelty really stands for continuity with the older ideas and values from which it is in reality breaking away. His are not the only NT writings that are vitiated by this need. We shall see in Chapter 2 how hard Luke tries in Acts to represent the church as really continuous with Israel and alienated from it only by perversity on the part of the Jews. The way in which he suggests this continuity in his gospel is equally unconvincing. The birth and infancy narrative of its opening chapter presents a Jesus who will fulfill the political and nationalist hopes familiar from the OT: an angel (no less) foretells that God will give him the throne of David to reign over Israel for ever (1:32–33). Zechariah, speaking in this same chapter not just as a pious Jew, but "through the holy spirit," tells of the promised one who will save God's people, who will "deliver us from our enemies" and "rescue us from their hands" (1:67–74). In the upshot, however, it transpires that the promises given to the fathers have been fulfilled not by achievement of any political and national aspirations, but in the fact of Jesus's resurrection (Acts 13:32–33), with salvation for those individuals— Gentiles as well as Jews—who believe in this event. The next verses in Acts show that this, and not political freedom, is the "forgiveness of sins" promised in verse 77 of Zechariah's benediction in the gospel. Far from Israel being delivered from its enemies, Jerusalem will be trampled down by aliens, since its inhabitants did not know "the time of its visitation," viz. that God has visited it in the activities of Jesus (Lk. 19:44; 21:24). Luke of course refrains from any clear admission that he is in fact radically reinterpreting the old traditions. As Räisänen puts it, "the old vocabulary is made to serve a novel cause" (1997, p. 63). I try to show in this book that this has happened time and time again in Christianity, sometimes with the novel cause being represented as not novel at all, and sometimes— particularly today, as we shall see in my fourth chapter—with frank acknowledgement that it is.

But I must return to Paul and consider the implications of his epistles. The Göttingen NT scholar Gerd Lüdemann, who in an earlier book declared that "a consistent modern view must say farewell to the resurrection of Jesus as a historical event," has now supplemented this with the judgement that "most of Paul," particularly his idea of God's plan for man's salvation in Jesus Christ, "belongs in the museum" (2001, pp. 221, 230). This supplementation follows naturally from the premiss that Jesus was not resurrected, for Paul himself told doubting Corinthians that "if Christ hath not been raised, your faith is vain" (1 Cor. 15:17). Paul's theology, Lüdemann says, is neither a *précis* nor a development of Jesus's teaching. He finds it significant that Paul never appeals to any words of Jesus about the law in order to defend his own teaching concerning it, that he never calls Jesus a teacher nor Christians disciples, and that he attaches more significance to the OT than to what Jesus taught (pp. 178, 192). Lüdemann nevertheless holds fast to the view that the supposedly risen Christ of Paul's preaching was the person who had been the Jesus of Nazareth of the gospels, and had been accompanied in his ministry by disciples who, shortly after his crucifixion, believed that they had experienced him as resurrected.

My view is that Paul knew next to nothing of the earthly life of Jesus, and did not have in mind any definite historical moment for his crucifixion. As we saw, holy Jews had been crucified alive in the first and second centuries B.C., but traditions about these events, and about the persecuted Teacher of Righteousness, could well have reached Paul without reference to times and places, and he need not have regarded their occurrences as anything like as remote in time as they in fact were. Whenever it was that Jesus had lived obscurely and died, he had, for Paul, returned promptly after death to heaven; and the evidence for this exaltation, and indeed for his whole religious significance, was his recent appearances to Paul and to contemporaries of Paul which signalled that the final events which would end the world were imminent (cf. above, pp. 7f.). Thus even if the death and resurrection were put at some indefinite time past, it remains quite intelligible that Christianity did not originate before the opening decades of the first century A.D. Nor need any supposed relevance to Jesus of the Wisdom literature have been appreciated earlier.

Had Paul believed that Jesus suffered under Pilate, he would hardly have said that the governing authorities punish only wrongdoers (Rom. 13:1–7). The author of 1 Peter, who regarded Jesus as without blemish, likewise declared that imperial governors "punish those who do wrong and praise those who do right" (2:13–14). Christian writers of later date, who did believe that Jesus had been brought before Pilate, are noticeably less positive in their assessments of governors. Thus the author of the Pastoral epistles, who declares at 1 Tim. 6:13 that Jesus "witnessed the good confession before Pontius Pilate," urges that supplications be made to kings and all other authorities "that we may lead a tranquil and quiet life" (2:1–2). (The Pastoral epistles, although ascribed to Paul in the NT, are generally admitted, for reasons set out in detail in *The Jesus Myth*, pp. 78–94, to be compositions of later date.)

I have discussed further how Jesus came to be linked with Pilate in *The Jesus Myth* (p. 104), and will touch on it again in the next section of this chapter. The view that Christianity began with a Jesus who was condemned in Pilate's Jerusalem surely persists because Paul's, indeed all the early epistles, continue to be read from knowledge of the gospels. Readers come first to the gospels in their printed NT, and if they go on to the epistles, they naturally fill out what is there so scantily said of Jesus's life from their knowledge of what the gospels say of it. This is all the more natural, as the epistles are addressed to situations in which this life was already past, so that readers can feel free to presuppose wherein it consisted and to interpolate into it information from other sources. In this way, the "rulers of this age" who are said to have crucified "the Lord of glory" because they failed to understand the hidden and secret wisdom of God (1 Cor. 2:8) can readily be equated with Caiaphas and Pilate—as if Paul would have regarded such petty officials (whom he in any case never mentions) as "rulers (*archontes*) of this world" (he uses 'this age' and 'this world' interchangeably) who are "coming to naught" (verse 6), when this and other terms (such as principalities [*archai*], powers, dominions) clearly for him designate supernatural forces which have long harrassed humanity but have now been subjugated by Christ's saving act. They failed to recognize him because his incognito lasted from his birth until his resurrection disclosed his true glory (cf. above, pp. 5f., 25f.). Paul's wording resembles the title given in the fourth gospel to the supreme demonic being, "the ruler (*archōn*) of this cosmos" or (RV) "prince of this world" (Jn. 12:31; 16:11). The early Christians knew that they themselves were "of God," whereas "the whole world is in the power of the evil one" (1 Jn. 5:19 RSV). At Ephes. 2:2 we read of "the prince (*archōn*) of the power of the air," to whom recipients of the letter used to be beholden. The same letter declares that "our wrestling is not against flesh and blood, but against the principalities, against the powers, against the world-rulers of this darkness, against the spiritual hosts of wickedness in the heavenly places" (6:12). Such passages, says Barrett (1968, p. 70), show that both Paul and many of his contemporaries conceived the present world-order to be under the control of supernatural beings whose power was coming to an end (1 Cor. 2:6), the power of the age to come being already at work (Hebrews 6:5). Even Ignatius, who does link Jesus with Pilate, does not confuse Pilate with the evil, supernatural "ruler of this age," whom he mentions in five of his early second-century epistles, and from whom he says (Ephesians 19), echoing Paul, "the death of the Lord was hidden."

archontes can indeed be used to designate human governing authorities, and Paul does use it in this sense at Rom. 13:3. But here, as we saw, he is arguing that such 'rulers' are to be respected and obeyed, because they punish only evildoers; and so they can hardly be equated with the kind of *archontes* who "crucified the Lord of glory." Theissen takes these latter to mean both supernatural and human forces, but primarily the human ones, that is "historical persons in authority who were heightened symbolically to demonic powers" (p. 373). I propose instead that the primary reference is to the demonic powers. Admittedly, there must also be some implication that human forces were involved, for the supernatural 'rulers' will have needed human agents to effect a crucifixion on Earth. But the fact that Paul gives no indication as to who these agents were suggests that he had no precise information on the subject. Theissen would fain believe that he had Pilate in mind, but has to allow that his unspecific wording is a general reference to earthly persons who had some power and authority, to "earthly rulers in general" (p. 366). This is surely just the vague way of speaking to be expected from a Paul who knew nothing more specific.

The idea that evil spirits instigated Jesus's crucifixion because they were ignorant of his true identity is not confined to the early books of the NT. It is clearly stated in the early Christian apocalypse known as the Ascension of Isaiah, which purports to foretell that when "the Lord, who will be called Christ, will descend into the world . . . the God of that world will stretch forth his hand against the Son, and they will lay hands on him and crucify him on a tree, without knowing who he is" (9:14). By "the God of that world," Satan is meant, for a later passage states that Christ's crucifixion was instigated by "the adversary" who "roused the children of Israel against him, not knowing who he was" (11:19).

I have dwelt on this matter because the relevant material in the NT epistles, instead of confirming anything in the gospels, is incompatible with them. Mark stresses that Jesus, far from living incognito, worked prodigious miracles which enabled supernatural demons to recognize him for whom he was (1:34 and elsewhere). Even some early commentators were worried by this contradiction. Tertullian, for instance, resolved it (in his *Adversus Marcionem*, V, 6,) by supposing that Paul must after all have meant the *archontes* of 1 Corinthians to be earthly rulers who can be identified from the gospels as Pilate and Herod Antipas. (Details in Werner, pp. 244, 246 and notes. In Luke's passion narrative, Antipas as well as Pilate is involved in Jesus's trial, but Caiaphas, the high priest, is not mentioned, and the Jewish element in the trial is altogether attenuated compared with Mark's account.)

Another epistolary text that has been interpreted from knowledge of the gospels is Paul's statement that three years after his conversion (and not until then) he paid his first visit as a Christian to Jerusalem, where he spent a fortnight with Cephas (Gal. 1:18), who at 2: 7f. is alternatively called Peter (although there are grounds for regarding this as a post-Pauline interpolation[3]). It

has been assumed both that Cephas had followed Jesus in
Galilee (although Paul says nothing to suggest this) and that
during the fortnight in Jerusalem he must have instructed Paul
about his master's teaching and biography. If this were in fact
so, it becomes more difficult than ever to account for Paul's
silences about both! Furthermore, Paul's actual concern in this
passage is to establish his independence of Cephas and of all
the other Jerusalem apostles: he did not go near them at all for
the first three years of his Christian life, and even then met only
Cephas and one other apostle, and that only briefly. In this same
epistle, he insists that he did not receive the "gospel" he
preaches from any human agency (1:11–12).

Paul names the other apostle he met on the Jerusalem occasion as "James the brother of the Lord," and at 1 Cor. 9:5 he
mentions a group called "the brethren of the Lord." As the
gospels supply Jesus with brothers, Paul is taken to be referring
to members of Jesus's family. But it is quite possible that he
meant members of a 'brotherhood', a group of Messianists
which included James (and was perhaps led by him) and
whose members were not related to Jesus but zealous in the
service of the risen Lord (brethren "of the Lord," not of Jesus).
In Acts, the Jerusalem Christians are called "the brethren," and
the James who led them is not called Jesus's brother, nor even
'the brother of the Lord', although he is clearly the person
whom Paul designated by this term (cf. below, p. 88). Whoever
he was, Paul's references to him show that he was able unmolested to preach in Jerusalem that Jesus was the Messiah at least
until around 60 A.D. This would be very surprising if he had
been the blood brother of a Jesus recently executed as a
Messianic pretender by the authorities there (see further my
1999a book, p. 69).

It is also of relevance that in two gospels that are independent of each other (Matthew and John), the risen Jesus is made
to call followers who are not his blood relatives "my brethren."
Since elsewhere Matthew seldom and John never make Jesus call
his disciples this, the two evangelists may well here be drawing
on a common source, a story in which the risen Jesus made some
statement about his 'brethren' in the sense of a group of follow-

ers. In his commentary on John's gospel, Lindars says that the words "go to my brethren and say to them" at this point in its resurrection narrative (20:17–18), considered together with Matthew's "go tell my brethren," "require the supposition that John was using a source which also lies behind Mt. 28:10" (1972, pp. 596, 607). This would be evidence for an early (pre-gospel) use of the word 'brethren' for a group unrelated to Jesus serving the risen Lord. In John they are to be told that Jesus is ascending, not (as in Mark and Matthew) that he will appear to them. This is surely drawn from an old ascension tradition.

In this connection it is of interest that Paul mentions a faction at Corinth whose members called themselves "of Christ" and who were not in full agreement with other Christian groups there, differently named (1 Cor. 1:11–13). If, then, there was a Corinthian group called 'those of the Christ', there may well have been a Jerusalem one called 'the brethren of the Lord' whose members were as little related to or personally acquainted with the pre-crucifixion Jesus as were the Corinthians. If we abandon the premiss that Paul, James, and Cephas worshipped a recently active Jesus whom the authorities had found worse than merely troublesome, and regard them instead as members of a then obscure Jewish sect worshipping a historically distant figure who was probably quite unknown to the authorities of the time, this will at any rate make it understandable that James was long allowed to survive untroubled. Acts' story of wholesale Jewish acquiescence in Christianity in the Jerusalem of the 30s is, as we shall see in the next chapter, obviously legendary, and the speeches by Peter which occasioned these mass conversions are not historical. The Christian community there will have been unobtrusive and as good as unnoticed (see below, pp. 89f., 113).

According to Paul, the risen Jesus appeared successively to Cephas, to "the twelve," to "above five hundred brethren at once," to James, and to "all the apostles" (1 Cor. 15:5–7). Commentators have repeatedly shown how poorly all this— even the mention of 'the twelve'—matches what is in the gospels.[4] As for teachings, NT scholars have shown that the few "words" or "commands" of the Lord mentioned by Paul can be understood either as community regulations made firm by being put into Jesus's mouth, or as words communicated to Paul or others by the risen Jesus. (I give the relevant details in *The Jesus Legend*, pp. 28–36, and *The Jesus Myth*, pp. 60ff.) That Paul received such communications is beyond doubt. 2 Cor. 12:9 is expressly said to be what the Lord said personally to him in answer to a prayer, and so the speaker must have been the risen Lord, for Paul did not know Jesus before his resurrection and, as persecutor of Christians, certainly did not then pray to him. The sayings of the Lord in Revelation, the final book of the NT, show how early Christian 'prophets' addressed congregations using the name of the Lord in the first person; and Paul himself tells that the "spiritual gifts" operative in early Christian communities enabled some to prophesy, others to make ecstatic utterances, and yet others to interpret them (1 Cor. 12:8–11; 14:3–4). He felt entitled to give ethical advice because he had "the Spirit of God" (7:40).

It is also striking that when, in his letter to Christians at Rome, Paul urges them to "bless those who persecute you," to "pay taxes" and to refrain from judging ("judge not"), he does not designate these precepts as teachings of Jesus, but gives them on his own authority. Apologists continue to claim that he is here 'echoing' what, according to the gospels, Jesus had taught. But I have repeatedly pointed out that it is much more likely that certain precepts concerning forgiveness and civil obedience were originally urged independently of Jesus, and only later put into his mouth and thereby stamped with supreme authority, than that he gave such rulings and was not credited with having done so by Paul, nor indeed by other early Christian writers. Lüdemann's detailed discussion (pp. 183–193) shows that none of the Pauline passages commonly claimed as reminiscent of gospel pronouncements can be regarded as derived from words spoken by the Jesus of the gospels, but are in many cases ethical commonplaces with numerous parallels in Jewish literature, or have imagery familiar from Jewish apocalyptic.

There remains the "tradition" embodied in 1 Cor. 11:23–25, which Paul says he "received from the Lord"—for Paul this must mean the risen Lord—and which is paralleled by Jesus's eucharistic words in Mark. (I compare and contrast the two passages in my 1982 book, pp. 27–29.) Paul here represents Jesus as instituting a cultic act which existed as a regular part of Christian worship in Paul's time. Once such a practice had been established, it would be natural to suppose that Jesus had ordained it. The Dead Sea Scrolls show that a cultic act of this kind already existed in the Jewish background to Christianity. J.C. VanderKam says of the ritual meal described in some of the scrolls that, however one interprets it, "its messianic character, the prominence of bread and wine, the fact that it was repeated regularly and its explicit eschatological associations do recall elements found in the New Testament treatments of the Lord's Supper" (VanderKam 1994, p. 175).

Further aspects of the question as to what Paul can be taken to have known of Jesus are covered in *The Jesus Myth* (pp. 49–78). Here I would note that one after another of the few epistolary statements which might seem to imply knowledge of the Jesus traditions underlying the gospels has been shown to be explicable in other ways, or even to require such alternative explanation. The latter is notably the case with 2 Cor. 5:16, where Paul (in literal translation) declares: "From now on we know no man according to flesh; if indeed we have known Christ according to flesh we no longer know him (thus)." It has been claimed that this means that Paul deliberately chose not to speak of the historical Jesus, but can be presumed to have been well acquainted with the details of his life. But Paul is not here referring to 'Christ in the flesh' (the earthly Jesus), for 'according to flesh' qualifies the verb 'known', not the noun 'Christ'. Paul means that he no longer has a carnal (unspiritual, wordly) conception of Christ. He is saying that, judged by worldly standards, Jesus, who lived obscurely and died shamefully, would be of no account, and that this shows worldly standards to be worthless. This meaning is brought out in the translation given to the passage in the New English Bible: "With us, therefore [or in other words, because Christ died as he did], worldly standards have ceased to count in our estimate of any man. Even if they once counted in our understanding of Christ, they do so no longer."

Similarly, the Revised Standard Version reads: "From now on therefore we regard no one from a human point of view . . ." To take Paul as meaning that he is no longer interested in Jesus's physical existence in history would entail imputing to him indifference also to the physical existence of everyone ("we know no man according to flesh"), and that would be absurd.

Most students of the NT will nevertheless continue to hold that there are hints enough in the early epistles—to be explained away only by special pleading—which betray that the authors of these documents worshipped a Jesus who had preached in Galilee and had died in Jerusalem at the behest of Pilate. Accordingly Lüdemann undertakes, in a book of nearly 900 pages—not his book on Paul to which I have earlier referred—to construct an outline of Jesus's life by determining what he takes to be authentic elements in the first three of the canonical gospels and in the apocryphal Gospel of Thomas. He claims that one of the "best-attested historical facts" concerning Jesus is "his activity in exorcising demons" (2000, pp. 27, 881f.). But we saw (above, p. 37) that Paul could not have spoken as he did of Jesus's having lived incognito, unrecognized by demon powers, had he accepted the kind of gospel traditions to which Lüdemann here appeals; nor is there anything in the other early epistles of the NT which points in this respect to the gospels.

Jesus traditions outside the gospels in the NT are treated in a chapter (devoted mainly to apocryphal evidence) contributed to Lüdemann's book by Martina Janssen. Her account, however, covers only the Pauline letters, and them only briefly. She admits that "the question of continuity between Jesus and Paul" is a "difficult" one, and that the kindred question as to what words of Jesus might be "concealed" in these letters is "to a considerable extent open" (p. 820). Thus do theologians casually allude to an issue which is really of prime importance to any study of Christian origins; for it is surely undeniable that not only Paul but also the other authors of early epistles in the NT give an overall portrait of Jesus which is very different from what is said of him in the gospels.

ii. The Transition to the Gospels and to Later Writings

All this leaves us asking how Jesus could have come to be depicted so differently in the gospels. As in my 1996 and 1999a books, I propose here that the disparity between the early documents and the gospels is explicable if the Jesus of the former is not the same person as the Jesus of the latter. Some elements in the ministry of the gospel Jesus are arguably traceable to the activity of a Galilean preacher of the early first century, who figures in what is known as Q (an abbreviation for *Quelle*, German for 'source'). Q supplied the gospels of Matthew and Luke with much of their material concerning Jesus's Galilean preaching. No copy of Q has survived, but much of Q can be reconstructed from what is common to these two gospels, yet does not derive from the gospel of Mark, the other source from which they both (independently of each other) drew. Q consists mainly of Jesus's sayings, supplemented however with two miracle stories and with his dialogue with the devil in the story of his temptation.

Christopher Tuckett's 1996 book gives a full account of recent work on Q and accepts the majority view that it originated between A.D. 40 and 70 in northern Galilee or nearby, for it assigns Galilean localities to Jesus's activities, and links him with John the Baptist, known from the Jewish historian Josephus to have been executed before A.D. 39. This Galilean Jesus was not crucified and was not believed to have been resurrected after his death. The dying and rising Christ—devoid of time and place—of the early epistles is a quite different figure and must have a different origin.

In the gospels, the two Jesus figures—the human preacher of Q and the supernatural personage of the early epistles who sojourned briefly on Earth as a man and then, rejected, returned to heaven—have been fused into one. The Galilean preacher of Q has been given a salvific death and resurrection, and these have been set not in an unspecified past (as in the early epistles), but in a historical context consonant with the date of the Galilean preaching.

Already in Mark, the oldest extant gospel, there are Q-type traditions, as any synopsis (where parallel passages in the first three gospels are printed in columns side by side) will show. De Jonge observes that, "although influence from Q on Mark cannot be excluded, we may, on the whole, assume that in these cases traditional material has come down to us through two independent channels" (p. 85).

The gospels' synthesis of the two different Jesus figures was something novel, and may well not have immediately appealed to all Christian communities, even assuming that communication between them was such that they all knew of it. Hence it is not surprising that some of the epistles written at this time continued to proclaim the earlier, Pauline view of Jesus, with no assimilation of Q or of Q-like material.

Earl Doherty takes a more sceptical view of Q. He agrees that, in the gospels, the Galilean tradition of the preaching of the kingdom, as embodied in Q, has been combined with the suffering saviour idea of the early epistles. But he regards the Q that can be constructed from Matthew and Luke as a late form of the Q document. His whole reconstruction of Christian origins relies heavily on distinguishing earlier and later layers in the documents—in the first epistle of John, in the gospels of Peter and Thomas and in the Didache, as well as in Q.

Doherty is of course not alone in attempting a division of Q into chronological layers, but draws on earlier attempts to do this (on which I have commented in Chapter 6 of *The Jesus Legend*). Doherty (pp. 146ff.) and others argue that the original Q is a collection of 'Wisdom' sayings like the OT book of Proverbs, with advice on life-style. This "sapiental" layer (designated Q_1) was later, so the argument goes, supplemented (to form Q_2) with prophetic and apocalyptic sayings, of seemingly totally different character, about a fearsome coming judgment of mankind, and only at this stage do Galilean place names (p. 155) and references to John the Baptist enter the document. At a still later stage, some stirrings of a biography of Jesus such as the temptation story were added to form Q_3.

Most scholars who divide Q in this way accept the posited original layer (if not the contents of the two later ones) as sayings of a historical Jesus. But Doherty disputes that this is true even of these earliest sayings. He regards them as a sayings collection perhaps designated as words of Wisdom herself (p. 173), but not ascribed to any one human individual, and certainly not placed in a ministry of Jesus. That is why, he says, Matthew and Luke could each place the individual sayings in different contexts in their respective gospels (p. 161). A founder figure, he holds, perhaps not even initially named as Jesus, was introduced as the speaker of the sayings only at a late stage in the development of the material. "Wisdom" eventually evolved into "Jesus" (p. 178).

Even at the Q_2 stage there was still, in Doherty's view, no mention of Jesus. Q_2 consists of narrow-minded Jewish sectarian apocalyptic sayings, directed against those who failed to respond to the Q_2 community's preaching of the coming of the kingdom, not to the teaching or person of a Jesus; and the kingdom is to be inaugurated, with cosmic catastrophe, by a supernatural personage called here "the Son of man." By the time we reach the gospels, these apocalyptic warnings about the imminent "coming of the Son of man" have been put into Jesus's mouth (as at Mt. 24:37, parallel with Lk. 17:26), and in such a way that we are to understand them as sayings about his own future role as judge. Nevertheless, as Doherty stresses (p. 167), this material has been imperfectly assimilated into the gospels, for the reference still seems to be not to Jesus, but to some other and supernatural personage about whom he is talking: "Even as Jonah became a sign unto the Ninevites, so shall also the Son of man be to this generation" (Lk. 11:30).

The Q_1 which Doherty and some others have posited was a foreign source, with scarcely any specifically Jewish ideas. Its sayings strongly resemble those of a specific Hellenistic preaching movement of the time, namely that of the so-called Cynic philosophers (pp. 158ff.)—itinerant preachers who rejected conventional values and were fearless towards authorities. Doherty argues that Jewish preachers with apocalyptic ideas discovered Q_1 and adapted it into Q_2 by adding these ideas to it (p. 164). Why they should have assimilated sayings from Q_1 which differed so much from their own outlook is unclear, and was done "for reasons which can only be speculative" (p. 232). Critics such as Tuckett, who question the division of Q into chronological layers, have focussed on this anomaly, and have argued that the apocalyptic message that the kingdom of God is at hand belongs to the original document, and that the allegedly Cynic sayings, rejecting the comforts of civilized life, are not really Cynic at all, but part of this urgent message. Tuckett allows that the Q_2 layer, with its polemical attacks on "this generation," represents a significant and distinctive feature of the Q tradition. But since Q_2 does adopt Q_1 one expects there to be "a firm measure of continuity" between the two, and so they should not be too sharply distinguished (1991, p. 214). He is unconvinced that there is a Q_3 layer to Q.

R.M. Price is in broad agreement with Doherty's view of Q. He gives reasons for thinking that its earliest form consisted solely of aphorisms and proverbs, with no narrative introductions (p. 163), and so presumably lacked references to time, place and circumstances. This inferred original collection conveys "not the personality of an individual, but of a movement, the sharp and humorous Cynic outlook on life." The maxims parallel those of various Cynic philosophers who lived in different centuries; and if these latter maxims "do not need to come from a single person, neither do those now attributed to Jesus" (p. 150). They will have originally constituted a collection which was either "unattributed" or else "ascribed to the Wisdom of God" (p. 163). Price explains the Jewish terms and concerns manifest in many Q sayings by supposing that the basic Cynic material of Q_1 came into the apocalyptic Jewish kingdom of God movement (represented in Q_2) via the "God Fearers"— those Gentiles who attached themselves to Hellenistic synagogues. (Arndt and Gingrich's Lexicon, art. sebō, describes them as "pagans who accepted the ethical monotheism of Judaism and attended the synagogue, but who did not obligate themselves to keep the whole Jewish law.") Jesus, to whom the later, expanded collection was in due course ascribed, may be "a fictive figurehead like King Solomon in the Book of Proverbs, the Wisdom of Solomon," and other works ascribed to him (p. 160). In sum, we can view the original Q as "a collection of originally anonymous Cynic sayings only later attributed to Jesus, just as the Cynic Epistles contain numerous Cynic teachings only subsequently given the names of famous Cynics including Crates, Socrates, and Diogenes" (p. 163).

This obviously incomplete account of the work of Doherty and Price perhaps suffices to show that they have both made a significant contribution to the question as to whether Q in fact justifies ascribing historicity to a Jesus who underlies some of the sayings material in the gospels. Their work is, of course, highly controversial. Even Q itself is not extant, but has to be reconstructed from the non-Markan material common to Matthew and Luke; and to divide it into multiple editions, specifying which of these are earlier and later, must be to some extent speculative. For J.J. Collins (as for Tuckett) the mixture of sapiental and apocalyptic material in Q does not mean that the former type must derive from an earlier stratum. He refers to texts which give "ample evidence" that the two kinds could be combined "in various ways." For instance, "the apocalyptic belief in eschatological judgment" can "provide a frame for ethical judgment by holding out the prospect of everlasting reward or punishment." Thus in the second Sibylline Oracle (a Christian adaptation of a Jewish oracle) sayings representing everyday wisdom have simply been inserted unadapted into an apocalyptic context, and made relevant to it with the words: "This is the contest, these are the prizes, these the rewards." This text, probably from the second century A.D., is "exceptional in many respects," yet "may serve as a warning that ancient writers could sometimes juxtapose materials that seem ideologically incompatible to us" (p. 228).

Particularly strong criticism of the stratification of Q has come from scholars like Ehrman who accept Schweitzer's view that Jesus was an apocalyptic prophet. Ehrman points out that "Q is chock-full of apocalyptic sayings on the lips of Jesus, sayings in which he predicts the imminent end of the age in a catastrophic act of judgement sent by God" (1999, p. 82). Naturally, those who accept such sayings as pronouncements of the historical Jesus do not take kindly to having them relegated to a secondary stratum of Q.

J.S. Kloppenborg Verbin, who has recently published a very full critical review of work on Q, is convinced that it can be divided into strata, but not because of any supposed incompatibility between 'prophetic' or 'apocalyptic' sayings and 'sapiental' ones (pp. 150f.). He also finds that at all levels the document presupposes a largely or exclusively Jewish audience (p. 256), and that "to suggest that the Q people might meaningfully be compared (*not* equated) with Cynics is *not* to deny their Israelite identity" (p. 443). Q, he says, "nowhere challenges circumcision (unlike Paul) or Sabbath observance (unlike Mark) and appears to assume as self-evident the distinction between Jews and Gentiles." The Q people thus probably "took for granted the principal distinguishing marks of Israelite identity," criticizing only those points that may well have been controverted in the Galilean population as a whole, namely "purity distinctions, tithing, and the role of Jerusalem and the Temple in social and religious economy of the north" (p. 256). Only at the final level of Q's stratification do the Torah and the Temple appear in a positive light (p. 213).

In *The Jesus Myth*, while recognizing that it is difficult to regard Q as all of a piece, I was prepared to work with an undivided Q as a datum, and it yielded a historical preacher in Galilee in the early first century. F.G. Downing, who likewise has not accepted any stratification of Q or "any sharp division between wisdom on the one hand and either prophecy or apocalyptic or both on the other," nevertheless insists (against Tuckett) that there certainly are Cynic, as well as Jewish elements in Q. Jesus, he says, maintained a rich heritage from "a diverse Judaism long open to Hellenism." It was, he adds, "a very eclectic age" (pp. 126f.).

It is not only the Q material (at any rate in its present form) that will have prompted the gospels' assigning of Jesus's life to the early first century. The evangelists will have known that Paul and his fellow apostles experienced their visions of the risen Jesus about the year 30, and so they naturally assumed that the crucifixion and resurrection had occurred shortly before. This was not expressly alleged by Paul, but it would seem plausible enough to evangelists writing outside Palestine, after earlier events there had been obscured from their view by the devastating war with Rome from A.D. 66. It was also easier to cope with deviant Christologies if Jesus's life could confidently be placed in specific historical circumstances. Gnosticism was describing Christ's redemptive work in mystical and quite unhistorical terms; and the so-called Docetes regarded flesh as sinful, and suffering and pain as incompatible with the divine nature. Hence they supposed that Jesus did not have a real human body, but lived on Earth as a phantom, incapable of any suffering. Against this, and against all kinds of gnosticism, it was helpful to be able to point to a quite definite historical situation in which Jesus had lived and suffered. It was in order to confute the Docetes that Ignatius of Antioch—the earliest Christian writer outside the canon to link Jesus with Pontius Pilate—insisted that he was truly born from a human mother, the virgin Mary, that he was dependent on food and drink, like any other man, and was "truly nailed to the cross" in the days of "Pontius Pilate and Herod the Tetrarch."

Once Pilate had been introduced to give the crucifixion a historical setting, most of the rest of the gospels' passion story was prompted by musing on what was taken for prophecy in the OT: "The details and individual scenes of the narrative do not rest on historical memory, but were developed on the basis of allegorical interpretation of Scripture" (Koester 1990, p. 224). The betrayal by Judas may serve as an example. Passages in the Psalms spoke of the righteous man as treated with brutal insolence by a close friend; and at Jn. 13:18 Jesus actually quotes Psalm 41:9 ("he that eateth my bread lifted up his heel against me") as "scripture" to be "fulfilled" by Judas. We recall that Paul had represented the crucifixion as effected by evil supernatural powers, the *archontes* (Satan and his acolytes), to whom God, not man, had delivered Jesus (above, pp. 2, 25f.). In the gospels, Judas is introduced as a human intermediary, but, as a residue from the original conception, Satan is said to have impelled him: "And Satan entered into Judas" (Lk. 22:3; cf. Jn. 13:27).

In my first books on Jesus, I argued that the gospel Jesus is an entirely mythical expansion of the Jesus of the early epistles.

The summary of the argument of *The Jesus Legend* (1996) and *The Jesus Myth* (1999a) given in this section of the present work makes it clear that I no longer maintain this position (although the change is perhaps not as evident from the titles of those two books as it might be). The weakness of my earlier position was pressed upon me by J.D.G. Dunn, who objected that we really cannot plausibly assume that such a complex of traditions as we have in the gospels and their sources could have developed within such a short time from the early epistles without a historical basis (Dunn 1985, p. 29). My present standpoint is: this complex is not all post-Pauline (Q, or at any rate parts of it, may well be as early as ca. A.D. 50); and—if I am right, against Doherty and Price—it is not all mythical. The essential point, as I see it, is that the Q material, whether or not it suffices as evidence of Jesus's historicity, refers to a personage who is not to be identified with the dying and rising Christ of the early epistles.

I remain critical of many of Dunn's arguments against me. He acknowledges what he calls a well-known "relative silence of Paul regarding the historical Jesus." But in this context of his criticism of me, he fails to note that it is not Paul alone who is thus silent, but all the earliest extant Christian writers; and he tries to account for Paul's silence by the familiar hypotheses that Paul "had little need or occasion to refer back to Jesus's earthly ministry," and could in any case take for granted that his addressees already knew all about it. To show that these explanations will not do was an important part of my task in *The Jesus Myth*, where I also had to counter (pp. 245ff.) the standard argument (often regarded as decisive, even by those who deprecate arguments from silence!) that, since ancient opponents of Christianity did not deny that Jesus existed, his crucifixion under Pilate can be taken as historical. What outsiders in the first century thought of Christianity we do not know, there being "no evidence at all for any views they may have held" of it (Downing, p. 142). Downing gives evidence that the first outsiders whose reactions are preserved for us in any detail regarded Christians as "followers of a Cynic philosophical lifestyle" (p. 145). It has repeatedly been noted that, by this time, men who were both teachers (Cynic or other) and miracle workers were familiar figures. Consequently, there was no reason why the historicity of anyone alleged to have been such a teacher should have been questioned.

When we come to Christian documents, in and outside the canon, which are known to have been written late enough for the gospels (or at any rate some of their underlying traditions) to have been current, then we do find clear allusions to relevant biographical material about Jesus in a way that is earlier unknown. These later documents, from the first half of the second century include, within the canon, 1 Timothy (one of the three Pastoral epistles ascribed to Paul but, as we saw (p. 35), generally admitted to be later compositions) and 2 Peter, probably the very latest of the twenty-seven canonical books. Outside the canon there are (as we saw) the epistles of Ignatius of Antioch, and also the short manual on morals and church practice known as the Didache, the epistles of Barnabas and Polycarp, the apocryphal Epistle of the Apostles, the Apology of Aristides and the surviving fragment of Quadratus's Apology— both these were addressed to Roman Emperors—the so-called second epistle of Clement (later than 1 Clement and by a different author), and the two Apologies of Justin Martyr. Justin, writing around A.D. 150, quotes from written gospels and is the first Christian writer to do so extensively.

Naturally, the documents in this large group do not all reflect the same elements or the same amount of biographical matter about Jesus, partly because their authors do not all have identical aims, and partly because older Christologies will have continued in some quarters when newer ones were emerging in others, particularly as we cannot assume complete inter-communion between different Christian centres. Nevertheless, significant biographical matter is present in all these writings. The epistle of Barnabas, for instance, states that Jesus was a teacher and miracle worker who appointed twelve to preach the gospel.

There is, then, no doubt that, in the first half of the second century, Christian writers refer to Jesus in a way quite unknown in the earlier documents. I have repeatedly insisted that, until this distinction is accepted as fundamental, there will be no adequate understanding of Christian origins.

Appeal is still sometimes made to Tacitus as having confirmed the gospels' story that Jesus suffered under Pontius Pilate. But the few pagan and Jewish references to Jesus are all too late to serve as such confirmation. The Catholic scholar J. P. Meier allows that Tacitus, and Pliny too, both writing ca. A.D. 112, "reflect what they have heard Christians of their own day say," and so are not "independent extracanonical sources." As for Jewish testimony, "no early rabbinic text . . . contains information about Jesus," and later ones "simply reflect knowledge of, and mocking midrash on, Christian texts and preaching" (p. 466). Meier does accept Josephus as an independent confirmatory source; but he too was writing the relevant book at a time (around A.D. 94) when at least some of the gospels were available, and at a place (Rome) where he could well have heard about Jesus from Christians. In any case, few allow that the obviously Christian words in the paragraph about Jesus in his Antiquities are from the pen of this orthodox Jew. Had he believed what is here ascribed to him, he would not have confined his remarks on Jesus and Christianity to a few lines (cf. the detailed discussion of both the Jewish and the pagan references in Chapter 4 of my 1999a book).

The theological world is now engaged in what is called "the third quest for the historical Jesus." Meier concedes that "all too often the first two quests were theological projects masquerading as historical projects" (p. 463). Critical theologians have long since ceased to accept that Jesus was born of a virgin and, as we shall see, a significant number of them no longer believe that he was resurrected. But that he 'suffered under Pontius Pilate' is still almost universally accepted as historical fact.

iii. Doing Without Jesus in the Second Century

We have seen that it is a significant fact that first-century Christian writers who pre-date or are early enough to be independent of the gospels fail to confirm what is said of Jesus in them. I have also noted that numerous post-gospel apologists—

Justin Martyr is an obvious example—defend Christianity in the way one would then expect, that is by drawing on gospel traditions about Jesus's birth, ministry, death, and resurrection. However, other apologists, also of the second century, write almost as if these traditions did not exist. Some of today's theologians (for instance, Wenham, p. 219) have seized on this as showing that the silence of the earliest Christian literature does not after all discredit these traditions. The argument is: if men who were writing when the gospels were certainly available can almost totally ignore their contents, then the silence of early missionaries about the traditions which are presumed to underlie the gospels need occasion no surprise; and so the gospel portraits of Jesus can still be taken as a reliable starting point for a reconstruction of Christian origins.

This reassuring finding can, however, be challenged by showing that, for the relevant second-century writers (who are in any case a minority in the way they ignore the Jesus tradition), Christianity was essentially a monotheistic philosophy, not a historically based religion. This is why some of them (Tatian and Theophilus, for instance) can—in marked contrast to the earliest (pre-gospel) missionaries with whom they are aligned in the argument I am criticizing—defend Christianity without even mentioning Jesus or Christ at all. A Jesuit scholar (quoted in Grant 1990, p. 69) has recorded with astonishment that nobody reading *Ad Autolycum* of Theophilus (ca. A.D. 180) would have the slightest idea that Christian doctrine had anything to do with the person of Christ. This alone shows how very different such writing is from the Pauline and most of the other pre-gospel literature; which, although it does not put Jesus into any specific historical situation, leaves one in no doubt that he is the person in whose atoning death and resurrection we are to believe

The earliest pagan critics of Christianity—Tacitus and Pliny—had regarded it as mere superstition, as, in the words of R.L. Wilken, "a foreign cult whose origin and practices stood outside of the accepted religious standards of the Greco-Roman world" (p. 79). But by the mid-second century it had begun to make an impact on some Greek and Roman intellectuals, so that, a little later, Galen could refer to it as a philosophical school among others of the time (Platonism, Stoicism, Epicureanism, etc.). Wilken observes that most of the second-century apologists were brought up as pagans and converted to Christianity only later in life, retaining as part of their thinking the intellectual world in which they had been educated (p. xv). He mentions a group of Christians in Rome in the late second century who sought a philosophic basis for their beliefs and who, as we learn from a document quoted by Eusebius, "put aside the holy scriptures of God" and sought instead for syllogisms (p. 78). Similarly, Justin Martyr's pupil Tatian offers—in his *Oration Against the Greeks*, his only work extant in full—a theory of creation and salvation that Drijvers has called "fundamentally philosophical, based on the anthropological concepts of contemporary Middle Platonism," the processes involved being accordingly "timeless" (p. 130). Hence he makes practically no appeal to the gospels; and when he mentions the incarnation—without naming Jesus, and saying merely that "God was born in the form of a man" (Chapter 21)—his purpose is only to defend its feasibility by comparison with pagan myths which he finds ridiculous.

Tatian of course knew the gospels. His *Diatessaron* consisted of chosen passages from them, beginning with the prologue to the fourth gospel. Even in his *Oration* he betrays knowledge of this prologue when he refers (Chapter 13) to "what was said" (*to eirēmenon*), namely "the darkness does not overcome the light." He here changes the past tense of Jn. 1:5 into the present because he characteristically takes the verse in a timeless sense, the darkness meaning man's ignorant soul and the light designating the Logos or Word of God.

Such indications that these apologists, although mainly silent about gospel material, were nevertheless acquainted with it, is another feature which sharply distinguishes them from first-century Christian writers other than the evangelists. It was of course the fourth gospel that most suited the philosophical leanings of the late second century. J.L. Houlden has noted (1973, p. 11) that this gospel came to be accepted from that time, not only because it had become associated with the name of a supposed eyewitness, but also because orthodox theology was increasingly being formulated in philosophical terms, which included in particular the Logos.

Athenagoras's *Plea for Christians* of ca. A.D. 177 typifies this tendency, in that it propounds a philosophical monotheism which accommodates the Logos and combines this with total silence about Christ, while nevertheless betraying knowledge of the gospels. Thus he declares that the Son of God is "the first begotten of the Father," but also "one" with him, being "the Word of the Father in ideal form and energizing power, for in his likeness and through him all things came into existence" (Chapter 10). At the same time, the author draws on the Sermon on the Mount (without naming it or saying who spoke it) for his specification of "the teachings on which we are brought up," namely: "I say to you, love your enemies, bless them who curse you, pray for them who persecute you, that you may be sons of your Father in heaven who makes his sun rise on the evil and the good and sends rain on the just and the unjust" (Chapter 11, reproducing Mt. 5:44–45). Again "it says"—the "it" can only be Mt. 5:28—that "he who looks at a woman to lust after her has already committed adultery in his heart" (Chapter 32). One certainly does not find quotations of this kind in the first-century documents. And it is really not surprising that Athenagoras should not own up even to the kenotic ('self-emptying') pre-gospel Christology of Paul (Phil. 2:7) and other early writers (who had made the earthly Jesus a Jew who lived and died in unspecified circumstances); for he was writing at a time when, as we know from Origen (*Contra Celsum*, 4:14), the pagan Celsus was castigating less philosophical Christians for believing in a deity who, although by definition immutable, nevertheless underwent change and alteration to live as a human being.

Even Theophilus, whose silence about Christ astounded the Jesuit commentator mentioned above, and who, in calling himself a Christian, explains the name as "being anointed with the oil of God" (*Ad. Aut.,* 1:12)—even he quotes gospel teachings, as when he reproduces Mt. 5:44 and 46 at 3:14: "The gospel says: Love your enemies, and pray for them that despitefully use you. For if you love them who love you, what reward have you? This do also the robbers and the publicans." He goes on to record that "it says: Let not your left hand know what your right hand doeth" (cf. Mt. 6:3).

The second-century apologist who carries furthest the tendency to dispense with any historical Jesus is Minucius Felix. His rigorous monotheism led him to ignore the scriptures altogether, and even to mount what is at best an equivocal defence of the crucifixion. Pagans had criticized Christians for worshipping as a god someone who had been born a man and died a death which would have shamed the lowest of mankind. Minucius Felix replies:

> When you ascribe to our religion the charge that Christians worship a crucified criminal, you are very far wide of the truth in supposing that a criminal deserved or that a mortal man had the right to be believed in as God. Pitiable indeed is the man whose hope is stayed upon a mortal man, with whose death all that he builds upon comes to an end. (*Octavius*, Chapter 29)

There is no mention here, or elsewhere in his Apology, of Christ's resurrection, even though the writer advocates the resurrection of the body and its future reward or punishment. Earl Doherty has pointed out[5] that the author even criticizes pagan beliefs with arguments which tell against cardinal Christian ones, as when he challenges pagans by asking: "What single individual has ever returned from the lower regions?" (Chapter 11). Again, criticizing the cult of Isis and Osiris, he asks: "Is it not absurd to mourn your object of worship, or to worship your object of mourning?" (Chapter 23).

Celsus's criticisms which I have mentioned suggest that apologists played down the human qualities and sufferings of Jesus because these were felt as an embarrassment—a point reiterated by E.R. Dodds.[6] Yet it was surely not all a matter of apologetic convenience. Deeply held convictions in a philosophical monotheism that must not be compromised were clearly also involved. Ramsay MacMullen (1984, pp. 21, 131n.15 and references) points in this connection to the example of the best known of all converts, the Emperor Constantine, for whom Jesus was "totally unimportant"—except in so far as he was God.

That a theocentric creed could—in contrast to a christocentric one—result in assigning a decidedly muted role to Jesus is evidenced even within the NT, in documents which, unlike those we have been considering, do name him and stress his importance. This is well illustrated by the contrast between the decidedly christocentric fourth gospel, and the theocentric epistles ascribed to John (not to be identified with the author of the gospel), particularly the first of these three letters, the only one of substance. Admittedly, it does state that Jesus Christ is our advocate with the Father, and is the expiation for the sins of the whole world, and that he is "the one who has come in the flesh," and "came by water and blood." Yet Judith Lieu's recent study shows how often statements in this epistle about 'him' are (in the Greek original, not necessarily in modern translations) ambiguous, in that they are as likely to refer to God as to Jesus (1991, p. 41). This ambiguity is present when, for instance, the writer insists on obedience to 'his' commands, in particular to the commandment to "love one another"—not as sublime as it sounds, as the context shows that only love of fellow members of the community addressed is implied, the cohesion of this community being the author's over-riding concern (pp. 55, 69). Professor Lieu finds that, while the writer insists that what is to be believed about Jesus is of fundamental importance, he gives little unambiguous indication of its substance. Belief in him as the Christ or the Son of God (two terms used as equivalents) is indeed "the recurring theme of the epistle. . . . Yet why this should be so and what it means is not clear." His "role in the life of believers is a remarkably muted one," and this is the reverse side of the epistle's "fundamentally theocentric expression of Christian experience" (1986, pp. 199f.).

Those who stress apologetic convenience as accounting for the theocentricism of the apologists can appeal to the manner in which Paul is represented in Acts as preaching to pagans. Whereas in his own letters he declares that the whole content of his preaching was Christ crucified (1 Cor. 2:2), his address to the Athenians (Acts 17:22–31) makes no mention of the cross, does not name Jesus, and is, as we shall see (below, p. 96), a monotheistic sermon, made only half-heartedly Christian by its conclusion.

I return to the starting point of this section. What has justly been called "the thinness of appeal to the Jesus tradition" in Pauline and other early epistles has been held by some not to militate against acceptance of that tradition, as it is represented in the gospels, since this thinness can be seen to continue in a significant number of second-century Christian writers who post-date the gospels. I have tried to show that these later writers were in an entirely different situation from Paul and other early Christian missionaries, and that most of the later writers, for all their unexpected silences, nevertheless betray an acquaintance with the Jesus tradition that is not to be found in the earlier ones.

iv. The Futile Appeal to Eyewitness Testimony

Conservative apologists continue to claim that the gospels' story is validated by eyewitness testimony. As the gospels are anonymous—indisputably so in the case of the first three—the claim can be substantiated only either by appeal to patristic statements about their origin, or by supposing that eyewitnesses, who both supplied the story and would have protested against invention, were around when they were written. The latter tactic is exemplified in Sir Norman Anderson's 1973 argument (which has lost none of its popularity) that Mark wrote when "a number of eyewitnesses must still have been alive, and many were still available who had heard the story direct from the eyewitnesses' own lips" (p. 44). This might be plausible conjecture if his gospel had been written in Palestine ca. A.D. 60. In fact it was not even addressed to Jews at all, but to an audience remote from Palestine (and so not in a position to evaluate what they were being told) to whom Jewish customs needed to be explained, and was authored by someone who himself had an imperfect grasp of them. Moreover, it was written at a time when the Jewish war with Rome (A.D. 66–70) had devastated Palestine, so that for an outsider to have gleaned anything like accurate information about someone who had preached there in the 30s would have been extremely difficult. Mark's ignorance even of Palestine geography is notorious.

Much of this can be found stated in almost any non-fundamentalist account of the NT. Kümmel, for instance, in his standard handbook, writes, criticizing the traditional view that this gospel was written by the Jerusalemite John Mark of Acts:

> The author obviously has no personal knowledge of Palestinian geography, as the numerous geographical errors show. He writes for Gentile Christians, with sharp polemic against the unbelieving Jews. He does not know that the account of the death of the Baptist (6:17ff.) contradicts Palestinian customs. Could a Jewish Christian from Jerusalem miss the fact that 6:35ff. and 8:1ff. are two variants of the same feeding story? (p. 97). What we can learn from the material that lies behind Mark and his composing of it in no way leads us back to eyewitnesses as the chief bearers of the tradition (p. 94). Mark is probably based on no extensive written sources. . . . More likely the evangelist has woven together small collections of individual traditions and detailed bits of tradition into a more or less coherent presentation. (p. 85)

B.D. Ehrman's recently published historical introduction to early Christian writings is equally instructive, and says of Mark:

> We do not know who the author was, only that he was a Greek-speaking Christian, presumably living outside of Palestine, who had heard a number of stories about Jesus (p. 60). The first readers of this Gospel appear to have been the Christians of Mark's community, most of whom would have been illiterate, and thus 'read' the Gospel by hearing it read. They evidently resided outside of Palestine and had Greek as their primary language. There are clues in the Gospel that most of them had not converted to Christianity from Judaism, the most striking of which comes in 7:3–4, where Mark has to explain the Pharisaic custom of washing hands before eating for ceremonial cleansing. Presumably, if his audience were Jewish, they would already know this custom, and Mark would not have to explain it. What is even more intriguing is the fact that Mark appears to misunderstand the practice: he claims

that it was followed by "all the Jews." We know from ancient Jewish writings that this is simply not true. For this reason, many scholars have concluded that Mark himself was not Jewish. (2000, p. 74)

Ehrman adds, as is normally reassuringly done in such writing, that "many of the oral traditions found in this Gospel must [sic] go back to the earliest followers of Jesus." But this is a far cry from authentication of key elements, such as the resurrection, by eyewitness testimony. Norman Anderson, however, believed, as James Barr says in criticism of him, that the NT gives such strong historical evidence for this event that "no one could question" its actuality except "biblical scholars who (apart from conservatives) have been indoctrinated with false presuppositions" (p. 257).

Anderson writes as a highly educated person whose learning is not in theology (he was a lawyer), and who, as Barr has said specifically of him, "has no understanding of what modern theology is about and hates everything to do with it" (p. 160). His present-day counterpart is Professor J.W. Montgomery, who mounts similar arguments and also, as I shall show, relies extensively on patristic statements about the gospels.

Montgomery is an internationally known barrister, and also a Lutheran minister. His numerous tapes, articles, booklets and books have had a strong impact. The well-known apologist Josh McDowell—whose *Evidence that Demands a Verdict* (reprinted many times since 1981) claims "over a million copies in print worldwide"—refers to him as "the one who has stimulated my thinking about history."

I have criticized Montgomery at length in *The Jesus Legend*, but am returning to him here because my purpose is to show how plausible what such apologists say can look if one comes upon it without detailed knowledge of early Christianity. Many convinced Christians will be glad to seize on such material and worried doubters will find it reassuring. Neither group is likely to put the arguments to much of a test.

Since so many modern theologians have voiced substantial criticism of the NT, Montgomery (writing in 1993 in the

American Catholic Journal *New Oxford Review*) deplores reliance on any of them, "whether liberal or conservative," for information about its reliability. He insists that we be beholden instead to the primary sources, the early Christian texts themselves. He does not allow that critical theologians have reached their conclusions from careful study of these very sources, but, like Anderson, thinks they have been led astray by irrelevant philosophical premises, such as the dogma that miracles cannot possibly occur. It is however to be noted that he himself nevertheless relies extensively on theologians—on the ones, namely, who have continued to defend the most traditional and conservative views of the documents (for example Theodor Zahn, the fundamentalist J.G. Machen, and F.F. Bruce). It is also noteworthy that when he appeals to what he regards as primary material, it sometimes turns out to be not primary at all, but to consist of statements by second-century bishops, notably Papias, who wrote around A.D. 130 (as Montgomery himself says in his 1971 Inter-Varsity Press booklet *History and Christianity*, p. 32), and Irenaeus, who is known to have written around A.D. 180.

Irenaeus is clearly too late to be plausibly regarded as a primary source. His desire to establish the continuity of Christian tradition is apparent when he says that Luke was "a follower (*sectator*) and disciple of the apostles." He inferred this probably from Lk. 1:3, where the evangelist claims to have "followed all (*pasin*) accurately from the first." Here *pasin* could grammatically be either masculine or neuter, and so might mean 'all people' or 'all things'. Irenaeus will have taken it in the former sense and so made Luke a disciple of all the apostles. But this does not fit well here with the adverb 'accurately'. It makes better sense to speak of following (meaning 'investigating') a series of events accurately than to speak of following people accurately. Hence the RV (together with other translations) renders the passage as: "having traced the course of all things accurately from the first"; and C.F. Evans, in his valuable 1990 commentary on Luke's gospel, concludes his discussion of Irenaeus's claim by calling it "plainly false" (p. 8).

Second-century and later tradition made Luke into a companion of Paul (wrongly, as we shall see in Chapter 2 below);

and both Irenaeus and Tertullian declared Luke to have committed to writing the gospel preached by Paul. Origen even held that, when Paul spoke of "my gospel" (Rom. 2:16), he meant the gospel of Luke. But the word 'gospel' did not come to signify a book until the middle of the second century. In earlier Christian writing it means "the proclamation of the saving message about Christ or the coming of the kingdom" (Koester 1989, p. 380). In any case, Paul's preaching, as embodied in his extensive epistles, has practically no overlap with the substance of Luke's gospel, and tells us practically nothing about the life of Jesus. Nevertheless, Montgomery—quoting Irenaeus *Against Heresies*, iii, 1, in his 1971 booklet, pp. 33f.—confidently declares that Luke's gospel derives from Paul.

For Irenaeus, the fourth gospel and the first of the three epistles ascribed in the canon to 'John' were authored by an immediate disciple of the Lord (iii, 16, 5). Montgomery concurs, quoting 1 Jn. 1:1 in support:

> That which was from the beginning, that which we have heard, that which we have seen with our eyes, that which we beheld, and our hands handled, concerning the Word of life . . .

"At first reading and traditionally," says Houlden, "this passage has always been taken as clear evidence that the Epistle is the work of an eyewitness of Jesus's life." But "in common with most modern critics," he finds that "this is not so" (1973, p. 52). Jesus is not here designated 'one whom we have heard, seen and touched', since the relevant pronoun is, in Greek, neuter, not masculine. "That which was heard, seen and handled is not Jesus, the Son . . . but that (thing: neuter) which was from the beginning . . . concerning the word of life" (Lieu 1991, p. 23). Lieu adds: "Most would see in that neuter a reference instead to the preaching which makes available the original witness experience." The reference, then, is not to Jesus, but to the truth about his life and work—an interpretation required also by 'concerning' (near the end of the verse). Strecker's recent commentary notes that the whole of this epistle—he calls it a "homily in the form of a letter"—"betrays no knowledge of any tradition about the life of Jesus" (1996, pp. 3, 5, 14), and so is certainly not what an eyewitness of it would have written.

I will deal in more detail with Papias, for Montgomery declares (in the May 1994 number of the *New Oxford Review*) that "Papias, a disciple of the Apostle John himself, informs us of the primary-source authorship of all four gospels as told to him personally by John." Readers are likely to assume that Montgomery knows of what he speaks. Let us see whether the evidence supports him.

Although Papias's writings have not survived, the early fourth-century bishop and ecclesiastical historian Eusebius knew them, and assures us that Papias himself, "according to the preface of his treatises, makes plain that he had in no way been a hearer and eyewitness of the sacred apostles." Eusebius goes on to show, by quoting him, that Papias obtained his information very indirectly: Jesus spoke to his disciples, they to presbyters (Elders), the presbyters to their followers, and these (at last) to Papias. They told him what the original disciples "had said" (i.e. way back in the past), and what the presbyters "were [now] saying." The contrast between the two tenses (in English pluperfect and imperfect, in the Greek aorist and present because of Greek conventions concerning reported speech) indicates that the original disciples were no longer alive to give witness, whereas the presbyters were still there to talk to their followers who, in turn, talked to Papias.[7] In this very indirect way he received a good deal of what even Eusebius considered to be very obviously legendary information about Jesus.

One reason why, in spite of all this, Montgomery manages to put Papias into direct contact with the apostle John is that he identifies the latter with one of the presbyters, whom Papias also names as John: "Papias writes on the basis of information obtained from the 'Elder' (Apostle) John" (*History and Christianity*, p. 32. Further page references to Montgomery are to this booklet). But Papias had distinguished these two men, as Eusebius goes out of his way to record. The following two passages from the latter's *Ecclesiastical History* (iii, 39) make this clear.

First, Papias himself, quoted by Eusebius:

If ever anyone came who had followed the presbyters, I inquired
into the words of the presbyters, what Andrew or Peter or Philip
or Thomas or James or John or Matthew, or any other of the Lord's
disciples, had said, and what Aristion and the presbyter John, the
Lord's disciples, were saying.

Now Eusebius's comment on this:

It is here worth noting that he twice counts the name of John and
reckons the first John with Peter and James and Matthew and the
other apostles, clearly meaning the evangelist, but by changing his
statement places the second with the others outside the number of
the apostles, putting Aristion before him and calling him a presbyter.

Montgomery feels entitled to ignore this distinction between
apostles and presbyters presumably because, although Eusebius
uses the word 'apostles', Papias does not, but calls both these
groups "disciples of the Lord" (see the above quotation), thus
enabling apologists to blur the distinction he has made between
immediate disciples and later ones.

As for the claim that the apostle told Papias about all four
gospels, there is no reason to believe that the latter knew anything of the gospels of Luke or John; for Eusebius (iii, 3)
promises to record what ecclesiastical writers had said about
canonical and other writings, yet gives no statements from
Papias about these two gospels, and tells us only what he had
said about the gospels of Mark and Matthew. (I have discussed,
in *The Jesus Legend*, the claims Papias made for them.) It is hard
to believe that Eusebius knew and withheld statements about
the other two. Papias knew of the apostle John as a link in the
train of tradition about Jesus, but not as the author of a gospel.
His concern to ascertain what John "had said" does not suggest
that he believed him to have written a gospel. Montgomery and
I agree that the gospel now called that of John existed well
before A.D. 130. But commentators have shown—I give the
details in *The Jesus Myth*—that it was not ascribed to John until

late in the second century, and was earlier widely ignored because of the use which gnostic heretics were making of it.

If we want a document which really links the fourth gospel with Papias, we have to turn to its so-called Anti-Marcionite prologue. Marcion was formally excommunicated in Rome in A.D. 144, and some manuscripts of the fourth gospel in the Latin Vulgate which date from the eighth century or later include a prologue which mentions him as a heretic and also states that Papias was a "dear disciple" of the apostle John and wrote his gospel at his dictation. I quote an English translation:

> The gospel of John was revealed and given to the churches by John while yet in the body, as one Papias of Hierapolis, a dear disciple of John, has reported . . . Indeed, he took down the gospel in writing while John dictated. But Marcion the heretic was justly cast out *by John* after having been disapproved by him because of his adverse opinions . . . (Italics added)

Scholars now date this prologue at around. A.D. 400 or even later, and its author obviously had no accurate idea of the second-century situation; otherwise he would not have said that Marcion was cast out—in the year 144!—by John, who was already a grown man ca. A.D. 30. Moreover, the gospel now ascribed to him was not written by Papias at its author's dictation: otherwise the silence of both Irenaeus and Eusebius as to any such thing would be inexplicable. Papias himself, as quoted by Eusebius, even declares that he was concerned to inform himself about Jesus from oral tradition rather than from books: "I did not suppose that information from books would help me so much as the word of a living and surviving voice." This makes it hard to believe that he was the person responsible for putting a substantial gospel into written form.

Conservative apologists have tried to salvage the Anti-Marcionite prologue by deleting the words 'by John'. If a radical scholar defended a position by such tampering with a text, the conservatives would be the first to protest. They nevertheless have here supposed either that the words 'by John' have erroneously crept in and replaced the name of a Roman bishop who effected Marcion's rejection, or that these two words have been gratuitously added to the original document which, without them, made Papias responsible for the rejection. Neither of these two proposals is convincing. They leave us asking why a prologue to the gospel of John should speak of Marcion at all if John was not supposedly involved in the Marcion affair.[8]

Montgomery does not, in the publications to which I have referred, give reasons for identifying the apostle with his presbyter namesake, or for the claim that Papias knew the apostle and was assured by him of the authenticity of all four gospels. These are simply stated as facts, and the unwary reader is unlikely to question them. He or she might in any case find it laborious to assemble and scrutinize the relevant material, as I have done here.

In the NT itself, as against what is said by second-century bishops, claims to be eyewitnesses (or close to them) are made only in the later of its twenty-seven books, although Montgomery tells us that such claims are made "time and time again" throughout it (pp. 29f. He seems incapable of putting his case without overstating it). They occur notably in the final, appended chapter to the fourth gospel, and in 2 Peter, which is almost universally regarded both as pseudonymous and as the very latest NT book, written only in the second century (cf. pp. 121f. below). R.T. France declares, in his 1993 survey of *Evangelical Anglicans*, that today few even among evangelical Christians would try to defend its Petrine authorship with any enthusiasm. (He obviously does not reckon with Montgomery and his like.) Appeal is often made to the Acts of the Apostles, where the Twelve are represented as having been eyewitnesses to Jesus's ministry—but by an author who, himself anonymous, was writing after the completion of the gospel now ascribed to Luke, which is itself later than Mark's, which is in turn later than the Pauline letters, which no one takes as eyewitness records. Moreover the claims in Acts to eyewitness authenticity are made notably in speeches put into Peter's mouth—speeches which, as we shall see (below pp. 90f.), suffice to convert large numbers of Jerusalem Jews in the 30s by presenting them with arguments based on passages from the Septuagint (the Greek translation of the OT), even though these distort the Hebrew originals—as if such an audience would have been impressed by mistranslations of its own scriptures.

D.E. Nineham notes, in the second of his three valuable 1977 articles on 'Eyewitness Testimony and the Gospel Tradition': "According to our sources, those who chiefly moved about among the Gentile churches and supervised their development were, apart from Paul himself," persons "such as Barnabas and Timothy, Titus and Tychicus, Priscilla, Aquila, and Apollos, none of them eyewitnesses and one at least [Apollos] not very well up in the tradition" (p. 47). He also notes that anyone who reads 1 Corinthians—one of the very earliest documents—cannot doubt that the members of the primitive churches were enthusiasts who received messages from the risen Christ exalted to heaven, and will have been little concerned with accurate information about Jesus's life on Earth. Like the modern Pentecostals who model themselves on them, they supposed that they "had the power, mind and spirit of the exalted Christ," were "inspired by him in all their activities" and hence surely also in "the preserving, telling and hearing of the tradition of his earthly life, death and resurrection, especially as that tradition was so closely connected with liturgy and cult."

If, however, we grant to Montgomery that the gospels and the epistles of Peter, John, and so forth were all written by people who recorded what they themselves (or those close to them) had seen and heard, then—so he argues (p. 61)—we cannot plausibly query their accounts; for if we do, we shall, he says, be obliged to accept one or other of obviously unacceptable consequences; namely either that Jesus himself deluded these authors by making excessive claims about his own status; or that they seriously misunderstood or deliberately misrepresented him. The latter was the position into which Reimarus felt himself driven in the 1770s. Because he held fast to the belief that the gospels were written by eyewitnesses, and because he yet saw that their resurrection narratives are teeming with contradictions, he decided that the disciples must have stolen the body from the grave and then circulated, with slender agreement, stories that there had been a resurrection. Strauss pointed out, as long ago as 1861, that it is absurd to suppose in this way that they knew that there was no word of truth in their accounts, and yet proclaimed them with a conviction that sufficed to change the world.

Conservative Christians are today very understandably vociferous in defending not only their doctrines but the whole lifestyle based on them that has, really quite suddenly, become seriously threatened. The sociologist Steve Bruce, commenting on the abrupt change in the American scene, observes: "Conservative Protestants of the 1950s were offended by girls smoking in public. In the late 1960s girls were to be seen on newsfilm dancing naked at open-air rock concerts" (1990, p. 22). My main concern in this section has been to show how conservative apologists can mount a seemingly strong case for their religious doctrines—provided one does not look behind the scenes, which they do not help one to do. Their arguments may well impress not only those who already believe, or half believe, but even many of the uncommitted who are perhaps worried about modern 'permissiveness' and ill-defended against evangelical lobbying because they know little of the NT (or of early patristic literature) and who do not respond to evangelical blandishments by studying it in detail and supplementing such reading with perusal of scholarly commentaries not written from exclusively conservative premisses.

v. The Believer's Predicament

If the average person is asked what is to be understood by 'early Christian testimony', he or she will most likely point to the gospels and to the record in Acts of the early church. My purpose in this chapter has been to indicate that this testimony is very questionable because it is neither the earliest nor confirmed by the earliest, with which it is in significant respects even at variance. Additionally, many theologians who would not dream of basing anything on the cleavage between the earliest testimony and that of the gospels—or even of accepting that there is such a cleavage—have shown, from scrutiny of the gospels themselves, how unreliable they are, although at the same time they are invariably accepted as providing some authentic information about Jesus. Morna Hooker, for instance, writing from the Lady Margaret Chair of Divinity at Cambridge, addresses the question "How much can we know about the historical Jesus?" in an article where she calls the gospels Christian "propaganda," and hence questionable as sources concerning Jesus's character and career. Yet she finds their "evidence" for his having performed healing miracles to be "overwhelming," confirmed as it is by what is said of him in the Talmud—admittedly only "several centuries later" (pp. 21f., 27). This whole argument betrays how necessary it is to distinguish between on the one hand the Jesus of the gospels (and of the Q underlying two of them, which does include two miracle stories and a general statement crediting Jesus with miraculous powers) and on the other the Jesus of the early epistles. In none of these latter (which are not so much as mentioned in Morna Hooker's article), nor in the letters of the earliest fathers (Clement of Rome, Ignatius of Antioch, and Polycarp of Smyrna), is there any suggestion that Jesus had worked miracles of any kind, even though in some of these documents, miracles are regarded as of great importance for the spread of the Christian message. Thus "the power of signs and wonders," "signs, wonders and mighty works," and "signs and wonders and manifold powers" are predicated of Christian missionaries (Rom. 15:19; 2 Cor. 12:12; Hebrews 2:4), and 2 Thess. 2:9 speaks of satanic counter-demonstrations with "all power and signs and lying wonders." Only when we come to Acts do we find this standing terminology applied to Jesus himself in Peter's description of him (2:22) as "a man approved of God unto you by mighty works and wonders and signs which God did by him in the midst of you." It would seem, then, that powers which from the first were accredited to the missionary preachers were only later ascribed to Jesus himself—surely as a result of a radical change in Christology, involving the abandonment of the Pauline view that he had lived an obscure life of inconspicuous humiliation. As for the late statement in the Talmud that he had been condemned for "sorcery," it is relevant to note that hostile commentators would meet allegations that someone had worked miracles by denigrating them in this way, not by denying that they had been worked at all, since belief in miracles was, in antiquity, part of the way in which reality was comprehended. As Morna Hooker herself points out, this is how Jesus's Jewish enemies are represented as responding to his miracles even in the gospels: "By the prince of the devils casteth he out the devils" (Mk. 3:22).

I have written in some detail on the gospels in earlier books, and here will note only that, as early as 1835, Strauss set aside as mythical Jesus's virginal conception and birth in Bethlehem, the star of Bethlehem, his temptation, his transfiguration, the miraculous cures, the resuscitations of dead people, the feeding of the five thousand, the turning of water into wine, the passion predictions, the details of the passion story (the triumphal entry, the scene in Gethsemane, the words from the cross, the spear thrust into Jesus's side, the burial in a tomb owned by Joseph of Arimathea, the setting of guards over the tomb), the appearances of the risen Christ (as mystical visions without a base in reality) and the ascension. All this was found shocking at the time, but the Finnish theologian Heikki Räisänen, commenting on it, observes:

> Today one could glean a very similar list from almost any non-fundamentalist book on Jesus, with the exception perhaps of the triumphal entry and the burial; and of course the interpretation of the Easter visions is a most controversial issue. (Räisänen 2000, p. 231)

That this latter controversy produces much that undermines the traditional creeds is apparent from recent contributions to it by Lüdemann[9] and by the Protestant NT scholars Leslie Houlden and A.J.M. Wedderburn. Houlden is in no doubt that, as we move from the resurrection story in one gospel to that of the next, we are "confronted by a process of development in the telling of a story"—a development clearly prompted not by uncontrolled imagination but by theological motives. Thus Mark's "young man" at the tomb on Easter morning becomes, in Matthew, an angel who rolls away the stone—in Mark the visitors found it already "rolled back"—and seats himself on it.

Matthew is concerned not only to give, in this way, "more impressive authority" for the claim that Jesus rose, but also, by introducing guards to the sepulchre, to "quell accusations from the ill-disposed that the disciples simply stole the corpse." The apocryphal Gospel of Peter, "written perhaps a few decades later," seeks to quell all doubt by including a description of Jesus emerging from the tomb escorted by angels, in the presence of the awe-struck guards. Such developments, says Houlden, illustrate that the gospels are not "plain history" but "theological history" (1991, pp. 35–37). The development, as one moves from earlier to later documents, of the traditions formative for Christian theology is something I am much concerned to illustrate in the present book.

Turning now to Wedderburn, we find him confessing that "the result of a historical investigation into the traditions of Jesus's resurrection seems to yield little that is of much use for Christian faith." He urges "a reverent agnosticism" as to "whether anything in fact happened at Easter above and beyond what went on in the minds of the followers of Jesus" (1999, pp. 95, 98, 112). In accordance with the title of his book, he wants to move 'beyond resurrection' to "a faith that is thoroughly this-worldly," which questions whether Jesus or anyone else can survive death (pp. 134, 167). This and much else in the book goes quite against what is witnessed in the NT; yet Jesus, as there witnessed, remains the author's "primary orientation point" (p. 108). It is not surprising that, as a result of such "wrestlings with faith and understanding," he finds "both God and reality most mysterious" (p. 216). It is surely because she knows what emerges from the kind of detailed study of the texts typified in Wedderburn's book that Morna Hooker retreats into faith, declaring that "no amount of historical investigation" can prove the church's proclamation of the resurrection to be true, and that "the living Lord is encountered only by those who believe" (p. 31).

Faced with the destructive results of such scrutiny of the records, the systematic theologian commonly resorts to two ploys. The first consists of psychological improvisation. John Macquarrie, Emeritus Professor of Divinity at Oxford, exemplifies this when he calls knowledge of persons fundamentally distinct from knowledge of things. It is not merely a question of knowing different entities (sometimes with more emotional involvement in the one case than in the other), but of quite different kinds of knowledge—a knowing which "involves the whole person" of the knower, as against "more detached and observational kind of knowing" (p. 82). He quotes Martin Buber: "The primary word I-Thou"—as opposed to "I-it" can only be spoken with the whole being" (p. 88). Two pages later the former kind of knowledge figures not as involving 'the whole person', but as "gained from what may be called the total human experience." It is held to provide more fundamental information than the other kind, to which "positivistic prohibitions . . . characteristic of the twentieth century" (p. 97) would fain restrict us. It includes "spiritual discernment," insights which "cannot be demonstrated by argument," but which nevertheless enable us to see "in depth beneath the outward phenomena to their inward constitutive meaning." By means of such insights we come to know "the inner or ultimate reality of Jesus" (pp. 81, 87), what it is in him which makes him more than merely human.

Spiritual discernment is also involved in the second ploy. Macquarrie needs it to counter his admission that some of the words ascribed to Jesus in the gospels were not spoken by him, but put into his mouth by the early church, and—even more damaging—that it is not now possible to know exactly which words fall into which of these two categories. But this "does not matter" (p. 86) because Michael Ramsey (Archbishop of Canterbury in the 1960s) assured us that "the fact of Christ includes the fact of the church" (p. 95). Macquarrie endorses this with the comment that "the church was the community of the risen Christ, dependent on his Spirit and speaking in his name" (p. 86). The argument is not felt to be impaired by some admitted questioning about 'the risen Christ' ("We do not know enough . . . to be able to explain what happened on Easter Day," p. 112). Moreover, the voice of the Spirit is of continuing importance: "Our assurance of the reality of Christ and of his saving power does not rest primarily on the testimony of the

New Testament witnesses, but on the present experience of Christ in his church" (p. 96). Charles Gore, who later became bishop of Oxford, had written similarly in 1889, and for the same reason, namely awareness that scholarly criticism of the scriptures could no longer be brushed aside. "Belief in the Holy Scriptures as inspired," he said, "requires to be held in context by [i.e. must be admitted to be dependent on] the belief in the general action of the Holy Spirit upon the Christian society and the individual soul." That my interpolation between the brackets is just is shown by his next sentence: "It is, we may perhaps say, becoming more and more difficult to believe in the Bible without believing in the Church" (p. 338). Historical criticism has certainly made the going rough, in so far as this going depends on the NT. So it is convenient to introduce 'the Spirit' to authenticate what we want. It is a long-standing practice. Irenaeus declared, in his *Against Heresies* (iii, 24.1): "Where the church is, there also is the Spirit of God," and "the Spirit is truth" (this latter proposition quoted by him here from 1 Jn. 5:7). Deviants from what was accepted as orthodoxy were dismissed as "sensual, having not the Spirit" (Jude, 19). Convinced of this, the church for many centuries enforced its doctrines by brutal and quite unspiritual methods.[10]

Reliance on the Spirit does however have the disadvantage that it makes the theologian of today almost defenceless against the excesses of Pentecostals. Theirs is not a movement with intellectual pretensions, but—as is charmingly stated in the Foreword to Dempster's recent symposium—"a tradition uneasy with the academic enterprise." It is pointless to argue with people who, insofar as they interpret scripture at all, do so, according to this symposium, "unencumbered by the quest for dispassionate objectivity," and whose main concern is personal encounter with the Holy Spirit, evidenced in their speaking with tongues and other ecstatic behaviour. "Tongues," the same authority tells us, "allow the poor, uneducated and illiterate among the people of God to have an equal voice with the educated and literate" (pp. 12, 18). At Toronto their responses to the divine afflatus are notorious, and are characterized in the symposium as "rather unusual and unprecedented in revival history"

(p. 266)—a very restrained allusion to the roaring like lions and barking like dogs which has distinguished the "blessing" of the Holy Spirit in the congregation there. The insouciance of such people to problems posed by scripture is coupled with supreme confidence in their own convictions. A Catholic observer of the Latin American scene notes, again in this symposium, that, whereas Catholics and their priests seem inhibited, "Pentecostals go audaciously from house to house." They are certainly a force to be reckoned with, and, with their 450 million adherents, now comprise almost half the number of Roman Catholics, who themselves form the largest Christian denomination (pp. 131, 140).

2

The Acts of the Apostles: A Historical Record?

i. The Author and His Book

The author of Acts begins by calling it a sequel to his "former treatise," and this latter is the gospel we know as Luke's, for (among other reasons) Acts follows Luke where Luke differs from the other gospels—for instance in alleging (4:27) that Jesus was tried by Herod Antipas as well as by Pilate. For convenience I shall call the author of both the gospel and Acts 'Luke', although we do not know who he was, since both books are anonymous.[1] That they are both dedicated to the same person (Theophilus) does not mean that they must have been issued with their author's name,[2] as one might reasonably expect if they had been letters (e.g. 'Luke to Theophilus, greetings'); and their ascription to the Luke who was supposedly a companion of Paul is dubious tradition.[3]

Harnack and others argued that Acts displays such medical knowledge that it must surely derive from "Luke the beloved physician" of Coloss. 4:14. But the American NT scholar J.H. Cadbury showed that Lucian of Samosata and Philo of Alexandria had more medical knowledge than the author of Acts, although they were certainly not doctors.[4] Many of the words adduced as medical in Acts could be used non-technically in the ordinary, unlearned discourse of those days. For instance, in the biblical language beloved of Luke—nearly ninety percent of the vocabulary of Acts is represented in the Septuagint—Paul is made to curse a magician: "Behold the hand of the Lord is upon thee and thou shalt be blind for a season." The text continues: "And immediately there fell on him a mist and a darkness" (13:11). *achlus* (mist) could, as a medical term, mean an inflammation of the eyes which clouds vision. But Haenchen, with characteristic humour, observed (1971, p. 400) that Luke was surely stylist enough to realize that, in commenting on Paul's solemn, biblically-worded curse, it would be inappropriate to say something like:

And then God immediately afflicted him with acute conjunctivitis.

Whoever wrote Acts was no companion of Paul, for its account, even of his movements, let alone of his theology, is quite incompatible with what we learn from Paul's own letters. The Zürich theologian P.W. Schmiedel pointed out, a full hundred years ago, that, although a companion might conceivably have had an imperfect grasp of this complex theology, he "would at least be familiar with the events recorded in the epistles— events with which the representation in Acts is inconsistent."[5] Acts is, for instance, unaware that Paul spent three years in Arabia and Damascus immediately after his conversion and prior to his first visit to Jerusalem as a Christian (Gal. 1:15–18), and this has very adversely affected its account of his relations with the Jerusalem apostles.[6] Acts is also unaware of his turbulent relations with the Christians of Corinth which led to several visits there.[7] As for Pauline theology, Kümmel thinks it perhaps hazardous to suppose that any of Paul's companions understood much of its complexities (p. 181)! Nevertheless, if Luke had known the epistles he would surely have understood it better than to represent Paul as not only helping to compose but also to distribute (16:4) a decree which made some stipulations of the Jewish law necessary for salvation. Barrett, as the author of the most recent critical commentary on Acts, is quite adamant that the real Paul could never have done this (1998, pp. xliv, cxv); and Kümmel agrees that the author of Acts is so totally misinformed about Paul that he could not have travelled with him.

Acts also trivializes Paul's reason for breaking with Barnabas. A companion would have known that Barnabas incurred his wrath for his "insincerity" (*hupokrisis*) in joining Cephas's withdrawal from table fellowship with gentile Christians at Antioch (Gal. 2:13). But according to Luke the two men parted because Barnabas thought John Mark a suitable companion for their next missionary journey from Antioch, and Paul did not (15:36–41). We need not suppose that Luke was suppressing what he knew to be an unsavoury truth. He knew that Barnabas and John Mark had worked together, earlier with Paul (13:5) and later without him; so he readily inferred that it was a disagreement about the suitability of this assistant that had divided the two leaders.

Luke never suggests that Paul had written any letters at all. That he knew the epistles but deliberately ignored them is very unlikely. As Vielhauer observes (p. 407), a writer who does so much to glorify Paul would hardly have acted in a way that would have discredited his letters. In some cases, as in the instance over Barnabas, Luke clearly had some relevant information, and made inferences from it which were quite reasonable for someone who had to make sense of it without access to the epistles. (Further examples—drawn from Haenchen's commentary on Acts, which is still by far the best—are given in my *The Historical Evidence for Jesus*, pp. 154ff.)

The accuracy of Acts has often been defended on the ground that the author was well informed about administration and travel conditions as they were in the Roman Empire of the first century. But as Barrett has noted, "oddly it is on Christian matters that he is most open to criticism" (1998, p. liii).

As for dates, Acts is a sequel to the gospel of Luke, which is itself a rewriting of Mark's gospel—a rewriting which introduces allusions to the siege and destruction of Jerusalem in A.D. 70, and even intimates that, at the time of writing, these events may not then have been very recent.[8] If Mark wrote around 70, Luke's gospel can be put at 80 or 90, and Acts at 90 or 100. With this, Kümmel (p. 186) and many others agree. A later date is not feasible, for Clement of Rome, Ignatius of Antioch, and Polycarp of Smyrna all knew Pauline letters, and if Acts were later than around 100, its author would have known them too.

Acts does not, however, cover church history up to the author's own time, but depicts only Christianity's path from Jerusalem to Rome, the heroic period when the church was still an ideal and completely harmonious community whose members initially shared possessions, were widely respected and to some extent safeguarded by a plenitude of miracles.

Such safeguarding is the point of the story of Peter's miraculous slaying of Ananias and Sapphira for trivial fraud (5:1–11)—a pericope altogether repulsive to modern sentiment, the more so because the penalty is implemented by one who, at Mk. 14:66–71 and its parallel in Matthew, had committed the greater crime of denying his master with curses. The fate of Ananias and Sapphira shows the church to be a realm of holiness which kills unholy people who lay hands on it (Conzelmann 1971, p. 22). This story also conflicts with the generalization of 2:44 that "all that believed . . . had all things in common"; for the couple were reproached on the ground that they should have handed over all the money from the sale of their goods or none at all, as the surrender was voluntary. The sharing of possessions was obviously not a feature of first-century Christianity as a whole. Paul's letters show that it was not established in his congregations; and Luke intended it only as an illustration of the ideal uniqueness of the very earliest days, not as a norm for his own time. He himself shows that it did not last, for when at 11:29 the disciples decide to send relief to the brethren in Judea, "there is no longer any suggestion of pooling capital . . . The Christians are engaging in business and some at least were prospering—*euporeito*, had plenty" (Barrett 1994, p. 565).

Luke's portrait of the church's earliest days was not conscious idealization, but was how he, and Christians generally of the early second century, will have viewed the original period. This picture is poles apart from that which emerges from the epistles of Paul, who was actually involved in the acrimonious factional strife which truly characterized those early days. As Barrett observes: when Acts was written, Paul, Peter, and James will all have been dead, and it must have been hard then to think that they had ever been bitterly divided (1999, p. 533).

For his gospel Luke had plentiful sources (Mark and Q at the very least), since memories of what Jesus had supposedly done were treasured. But what early Christians had done after his death was not nearly so important, and less likely to have been recorded and preserved, particularly as much of it will have been mundane. Hence for the period covered by Acts (Easter to the Roman imprisonment of Paul) Luke's material will have been sparse. He certainly made the best of it. Nevertheless, as apostles' doings mattered so much less than deeds of Jesus, Acts did not carry the authority of Luke's gospel and was long ignored. Justin Martyr may have known it, but Irenaeus, who quoted substantially from it around A.D. 185, is the first of those who can be said definitely to have known it. The oldest papyrus manuscript so far discovered which includes part of it (papyrus 45) is dated in the early third century (Metzger, p. 252). Yet as late as ca. A.D. 400 Jerome could say that it was of no interest to many of his time; and his contemporary Chrysostom, author of the first extant treatise on Acts, declared that many "are not even aware that there is such a book in existence" (Quoted by Cadbury 1955, p. 159).

Acts' lack of authority is clear also from its textual history. In no other part of the NT are textual variants so many and so free (Barrett 1998, p. lxix). The so-called 'Western' text of Acts is even some ten percent longer than its Alexandrian or 'neutral' equivalent, and introduces a theological agenda of its own. Its principal uncial witness, the Codex Bezae, frequently contradicts the text it was revising, and imports numerous anti-Jewish and pro-Gentile readings. For instance, whereas the neutral text, while emphasizing the guilt of the Jews over the crucifixion, allows that they acted in ignorance (an idea peculiar to Luke), the Western text all but eliminates this excuse. Epp's detailed study endorses (p. 70) D. Plooij's "strong conclusion" that "the Western reviser was not merely a stylistic redactor but a man of distinct dogmatic convictions" who "did not hesitate to correct the text according to what he thought to be the truth."

ii. Christianity and Judaism

When Acts was written, Christianity was no longer within Judaism; and it is because most Jews had by then refused the new faith that the book represents Paul as turning in despair from them to the Gentiles on three occasions—in Asia Minor (at the Pisidian Antioch, 13:46), in Greece (at Corinth, 18:6), and, with final solemnity, in Rome (28:28), with the last words he speaks in the book. After the first two of these three repudiations, he nevertheless continues to missionize in synagogues in the next town in which he preaches. Wilson surmises that he is made to do this probably because the repudiations represent the situation that obtained in Luke's own day, when the church was predominantly gentile and Jews were hostile, whereas the further approaches to synagogues reflect earlier circumstances, as they were in Paul's time. Luke was thus "torn between historical and parenetic motives." He wished to be true to the historical facts, but also to interpret them for the church of his day (1973, p. 232).

In spite of this discrepancy, Paul's dismissal of the Jews does cover the whole missionary field in which he was active. The real Paul of the epistles had still hoped that the Jews would finally convert (Rom. 11:25–26). Any companion of his would have known that a major factor in causing the break was the Jews' insistence that Christianity cannot claim to be still within Judaism and yet at the same time admit Gentiles without requiring them to conform to the Jewish law. As Paul himself had said: the Jews "were forbidding us to speak to the Gentiles that they may be saved" (1 Thess. 2:16). Orthodox Jews could not countenance a Paul who had declared that "the law worketh wrath" (Rom. 4:15), that it leads not to salvation but to sin (1 Cor. 15:56), and that "Christ is the end of the law unto righteousness to everyone that believeth" (Rom. 10:4). For Gentiles to turn to it as a means of salvation would, he implies, be equivalent to returning to their previous slavery to the elemental cosmic powers (Gal. 4:8–10). His only concession was that he did not encourage Jews to abandon the law: every man should remain in the circumcised or uncircumcised state in which he was "called" to the new faith (1 Cor. 7:17f.); for what matters is not circumcision or its absence, but "faith working through love" (Gal. 5:6).

That it was Paul's attitude to the law that caused his difficulties with the Jews shows through at times in Acts. Thus Christian Pharisees demand the circumcision of gentile Christians (15:5); Jewish Christians of Jerusalem complain that Paul teaches Jews of the Diaspora to forsake the law (21:20f.); and Ephesian Jews on pilgrimage to Jerusalem attack him in the Temple because he everywhere teaches against the law (21:28). But for the most part Acts grasps at all traditions which depict him as a law-abiding Jew, and traces Jewish hostility to Christianity not to any specifically Pauline doctrine, but to the general Christian message that, as the first fruits of a general resurrection of the dead (26:23), a man crucified as a criminal had been resurrected as Lord. It is this doctrine which makes "the priests and Sadducees sore troubled" (4:2) and which angers the Sanhedrin: for if Jesus had been rehabilitated by resurrection, they will have been guilty of judicial murder. Hence they complain that the apostles "intend to bring this man's blood upon us" (5:28).

Luke insists that this Christian doctrine is not really incompatible with Judaism at all, since the Pharisees believe in resurrection. What they expected was, of course, a general resurrection of the dead at the end of the aeon, not the death and resurrection of the Messiah in the present. Nevertheless, Luke represents them as speaking up for Christianity (5:34–39) and as shielding Paul (23:6, 9). He even makes Paul tell the Sanhedrin that he himself has not ceased to be a Pharisee; whereas the real Paul regarded his one-time Pharisaism as "dung" (*skubala*, Phil. 3:8) from which he turned away to Christ. We cannot defend Luke's narrative here by supposing that Paul was ingratiating himself with the Sanhedrin by lying; for even if he had stooped to this, the Sanhedrin would not have permitted itself to be led astray. Rather must we allow, with Haenchen (1971, p. 121), that here Acts is so grotesque that such thinking is comprehensible only in a writer of the post-apostolic generation who no longer had any notion of Paul's real conflicts. It is part of Luke's attempt to show that Jewish opposition to Christianity is unwarranted and irrational.

If, then, it was the proclamation of Jesus's resurrection which the Jews, unreasonably, found so obnoxious, the first thing Acts must do is to show that this doctrine is incontrovertibly true. Hence the book begins with the risen one giving "many proofs" over a period of forty days that he is alive and well, before he finally ascends to heaven. In the Ascension of Isaiah, a composite Jewish and Christian writing of the second century, the forty days are expanded into eighteen months; and in the Pistis Sophia, a product of third-century Egyptian Christianity, they become eleven years. The motive there is to accommodate secret gnostic teachings from the resurrected Jesus—an idea quite foreign to Luke.

Yet even Acts' forty days are out of line with Luke's own gospel, from which one gathers that the ascension occurred on Easter Day. A number of appearances of the risen Jesus to his disciples on that day culminate there in his statement (24:49): "Behold I send forth the promise of my Father upon you." This is followed by his instruction, in the same verse, that they are to remain in Jerusalem until they receive this promise, until, that is, they are "clothed with power from on high." All this sounds very solemn and final; and then, in verse 50, with no suggestion of any interval of time, he "led them out" to somewhere near the neighbouring locality of Bethany, and "parted from them and was carried up to heaven" as he solemnly blessed them with uplifted hands. Tyson (p. 94) is among those who suppose that, although no interval is indicated between the instruction of verse 49 and the final parting of verse 50, we can nevertheless accommodate between them the forty days and all that Acts records of them. It is, however, more usual to admit—albeit in suitably guarded language—that there is a real discrepancy here. Thus Talbert accounts for what he calls "the different slants" of the two books on this matter by saying (what is quite true) that "in Luke 24 the instruction and the ascension function to close the time of Jesus's earthly ministry"; whereas in Acts 1, where the instruction to remain in Jerusalem is repeated, they "function to lay the foundation for the ministry of the church that is about to begin" (p. 20). We should not, however, over-look the fact that an author's concern to depict different 'functions' of an event gives him no ground for assigning different dates to it.

The apostles are, then, to remain in Jerusalem until they have been "baptized with the Holy Ghost" (Acts 1:4–5)—a baptism which follows at Pentecost in the next chapter. The Holy Spirit is necessary for their preaching, and they must wait for it before they start work. At every turn in Acts, the Christian mission is promoted by supernatural forces, whether by the Spirit, or by angels, visions or directives from the exalted Jesus, sometimes making the human agents little more than puppets.

That the work is to start in Jerusalem is Luke's repudiation of Mark's view that the disciples returned to Galilee after the resurrection, or at least were directed to do so.[9] Mark's idea was surely that they should establish themselves there, some seventy miles from Jerusalem, as a Christian community. Luke replaces this with a Jerusalem-oriented mission partly because, for him, Jerusalem represents continuity between Israel and the church. The initiation of the church there shows that Christianity had not broken readily or lightly from its Jewish roots; indeed, for Acts, the eventual rupture was entirely the Jews' fault. Thus the apostles initially frequent the Temple and even convert the Jews of the city by their thousands.[10]

iii. Eschatology and Relations with Rome

During the forty days, Jesus speaks to the apostles also about "the kingdom of God." Notwithstanding the length of this course of instruction, his pupils ask him at the end of it whether "at this time" he intends "to restore the kingdom to Israel." To take this narrative as historical would imply either that he had been a very poor teacher, or that his pupils were very obtuse. But of course their question is not history, but simply a means of introducing the proposition couched in his reply, namely that it is none of their business to know about the timing: their task is to get on with propagating Christianity "unto the uttermost part of the Earth" (1:8). Either this advocates (with Lk. 24:47) the gentile mission (somewhat prematurely if we are to find Peter's later reluctance to have any contact with Gentiles at all plausible), or it can be understood as enjoining mission work only in the Jewish Diaspora. In any case, it is Luke's way of saying to his readers: forget all those earlier Christian ideas about an imminent second coming and judgement[11]—ideas which were still to some extent represented in his own gospel.[12]   For Acts, there will undoubtedly be a judgement, but not yet. This changed position suggests that Acts may well have been written more than just a year or two later than Luke's gospel, and at a time when the situation facing the author was no longer quite the same.

There is, however, one passage in Acts which harks back to older eschatological notions, namely 2:16–21, where the Pentecost miracle which confers the Spirit is linked (by means of a quotation from Joel) with "the last days" and the catastrophes which will characterize them. These verses certainly form an erratic block, although commentators are apt to dismiss them by saying that the formula 'in the last days' had "become a stereotyped expression," no longer denoting any expectation of an immediate end (Conzelmann 1987, p. 19). It would perhaps be better to admit that hardly any book in the NT is completely consistent in its theology.

There were two ways in which Christians of the late first century could cope with the failure of the 'end-events' to occur. They could suppose either that these events were being realized in the present, or that the end would come at some indefinite future. As Haenchen has noted (1971, pp. 95f.), both alternatives are represented in the literature. The fourth gospel says that eternal life can be enjoyed by believers here and now.[13]   Acts takes the other course and allows for a period between Jesus's resurrection and his parousia, his second coming, during which the church exists and grows. One is reminded of Loisy's famous remark: "Jesus announced the kingdom, and it was the church that came."[14]   It is a church which, although without the parousia, is continually forwarded by the activity of the Holy Spirit.

Barrett notes that, in Acts, "references to the Spirit are as frequent as references to the parousia are few" (1998, p. lxxxiii).

Meanwhile, Christianity must settle down in the world, and this means: learn to coexist peacefully with the Roman imperium. This, for Luke, was of great importance. Walaskay (p. 58) has plausibly suggested that he may well have been concerned to counter the kind of anti-Roman sentiment expressed in the book of Revelation (usually dated in the 90s) and have recognized such provocation as a danger to Christianity. If, as Acts argues, Christianity gives the true interpretation of the Jewish scriptures, then Rome should tolerate it, as it did Judaism. Jews in the Empire were, for instance, exempt from military service and could not be summoned to court on a sabbath (Schürer, pp. 362f., 379f.). The Roman state may have threatened Christians in Luke's time, as it did in Mark's. But in his gospel Luke tones down some of Mark's references to persecution,[15] perhaps in the hope that the stormclouds had passed. He certainly did not want Christians actively to seek martyrdom. As Maddox puts it (pp. 96f.), they should not play the hero, but try to live at peace with the sovereign power. Hence Acts represents Christianity as politically innocuous, as contravening no Roman laws, and repeatedly claims that Roman officials themselves properly acknowledge its harmlessness. (Paul's difficulties with them in Philippi are only an apparent exception.[16]) Thus Gallio, Proconsul of Achaia, rejects the Jews' complaints about Paul as of no concern to Roman authorities (18:14–16); and the governors Felix and Festus both refuse all Jewish requests for his condemnation.

Luke would even have us believe that what the Romans really wanted was to have Paul released, and he goes so far as to make Paul himself say as much: "The Romans, when they had examined me, desired to set me at liberty" (28:17–19). In fact, in Luke's own account, only those Romans who do not have authority to decide his case are represented as favouring his acquittal. Claudius Lysias found him innocent (23:29), but as a subordinate official was obliged to send him to the governor Felix for trial. Felix had the power to acquit or condemn, but adjourned the case; and his successor Festus, who declares Paul innocent (25:18, 25; 26:31f.), does so only after the appeal to Caesar has taken the case out of his hands. It is, then, clear what Luke wishes us to believe, and equally clear that he does not make the evidence quite add up to it.

At the very end of Acts, the Romans are represented as allowing their prisoner to preach in the capital for "two whole years," "unhindered"—the very last word in the Greek text, and one which manages to say something nice about the Roman authorities. In specifying a precise period of two years when Paul was allowed to missionize in Rome, Luke obviously knew that it was followed by a change in his circumstances. He knew that Paul had come to trial there, for, in Acts' account of his voyage to Italy, an angel tells him that God has decreed that he must survive this journey to "stand before Caesar" (27:24). Moreover, Luke clearly knew that the outcome of the trial was not an acquittal; for earlier he makes Paul predict—in a farewell address to Asian clergy, his last speech before his arrest in Jerusalem—not only that imprisonment and affliction await him, but also that he will never return to the areas where he has missionized—a sorrowful pronouncement emphasized by being repeated (20:25, 38). Luke, then, knew that Paul had stood before the Emperor and did not return to his congregations. But he could hardly say outright that he died a martyr. For him, Paul was the bearer of the triumphant and invincible word of God, and in Acts is given a career which reflects this triumph. In any case, to have narrated the death of his hero at Roman hands would have spoiled his portrait of harmony between Rome and Christianity. Barrett comments, appositely, on the ending of Acts:

> The promise and commission of 1:8—"ye shall be my witnesses . . . unto the uttermost part of the Earth"—are fulfilled by Paul's preaching in Rome; they would not be more completely fulfilled by his death. Again, Luke was writing a work of edification; Paul's death may not have been an edifying story. He may have been deserted, even betrayed, by those who should have stood by him. 2 Tim.4:16 ["all forsook me"] may or may not be historical, but it is more likely to rest on tradition than on fancy. . . . Perhaps there was no dramatic scene; the Romans locked him up and left him to rot. (1998, p. xliii)

iv. Missionary Speeches: The Twelve Apostles and Paul

The names of the Twelve as listed in Acts (1:13) agree, as is to be expected, with the list in Luke's gospel (6:13–16). Both include a second Judas ("son of James") who does not figure in the corresponding lists in Mark and Matthew, which have a "Thaddeus" in his stead. That the four lists fall short of full agreement underlines the fact that most of the Twelve are insignificant in the gospels' story. As so often with personal and place names in them, there is considerable manuscript variation, as scribes tried to harmonize or otherwise make sense of the data. In the fourth gospel the names of the Twelve are not even listed, and significant roles are given to disciples unmentioned in the other three (such as Nathanael and Nicodemus).

Of nine of the Twelve, Acts tells us nothing more than their names. The remaining three are Peter, who is prominent in the first half of the book, James the son of Zebedee—of him we are told only that Herod Agrippa I had him killed (12:2)—and his brother John, who is worked only as a silent supernumary into stories about Peter. For instance, in the account of the cure of the lame man in Chapter 3, Peter, "fastening his eyes" on the patient "*with John*," said "look on us." He then cures the man by invoking the name of Jesus, while John remains a silent observer. The patient then took hold of "Peter *and John*," whereupon Peter delivers a long speech and John is silent as before, remaining so for the rest of the narrative. The words I have italicized suggest that John has been worked into a story which was originally only about Peter. Dunn, while allowing that it is here "Peter who carries the action, with John as a more shadowy accompanying figure," finds in this pericope an example of the strong emotional appeal of Acts, "the most exciting book in the New Testament" (1996, p. ix): the story has "a beautiful and moving simplicity . . . which both tugs the heart strings and gives delight" (p. 39)!

Clearly, Peter was the only one of the Twelve who figured to any extent in traditions on which the author of Acts could draw. That a group of twelve were leaders in post-resurrection

Jerusalem at all is not easy to harmonize with what Paul says about his dealings with the leadership there. Chapters 1 and 2 of Galatians show that, when he went to Jerusalem to argue with "them that were apostles before" him, he had to put his case not to any twelve, but to Cephas, John, and "James the brother of the Lord." Even in Acts the Twelve are dropped altogether in the middle of the book. (They are last mentioned at 16:4.) There is no suggestion that they appointed the "Elders" who first overlap with them in Jerusalem (11:30; 15:2) and then replace them there; and the identity of the 'James' who shares power with the Elders is not indicated. He enters the narrative abruptly at 12:17 and plays a decisive role at the Jerusalem conference in Chapter 15, and again later in the incidents leading to Paul's arrest there. He is not the son of Zebedee, who has already been executed (12:2), and is not said to be 'the brother of the Lord', although he is obviously the person whom Paul so designated in Gal.1:19. Nor is he said to be the brother of Jesus; for neither in his gospel nor in Acts does Luke suggest that Jesus had a brother of this name, although he must have known that this is alleged in Mark's gospel. (I discuss this whole complicated issue in detail in Chapter 8 of my 1982 book.)

The Muratorian Canon—a list of sacred books long dated to around A.D. 200, but which Hahneman (1992) and others now assign to the fourth century—calls Acts "the Acts of all the Apostles." This is wishful thinking if ever there was, and indicates what Christians wanted to find in the book. The risen Jesus does indeed instruct the apostles, as we saw, to be his "witnesses unto the uttermost part of the Earth" (1:8). But Acts' own account limits their activity outside Palestine to temporary absences of Peter and John in Samaria, and leaves wider missionary work to Paul and his associates. If the author had known anything of foreign missions by any of the Twelve, he would gladly have recorded it as fulfilling Jesus's instruction to them. Nevertheless, by the mid-second century, Christian writers were claiming that these Twelve had gone out from Jerusalem to convert the whole world (Details in Haenchen 1971, p. 144n.1).

Acts' first chapter concludes with Peter's speech which leads to replacing the deceased Judas Iscariot by Matthias. The NT has two different traditions about Judas's death. Matthew points to the horror of remorse which will befall the faithless, and makes Judas say: "I have sinned in betraying innocent blood," as he throws the pieces of silver into the Temple and then hangs himself (27:4–5), whereupon the chief priests used the silver to purchase a field which became known as "the field of blood." In Acts, however, it was Judas himself (so Peter tells) who bought this field with the money, but he then fell headlong to his death, his bowels bursting open. Both stories serve to admonish potential traitors within the Christian community, but this purpose is all that they have in common.

In Acts Peter tells his story of Judas's end to an audience of 120 Jerusalem Jewish Christians, as if it were an event of the distant past, about which they knew nothing and needed to be informed. In fact, even Good Friday, let alone Judas's death, was only a few weeks back, and the story is told only for the benefit of Luke's readers. And what a speech this is! One would think that Peter was talking not to Aramaic-speaking Jews at all; for he solemnly explains to his audience that the word 'Akeldama' means 'field of blood' "in the language of the inhabitants of Jerusalem"—as if this were not the language of the people he is addressing. Having elucidated this word in Greek for their benefit, he goes on to present them with what he regards as prophecies about Judas. Christian writers from the late first century onwards supposed that the Jewish scriptures are full of references to Jesus's biography, to incidents such as his betrayal, death, and resurrection. From this premiss, Peter interprets Psalm 69, where a pious Israelite, cursing his enemies, says: "Let their habitation be made desolate." To make this refer to Judas, Peter, quoting the Septuagint (the Greek translation of the OT), has to alter it to: "Let his habitation be made desolate." Jewish rabbis gave fantastic interpretations enough of their own scriptures, but they never tampered with the actual wording of the texts.

Speeches make up nearly a third of Acts, and they often adduce Septuagint passages which actually mistranslate the original—as if the Jewish audiences addressed would have been impressed by distortions of their own scriptures. In Chapter 2, for instance, Peter quotes, as a prophecy of the resurrection, the Septuagint of Psalm 16. In the Hebrew, the Psalmist says: "My flesh shall dwell in safety," meaning that he will not die prematurely. He has been delivered from peril and is thereby permitted to live a little longer. Only in the Greek version does he speak of living not 'in safety', but "in hope"—hope namely of a deliverance from the corruption (*diaphthora*) of death; and it is this that allows Peter to adduce the passage as relevant to the resurrection.

Such speeches were surely never made in the early Jerusalem church. They were concocted in a Hellenistic community which ascribed to the apostles its own understanding of the scriptures. Perhaps the crassest example is at 15:16–18 where James appeals to Christian Jews of Jerusalem with a Septuagint distortion of Amos 9:11–12, when his purpose—with this Jewish audience—is to justify the circumcision-free mission to the Gentiles! In the Hebrew original, Yahweh promises to restore the Davidic kingdom to its former glory, so that his people may then possess what is left of the neighbouring kingdom of Edom, and also "all the nations that were once named mine." In the Septuagint quoted by James, this promise of conquest is transformed into a universalist message, reversing the nationalist implication of the original: Yahweh declares that the kingdom's restoration will enable "all the Gentiles upon whom my name is called" earnestly to "seek me." We cannot defend this narrative by supposing that James quoted some hypothetical Hebrew text which is accurately rendered in the Greek, for commentators have shown that the Septuagint has here simply misunderstood two words in the standard Hebrew text. Altogether, attempts to trace elements of the speeches in Acts to underlying Aramaic *ipsissima verba* of the apostles have not been successful (cf. Chapter 6 of my *The Historical Evidence for Jesus*).

Peter's speeches in the early chapters of Acts go down extraordinarily well. He declares that "God foreshewed by the mouth of all the prophets that his Christ should suffer" (3:18). One might expect Jews to regard this as stretching their scriptures more than a bit. But no, Peter's audience accepted it in their thousands (4:4). This speech, and his previous one at Pentecost, have sufficed to Christianize what has been calculated as one fifth of the then population of Jerusalem.

This again is not history. It is part of Luke's concern to show that Christianity was no hole-and-corner business ("not done in a corner," 26:26). To this end he likes to portray not only mass conversions but also sympathetic responses in high places. The Roman Proconsul of Cyprus is said to have "believed" (13:12). At Ephesus the Asiarchs, men concerned to promote the cult of the Emperor, appear as Paul's friends (19:31), and the town clerk declares the Christians innocent of sacrilege and blasphemy (19:37). The Jewish king Agrippa II, great-grandson of Herod the Great, comes near to being a convert (26:28). It all serves the thesis that Christianity is essentially God-driven, propelled to success after success by the divine power behind it.

But I revert to Peter's very first speech. Judas, he says, must be replaced "as a witness to Jesus's resurrection" by someone who, like the surviving eleven, had been with the Lord from his baptism to his ascension (1:22); for only someone thus qualified can testify reliably that he really was resurrected, that the person who appeared after the crucifixion was the same as the person who had preached in Galilee. For Luke, to be an apostle is to be thus qualified. It follows that, for him, there can be no apostolic succession; for men of a later generation cannot have been companions of Jesus.

In *The Jesus of the Early Christians* (Wells 1971, p. 136) I wrongly followed commentators who have suggested that Acts' story of replacing Judas was an expedient to meet the difficulty that his misconduct had subtracted one from the Twelve who had been promised seats "in the kingdom" on twelve thrones as judges of the twelve tribes of Israel (Lk. 22:30). This interpretation overlooks the fact that Acts has dropped the apocalyptic expectations still evidenced in Luke's gospel. The clear statement in Acts is that the full complement of twelve is required in the early Jerusalem church as properly qualified witnesses to the truth of the doctrine of Jesus's resurrection. As most of the Twelve nevertheless have no further role in Acts, it is perhaps not surprising that neither Matthias, who is elected to replace Judas, nor his rival candidate in this election ("Joseph called

Barsabbas who was surnamed Justus," 1:23) are ever mentioned again.

Even Paul is, on Luke's definition, not an apostle. Luke does not give this title to anyone who is not a member of the Twelve, except at Acts 14:4 and 14, where Paul and Barnabas are, by way of exception, called apostles, possibly because at that point they are envoys sent out by the church of Antioch, i.e. messengers of a church in the sense in which Paul himself had used the term *apostoloi* at 2 Cor. 8:23. The word is never again used of Paul in Acts, for in its later chapters he is an independent missionary no longer reporting back to Antioch; and Barnabas is dropped altogether after Chapter 15.

The church of Antioch is prominent in Acts. It was there that converts were first both sufficiently numerous and sufficiently distinct in their faith from Judaism to be called 'Christians' (11:26), equivalent to the slang 'Christ-wallahs'. The term implies that 'Christ' was understood as a proper name, not as a title ('Messiah'), for to have called them 'Messiah-wallahs' would not have distinguished them from orthodox Jews. The appellation came presumably from outsiders, but by the time of Ignatius of Antioch (the early second century) it had been accepted by Christians as a self-designation.

Because, then, the church in this Syrian Antioch was so important, Luke will surely have had access to some of its traditions. Hence he may have drawn what he says in Chapter 14 from Antiochene material in which Paul and Barnabas were called apostles, and allowed this designation to stand. Barrett mentions this possibility, and says too that in this chapter we see something like the apostles of the Didache (11:3–6), wandering preachers who were certainly not of the Twelve (1994, p. 557).

All this does not alter the fact that Paul is not an apostle, as Luke has defined the term. Paul did indeed claim to be one, in Galatians and elsewhere, on the ground that he was called directly by the risen Jesus, no human agency being involved in his conversion. In Acts he is, of course, likewise called by the risen Jesus, but this, for Acts, does not make him an apostle. Acts even makes Paul himself refrain from claiming to be a witness of Jesus's resurrection when he says that the relevant witnesses are "those who came up with Jesus from Galilee to Jerusalem" (13:30f.). The fiercely independent real Paul, who repeatedly stressed the importance of the resurrection appearance made to himself (1 Cor. 9:1; 15:8; Gal. 1:12, 16), would not have deferred to them in this way.

In later Christianity we meet the idea that the apostles, as witnesses of the whole span of Jesus's activities on Earth, are guarantors of true and pure doctrine, going back to Jesus himself and uncorrupted by heresy. Luke does not put them to this use. He says little about heresy and is more concerned to stress the idyllic unity of the early church. For him, the great enemy is not the heretic but the Jew. He does betray that heresy had begun to appear in his own time, but it is Paul, not the apostles, whom he makes warn that it will be a future problem. In the relevant speech Paul declares that he himself has delivered the true doctrine, "the whole counsel of God," and is not to be blamed for future divisions:

> I know that after my departing grievous wolves shall enter in among you, not sparing the flock; and from among your own selves shall men arise, speaking perverse things, to draw away the disciples after them. (20:27–29)

The reference is obviously to gnostic heresies of Luke's own time. Barrett observes: "This prediction—or *vaticinium post eventum*—corresponds with surprising exactness to events that are described elsewhere in the NT"—in epistles which are dated in the late first century: "Faced by the failure of the Christian mission (for 'the world does not listen to us') some members of the Johannine community had 'gone out' into the world; they had learned to speak out of the world's vocabulary (*ek tou kosmou*), and accordingly the world paid attention to them" (1 Jn. 4:1–6), and to their gnostic doctrine which was "drawing disciples after them" (1998, p. lxiii). Luke specifies the audience of Paul's warning speech in Chapter 20 as "Elders" from Ephesus, thus indicating a more elaborate church hierarchy than in fact existed in Paul's time, for he never refers to 'Elders' in those of his epistles today accepted as genuinely from his hand. Dunn notes that this in itself "suggests that Luke more than half consciously wrote with an eye to the churches of his own day" (pp. 269f.).

Luke does not mean to denigrate Paul by defining 'apostle' so as to exclude him. He is not so much concerned to subordinate him to the Twelve as to convince us, against what we know from Galatians where Cephas is called a hypocrite, that they all worked in harmony. However, a certain subordination to Christianity as it was already established has often been seen in what Acts has to say about Paul's conversion; for, against his own account in his epistles, a man who was already a Christian played some mediating role in it. This mediator is Ananias, a pious Jew of Damascus (not to be confused with the Jerusalem Ananias who, with his wife Sapphira, was miraculously slain by Peter). Whether Acts, by introducing him, means to subordinate Paul is not readily discernible, as his conversion is related in three separate accounts which are not consistent in the role they assign to the mediator. In the first of these, the risen Jesus tells Paul to go to Damascus, where he will be "told what do do" (9:6). The Lord then instructs Ananias to go to him, for he has been chosen "to bear my name before the Gentiles." Ananias does not pass this information on to Paul, but merely lays his hands on him so that he is cured of the blindness occasioned by his encounter with the risen one, and filled with the Holy Spirit (9:17). Later, where Paul is made to give an account of his own of these incidents, he confirms that he was initially told to go to Damascus to be instructed (22:10), and adds that Ananias did there tell him the purpose for which he had been converted, namely "to be a witness" for the Lord "unto all men" (22:15). Nevertheless, his explicit call to the gentile mission is reserved for the Lord himself, in a vision Paul had—so he here claims in retrospect—in the Jerusalem Temple a little later (22:17–21. Of this nothing was said in Chapter 9). Finally, when he repeats his account in Chapter 26, he makes no mention of Ananias at all, and says he was told to go to the Gentiles directly by the Lord on the Damascus road at the time of his conversion (26:16–18).

From all this, it looks as though, if Luke was concerned to subordinate Paul to the established church at all, this was not his overriding purpose. Ananias himself is not subordinated to the

Twelve, but appears suddenly as a resident of Damascus, with no suggestion that he owes his Christianity to them. Wilson draws the conclusion that he is, for Luke, a representative of God: God calls Paul and Ananias is his instrument (1973, p. 165).

It is surprising, however, that it is not Paul, "an apostle of Gentiles," as he had called himself (Rom. 11:13), but the Jerusalemite Peter who in Acts establishes the principle of admitting Gentiles without circumcision. Here it is "the apostles and the brethren in Judea" (11:1) who lead the way, while Paul only follows. In the longest account of a single incident in the whole of Acts (10:1–11:18), Peter converts, in Caesarea, the Roman centurion Cornelius, together with his family and friends, and then obtains Jerusalem's approval for not having required their circumcision. That it was Peter, not Paul, who gave the lead in this matter is reflected in the account of the Jerusalem Council in Acts 15. The Council has been called to decide whether to allow the circumcision-free mission which, by then, Paul and Barnabas were practising. But what these two say at the Council is barely mentioned, whereas the speeches of Peter and James, both of which make reference to the earlier Cornelius incident, are given *in extenso*.

In the Cornelius narrative, Peter declares that God is not partisan (10:34f.) and has no special love for one race against another. This radical denial of the whole Jewish idea that Israel has a privileged relationship with God suggests that what we have here is not anything that could have been said by the Cephas (Peter) of the Pauline letters, but the thinking of gentile Christians of Luke's day.

That the gentile mission began with such a single dramatic incident is altogether very unlikely. Probably Gentiles were admitted haphazardly in various churches and, then or later, some theological justification was found, such as: circumcision of the heart is more important than circumcision of the flesh (see Räisänen 1987, p. xviii). Their admission was facilitated because, in the Diaspora, some Jewish Christians themselves no longer observed the law strictly. This is obviously true of those whom Paul had persecuted before his conversion; for his hostility to them was prompted by his own strict acceptance of his native traditions (Gal. 1: 13f.; Phil. 3:6). His vision of Jesus which terminated this persecution naturally led him to adopt the liberal attitude to the law of his former victims (see the discussion in my 1986 book, p. 35).

The missionary speeches in Acts mostly follow a recognizable pattern. First, Jesus's life, Passion, and resurrection are outlined, often with emphasis that the apostles had witnessed these events; then proofs of his status are adduced from the OT, and finally there is a call for repentance. Two striking exceptions to this pattern are Paul's speeches in Lystra and Athens which eliminate, in the manner of second-century Christian apologists to pagans, what in Christology was likely to alienate these gentile audiences. Whereas in his own letters Paul had declared that the whole content of his teaching was Christ crucified (1 Cor. 2:2), his address to the Athenians (Acts 17:22–31) makes no mention of the cross, does not name Jesus, and concludes with what Barrett calls "an obscure reference to a man authorized to act as judge of mankind by the fact that God raised him from the dead" (1999, p. 528). It is a monotheistic sermon, made only half-heartedly Christian by its conclusion. Dibelius commented that the author's primary purpose here was "to give an example of how the Christian missionary should approach cultured Gentiles" (p. 79). We can perhaps be thankful that, in this appeal to Greeks, Jesus is omitted rather than adapted to their philosophies in the manner of later Trinitarians, who argued endlessly about his *anhypostasia*, his *enhypostasia* and other supposed aspects of the relation between his human and his divine self. One sympathizes with Harnack's wearied comment that "the hundred and one 'doctrines' which floated around the Trinitarian and Christological dogma were as fickle and uncertain as the waves of the sea" (p. 336).

v. Miracles and the Spread of Christianity

Acts' story of the great turning point represented by the Cornelius episode simply teems with miracles. Their purpose is to convince us that it was God himself who ordered the gentile mission. Peter is represented in this incident as reluctant to have any dealings with Gentiles at all, but as forced to do so by the clear will of God manifested to him in a vision. Paul is likewise portrayed throughout as a strictly orthodox Jew, but as compelled to become a Christian by irresistible supernatural pressure. We are told three times in three different chapters of Acts that his commission to go to the Gentiles derives from the risen Jesus himself (9:15; 22:21; 26:17). This emphasis on having to do what has been supernaturally ordained runs the risk, as we saw, of reducing the human agents to puppets.

Altogether, the profusion of miracles throughout Acts is something that does not inspire confidence—the Spirit providing transport for missionaries (8:39), angels ordering them about (8:26) and releasing on one occasion the apostles (5:19) and on another Peter (12:7–10) from the securest of prisons. Such stories of prisoners being supernaturally released were popular in the literature of the time. The apostles themselves work miracles ceaselessly. The Jews have their own magicians but they are always worsted when up against Peter or Paul (8:9–24; 13:6–11). Already by Chapter 2 the apostles have performed "many signs and wonders" (2:43); and in Chapter 5 "the multitude from the cities round Jerusalem"—there were no 'cities' round it: Luke had a poor grasp of Palestinian geography—bring sick folk, "and they were healed every one" (5:16). They thought they might be cured if only Peter's shadow fell upon them (5:15), just as, later, contact with Paul's handkerchief in fact suffices to make sufferers well (19:12). When Peter raises Tabitha from the dead (9:36–41), the obvious parallel with what both Elijah and Elisha had done (1 Kings 17:17–24; 2 Kings 4:18–37) betrays that Luke's intention here was to show that the apostles were in no way inferior to the prophets. But the more general overall purpose of the miracle stories is to demonstrate that the growth of the early church was God-driven.

Quite apart from this questionable supernaturalism, the spread of Christianity was surely in reality not effected simply by a series of dramatic incidents involving known Christian leaders. In Corinth, Paul may well have been the first actually to missionize. To have admitted that Christians were there before him would "fit poorly into the Lucan historical picture" (Haenchen 1971, p. 533n.4). But Aquila was there before he arrived (18:1f.) and, as Haenchen adds, "if he had been first converted by Paul, this would certainly have been handed down *ad maiorem Pauli gloriam.*" The communities at Damascus, Antioch, Ephesus, and Rome were all founded by unknown persons, as is clear from Acts itself. Let us look at these four cases.

Ananias is introduced as a member of a Jewish-Christian church already existing in Damascus before Paul is converted and missionizes there (9:10; 22:11–13). The mixed Jewish-Gentile church at the Syrian Antioch was started by unnamed Greek-speaking Jews (Acts calls them 'Hellenists'), driven by persecution from Jerusalem (11:19–20). Luke does indeed allege that it was the whole Christian community except the apostles that was driven from the city following Stephen's martyrdom (8:1). But commentators have shown that he is unable to sustain this thesis, and that it was only the 'Hellenists' who were expelled. They incurred the wrath of orthodox Jews doubtless because they were less respectful of the Jewish law than were the 'Hebraist' (Aramaic-speaking) Christians, who remained unmolested (cf. my 1986 book, pp. 129–131). Luke of course envisaged the Jerusalem church as a harmonious unity, not as divided into 'Hellenists' and 'Hebraists' who followed different doctrines. He makes these two groups differ only over a triviality which is soon settled (6:1–6). His account is all the more difficult to follow because in different contexts he uses the term 'Hellenists' to denote different groups: at 6:1 it means Greek-speaking Jewish Christians; at 9.29 it denotes orthodox Hellenistic Jews, and at 11:20 Gentiles.

As for Ephesus, it is only by means of a clumsy insertion that Luke can suggest that it was Paul who delivered the first Christian sermon there. Without the insertion, the text, recording the arrival of Paul with the married couple Priscilla and Aquila, would read:

> And they landed in Ephesus and he [Paul] left them [the couple] there, but he himself set sail from Ephesus.

With Luke's insertion, it reads:

> And they landed in Ephesus and he left them there, but he himself
> [entered into the synagogue, and reasoned with the Jews. And
> when they asked him to abide a longer time, he consented not, but
> taking his leave of them, and saying, I will return again unto you
> if God will, he] set sail from Ephesus. (18:19–21)

It does not make sense to say: he left them there (in Ephesus),
but he himself went into the synagogue—as if the synagogue
were not in Ephesus. There is also no reason why the pious
couple should not have gone into it with him: they are there a
few verses later (18:26), and the next verse after that shows that
there was already a Jewish-Christian community within this synagogue. Earlier in Chapter 18, Luke, as we saw, allows Aquila
less importance for Christianity in Corinth than is likely to have
been historically the case. The truth seems to be that "Aquila
and Priscilla were so important for the history of the Christian
mission that Luke could not overlook them" (Haenchen 1971, p.
539), although he minimizes their contribution.

Finally, concerning Rome, both Acts and Paul's letter to the
Romans show that there were Christians in the city before he
arrived there, although Luke again fudges the evidence somewhat, and would clearly like us to believe that it was the great
missionary himself who founded the Roman church. Having
recorded Paul's arrival (28:14), Acts represents (verse 15)
Christians as setting out from the city to meet him (still on his
way there) at Forum Appii and Tres Tabernae (two well-known
stopping places on the Via Appia between Naples and Rome, 63
and 49 km respectively from the city). That Luke inserted this
verse into a story drawn from one of his sources is betrayed by
the fact that the following verse reverts to the situation reported
at the end of verse 14 (Paul's arrival in the capital). The insertion briefly acknowledges the existence of Christians in Rome,
but Luke never mentions them again, and says nothing of a
church there. Instead, he makes Paul summon—such a person
of authority is he for Luke—the leading Jews of the city, who
ask him to explain Christianity to them, since they know noth-

ing of it, except that it everywhere meets with opposition (28:22). From Paul's own epistle it is clear that a sizable Christian community existed there, and the leading Jews could not have remained indifferent to and ignorant of Christian Messianism, as Luke suggests.

In Acts, even Paul's fellow missionaries are mostly made into mere travelling companions, without the responsibilities which we know from the epistles that they had. Or they are not mentioned at all. For instance, Titus, who on several occasions went to Corinth as Paul's delegate and is mentioned nine times in 2 Corinthians, is unmentioned in Acts.

Barrett has said that not only we, but probably also Luke himself, would gladly have known more about the beginnings of Christianity in the various locations (1999, p. 531). He was doing his best with sparse material, and trimming it a bit to his own ends. Of course we cannot reconstruct his sources, any more than we could reconstruct Mark's gospel from Luke's if Mark's were not extant. But we can ask how he will have come by his material. Haenchen has suggested (1971, p. 86): he could have visited important Pauline communities, such as those at Philippi, Corinth, Ephesus, and the Syrian Antioch. Or other visitors to these places could have made inquiries for him. Or he could have written for information. The long Cornelius story certainly looks like an account from the church in Caesarea as to how its mixed Jewish-Gentile community was founded by Peter, and how in the upshot it managed to obtain Jerusalem's recognition that the admission of Gentiles without circumcision had been a proper step. As Herder said already in the eighteenth century, many a local church will have claimed foundation by an apostle. This particular story, packed with miracles, is the kind of colourful narrative one would expect from a community wishing to celebrate its own origin. That it reached Luke originally as an independent unit is suggested by the fact that it does not fit at all well into the sequence of events in Acts; for if Jerusalem had already conceded that it was proper to allow in the uncircumcised (11:18), the later conference there in Chapter 15, which has to decide this very issue, would have been unnecessary. Another unevenness is that we might well suppose from

8:40 that Caesarea's Christianity had been initiated by Philip the Evangelist, well before Peter.

The best known of all the miracles evidenced in early Christian communities is 'speaking with tongues', for this is replicated in modern Pentecostal churches. It comprises utterances which are unintelligible except to a gifted interpreter. In 1 Cor., Paul includes such speech among the gifts of the Spirit; and in Acts it occurs on two occasions as an unmistakable sign that the Spirit is at work. Thus when Peter and his Jewish companions heard Cornelius and his family "speak with tongues and magnify God," they realized, with amazement, that "on the Gentiles also was poured out the gift of the Holy Ghost" (10:45f.); and when Paul baptized converts at Ephesus, "the Holy Ghost came upon them, and they spake with tongues and prophesied" (19:6).

In the Pentecost narrative of Chapter 2 of Acts, the very first coming of the Spirit is depicted. Fifty days after Easter it comes upon the disciples—by then 120 in number—like a mighty wind from heaven, and in this instance occasions not glossolalia but xenoglossia, namely the ability to speak "other tongues" which are recognizable as familiar languages, yet are not the native tongue of the speakers, nor languages they have learnt. Barrett suggests that Luke was here adapting the supernatural phenomenon of glossolalia to his desire to show that the church was, from the beginning, universal (1994, p. 109).

The fourth gospel gives a very different account of the coming of the Spirit. In the farewell discourse put into Jesus's mouth in its Chapter 14 he foretells not cosmic catastrophe and judgement, as in the other gospels, but the advent of "another Comforter," namely "the Holy Spirit" who "will teach you all things" and will, as he had earlier said (7:38f.), be available to all believers after he himself has been "glorified," that is, crucified and raised from the dead. He actually imparts it to his disciples when he appears to them on Easter Day, in an incident contrived by the evangelist's sophisticated use of the OT: just as God made man into "a living soul" by breathing into his nostrils "the breath of life" (Genesis 2:7), so too Jesus's disciples had their whole being transformed when he "breathed on them and saith unto them, Receive ye the Holy Ghost" (Jn. 20:22). In sum, this gospel combines Easter and Whitsun into a single day, and makes the imparting of the Spirit into something very different, and not only in date, from what it is in Acts. All that the two accounts have in common is an underlying conviction that there was a clear division between the time of Jesus's earthly life and the time when the Spirit was available to the disciples. That the divide is portrayed in such different ways does not suggest that there was a real, underlying historical occurrence.

In 1981 the then Head of Religious Studies at Aberystwyth, C.G. Williams, published a survey and appraisal of modern instances of glossolalia and xenoglossia. In cases of the former, he noted that the interpretations of the utterances are "vague in content and often cryptic," comprising little more than exhortations to the congregation to "pursue the spiritual path and avoid the doom which will befall the godless." He noted too that no explanation is given as to why such basic, not to say banal information needs to be imparted in such a roundabout way (pp. 82ff.). As for xenoglossia, he found that no modern claims have been verified by competent linguists, while Pentecostals retort that the chances against recognition are enormous, since some 2,800 known languages and dialects are today spoken, many more are extinct, and there are also unknown tongues spoken by supernatural personages (pp. 34ff., 183).

Christian critics of glossolalia may attribute it to demonic possession, or warn that ecclesiastically uncontrolled utterances can pose a threat to established doctrine. But they cannot deny that, according to Acts, the Spirit manifested itself in the early church in the form of visions, prophetic sayings and speech in tongues. And the future of Christianity may well lie with those who allow Acts to guide them into believing that such phenomena are still present-day realities; for, in the course of the twentieth century, Pentecostalism has developed from insignificance into a world-wide movement estimated in Dempster's 1999 symposium at some 450 million strong (p. xiii). Many Pentecostal churches are in the Southern hemisphere, to where Christianity's centre of gravity is accordingly shifting. Hence "what could not be achieved by almost two millennia of European missionary enterprise is being brought about within a century of the birth of the Pentecostal movement" (MacRobert, p. 119).

vi. The 'We' Source and Paul's Travels

a. THE CROSSING INTO EUROPE

Of all the sources of Acts, the so-called 'we' source is the most controversial. In three sections concerned with Paul's sea voyages the author writes of 'we' or 'us' as if he had himself been there. But that he was a companion of Paul is surely excluded by the portrait he gives of him throughout the book. Perhaps, then, he drew the 'we' passages from a travel account of some other person who had accompanied Paul. If so, it is necessary to explain why he left the original author's 'we' standing.

It has alternatively been argued (by Robbins, pp. 221, 228, and others) that Luke is here merely following a convention of Hellenistic literature which required sea voyages to be related in the first person, whether or not the author had actually participated in them. Conzelmann illustrates this by printing, as Appendices to his 1987 Commentary on Acts, relevant passages from Lucian of Samosata's *Verae historiae* and from the *Adventures of Leucippe and Cleitophon* by Achilles Tatius, both of which were written in the second century A.D. The literary convention exemplified in such narratives served two purposes. First, it suggested that the people on board felt themselves to be a community, all involved together in the voyage's dangers. Something like 'We thought we were lost, but we all did what we could and came through in the end' would express the idea. Second, the 'we' encourages readers of the story to feel that they themselves are directly involved in its incidents.

If, as is proper, the Western text of 11: 28 is discounted,[17] the first 'we' in Acts appears abruptly at 16:10 and is sustained for only eight verses. It enters the text apropos of a decisive question in Paul's gentile mission, namely whether to cross from Asia into Europe. That he did so resulted in extensive work throughout Macedonia and Greece for practically all the remainder of this second of his three missionary journeys. So far, "the Holy

Ghost" has directed him and his companions to go westwards across Asia Minor, almost non-stop and without deviations, to Troas, on its west coast (16:6–8). The purpose of mentioning directives from the Holy Ghost and "the Spirit of Jesus" is to establish that Paul himself did not choose destinations, but was propelled to a goal chosen by the Deity. The decision to cross from Troas into Europe is motivated by further supernatural-ism—by a vision vouchsafed to Paul, whereupon "straightway we sought to go forth into Macedonia"—hitherto, the party as it crossed the land mass of Asia Minor, has been designated as 'they'—since we "concluded that God had called us" to preach the gospel there. Luke's idea seems to be that this crucially important vision, leading as it does to missionary work spread over two whole chapters, was authenticated by someone present on the occasion. Paul was sent into Europe by God, and a witness has testified to this fact.

The 'we' continues for a few verses until Paul reaches Philippi, where it is—obviously quite deliberately—phased out so as to concentrate attention on him. When first introduced at 16:10, the 'we' means 'Paul and his companions'. After seven such verses it is stated that, in Philippi, a slave-girl followed "Paul and us." Here he is distinguished from 'us', who include only his companions. There follows a story with no 'we' at all, about how he exorcized the slave-girl of a demon, was mal-treated, imprisoned and released when, in answer to his prayers, an earthquake opened all the doors of the prison, did little dam-age elsewhere, but made the fetters fall from all the prisoners (16:26). At this, the jailor, recognizing that Paul commands supernatural powers, accepted baptism, as did his whole family. Haenchen's detailed analysis of the whole episode leads him to conclude that it is "such a nest of improbabilities that it must be struck out as unhistorical. Its absence does not produce any gap whatever" (1971, p. 501). But my concern here is to draw atten-tion to the way in which the 'we' is phased out in this account of Paul's mission in Philippi, and also to note that the same sequence recurs when the 'we' reappears at 20:5. First it means 'Paul and the others', then he is mentioned additionally to the 'we', and finally there follows a story about him with no 'we'.

Thus the 'we' is restricted to sections which report no special acts of Paul.

I turn now to this second of the 'we' passages and to the whole narrative of chapter 20.

b. THE RETURN TO JERUSALEM AND THE MONEY COLLECTION

When the 'we' returns at 20:5, Paul is again in Philippi, but this time, years later, not on an outward journey to Greece, but on his way back to Jerusalem from a later, his third missionary journey. If the 'we' passage in Chapter 16 authenticates a vision, the corresponding passage here in Chapter 20 seems to have the function of making the reader feel directly involved in this, Paul's last journey as a free man. Why he is travelling to Jerusalem is not clear from Acts, which in its usual way says no more than that "the Spirit" prompted him (19:21; 20:22). Only from his letters is it clear that his purpose was to hand over to the Jerusalem church the money he had taken enormous trouble to raise from his gentile churches so as to honour the agreement he had made with James, Cephas, and John to support the Christian poor of Jerusalem (Rom. 15:25–27; 1 Cor. 16:1–4; 2 Cor. 8 and 9; Gal. 2:10).

Because the 'we' was dropped at Philippi (16:17) and is resumed at this same place (20:5), the impression may be given that both sets of 'we' verses derive from the same writer—from someone who had remained in Philippi on the outward journey of Chapter 16, instead of going on through Macedonia into Greece with Paul, and who rejoined him on his return there from his later and final missionary journey to Greece. (He had not touched Philippi on his return from the second missionary journey, but had travelled to Palestine by ship from Greece.) However, Haenchen (1965, pp. 253f.) has shown that Luke's narrative in Chapter 20 is influenced by his inability or unwillingness to disclose the reason for Paul's final journey back to the east. The epistles tell that he was accompanied, doubtless for his protection, by delegates of churches of Greece, Macedonia, and Asia Minor which had contributed the money he intended for

Jerusalem. The epistles also show that the journey began in Corinth, to where he had gone from Ephesus because of some dispute about his authority. That had been settled, and he remained in Corinth for some months until the money had been brought to him from the other churches which were contributing. The plan was obviously for the men who brought it to travel with him by ship from Corinth.   From this point we have only the evidence of Acts, according to which he changed his mind and decided to begin the journey by land, going northwards through Greece and Macedonia, and only from there by ship to Asia Minor and onwards. Now it is probably because Acts makes no mention of the money collection that its narrative of Paul's movements from Ephesus into Europe and back into Asia Minor is both brief—a mere three verses—and vague. It is not said that he went to Corinth, but only, via Macedonia, to "Greece" and then determined to "return through Macedonia" (20:1–3). As his travel companions are not, in Acts, guarding him and money, they can be no more than some kind of guard of honour; and Luke does not mention them at all until, having listed their names, he says that "these"—presumably the two Asians named at the end of the list—were sent ahead from Macedonia to Troas in Asia Minor, "and were waiting for us" there (20:5. It is here that the first person pronoun reappears). The two Asians will have been familiar with travel in Asia Minor and will have been sent ahead to find a ship which would take the whole party eastwards from Troas without calling at Ephesus, which Paul was anxious to avoid. It was obviously from Philippi in Macedonia that they had been sent ahead, for verse 6 reads: "And we sailed away from Philippi . . . and came unto them at Troas."   In this way, the impression may be given that it is someone who had joined the party only at Philippi who is speaking of 'we' or 'us' at this point.

When Paul has reached Jerusalem and is pleading his case before the governor Felix, he says that his reason for travelling there was "to bring alms to my nation and offerings" (24:17). This is often understood as an allusion to his money collection—if indeed the only one in Acts, and one which readers ignorant of the epistles could not possibly understand to be such. But the reference here is to gifts and offerings which are related to Judaism, not to money for poor Christians—money which moreover is not a personal gift from Paul but was raised by his gentile churches (Rom. 15:25–27). The next verse in Acts shows that the "offerings," if not the "alms" as well, in fact refer to the money needed to defray the expenses of four poor Nazirites. Paul had, on arrival in Jerusalem, agreed to James's request (21:23f.) that he should do this in order to clear himself of any suspicion that he was hostile to Jewish practices. He could of course not have foreseen that James would ask this of him; and so his purpose in going there could not have been to meet the costs of acceding to such a request.

In Chapter 11, Acts states that a collection was made at a much earlier date, and only at Antioch, for the "relief" of Judean Christians, in view of an anticipated world-wide famine, and that Paul and Barnabas took the money to "the Elders," presumably of Jerusalem (11:28–30). This is surely not historical. Galatians speaks of only one journey of Paul and Barnabas to Jerusalem, and it was clearly the one made to discuss the circumcision question with James, Cephas, and John, as recorded in Chapter 15 of Acts, where both these persons involved and the question at issue are the same as in Galatians. Paul would not, in this epistle, have suppressed mention of an earlier journey with Barnabas; for his purpose in that letter was to repudiate the charge that he was subordinate to Jerusalem. To this end he stressed how seldom he had been there and had had dealings of any kind with the apostles there. If he had failed to mention any visit, particularly such a significant one as is alleged in Acts 11, he would have played into his enemies' hands, enabling them to say that his case for his independence was based on a lie. Acts, then, has made two visits out of one. Barrett (1998, p. lx) shows how this probably came about. Galatians tells that Paul's law-free gospel was confirmed in Jerusalem provided he remembered the poor there. Luke had a tradition about a meeting there at which this gospel was confirmed, and another tradition that Paul brought relief for Christians there. He concluded, wrongly, that two different purposes meant two visits, two meetings.

I revert now to Paul's journey to Jerusalem, to the point where he had reached Troas. There he resuscitates a young man who had dropped three floors from a window as a result of falling asleep while listening to Paul's interminable sermon (20:9–12). 'We' are said to be present at the sermon (verse 8), yet there is no 'we' in the story of the young man, not even at its conclusion, where only 'they' (Paul's local audience), and not—as one would expect from verse 8—both 'we' and 'they' of that place, are said to rejoice at the happy issue of the accident (verse 12). Once again there is no 'we' in sections which report special acts of Paul.

The 'we' returns as the voyage continues to Miletus, but drops out there for a while as Paul delivers his farewell speech as Christian missionary for the rest of Chapter 20. He has summoned the church Elders of Ephesus, 50 km away, to hear him say that he has completed his career, hint that martyrdom awaits him, and warn that, after his departure heresy, for which he is in no way to be held responsible, will rend the church. The speech does not fit its context well. It is not clear why these Elders, whom he has last seen only a few months previously, should have to travel 50 km to hear not only this, but additionally a good deal of self-justification from Paul, who recalls how he had worked himself to the bone for three years in their midst, had sponged on none of them, and is altogether the ideal missionary, "pure from the blood of all men." (Had he forgotten that, before his conversion, he had persecuted Christians "unto the death," 22:4?) Even the motive Luke gives him for summoning the Elders to hear him—namely that he is too short of time to go to Ephesus himself—is unconvincing, as getting them to Miletus from such a distance would have delayed him considerably. 1 Cor. 15:30–32 and 2 Cor. 1:8–10 betray that his real motive for avoiding Ephesus will have been that he feared for his life in that city where he had earlier been so severely persecuted.

In sum, what Acts gives is not a speech by the real Paul, but Luke's assessment of his significance, the image of Paul that he wants his readers to retain. Dunn calls the speech "the testament of Paul," and notes that the "genre of testament," characteristically warning of evil times ahead, was already well established in Jewish circles (1996, p. 269).

c. THE FINAL VOYAGE TO ROME

After the valedictory speech at Miletus, the 'we' is resumed (21:1) until the voyage ends at Caesarea, indeed until Paul reaches Jerusalem (21:18). But from that point the interest centres on him—on his arrest and his various defence speeches— and there is no more 'we' until Chapters 27 and 28, the two final chapters of the book which depict the voyage of prisoners, including Paul himself, from Caesarea to Rome, guarded by a centurion and soldiers. Barrett is quite right to say that, whoever was responsible for the substance of Chapter 27, with its many technical terms, was certainly "familiar with the sea and with seafaring, in particular with conditions and places in the Mediterranean and the Adriatic" (1998, p. 1178). Greek literature has novels enough about perilous sea voyages, but these do not characteristically include the kind of prosaic nautical data of Acts 27—data which would have bored readers of novels. Even the storm at sea in this chapter is not described in the exaggerated horrific manner of such tales.

It is, then, quite possible that Luke based this account on reminiscences of the transport of the prisoners written by someone not himself a prisoner who had travelled on the same ship and who, unlike the prisoners (who were probably chained and below deck), was in a position to experience the nautical measures taken, and knew enough about seafaring to record them later—not at the time, for a diary would not have survived the shipwreck. The writer of such a straightforward, unadorned account would have referred to the prisoners as 'they', to himself as 'I', and to the crew and himself as 'we'.

If Luke is here drawing on such a report, he did not use it unaltered. First, he has introduced a 'we' inappropriately at the beginning. 27:1 reads: "And when it was determined that we should sail for Italy, they delivered Paul and certain other prisoners to a centurion named Julius." No ship had at that point been found for the transport; and what had been decided was to send prisoners, not additionally some further person who is here distinguished from them. In verse 6, the centurion, having by then "found a ship of Alexandria sailing for Italy," is said to put "us" on board. Luke's purpose with the 'we' in these verses may well have been to suggest to the reader that the whole narrative derives from an eyewitness.

In fact however—and this is the second way in which the source material has here been manipulated—Luke has inserted a number of incidents glorifying Paul which are easily detachable from the rest and are obviously fictitious.

The first such insertion comprises verses 9–11, where there is no 'we', and where Paul advises not to proceed further with the voyage because it is too late in the year. The centurion then decides the question by heeding the advice of the captain and the ship-owner and discounting that of Paul. In reality, the centurion would have had no jurisdiction concerning nautical problems; and Paul, as one of the prisoners, would not have been accepted by any of the three as a partner in such discussions, particularly as he speaks as a Christian prophet, not from maritime experience. He has never even travelled this route before. If these three verses are deleted, the text runs on naturally from verse 8 to verse 12.

The second inserted episode comprises verses 21–26. When they are removed, verse 27 follows on from verse 20. In the insertion, Paul, having "stood forth in the midst of them," like an orator indicating that he is about to speak, bids all take heart, as if he were preaching in a synagogue, instead of standing on deck in a hurricane. He again speaks as a Christian prophet. The inevitable angel has told him, so he says, that he will survive to stand before Caesar, and that all will survive with him, although "we must be cast upon a certain island." At verse 42 the soldiers advise killing the prisoners lest any should swim away from the doomed ship and escape to the nearby land. But (verse 43) "the centurion, *desiring to save Paul*, stayed them from their purpose, and commanded that they which could swim should cast themselves overboard and get first to land." The four words I have italicized—they are four also in the Greek—are another insertion. That Rome should intervene purely to save this one particular captive fits Luke's conception of how the authorities should treat Christians.

By the beginning of Chapter 28, all have safely reached "the island . . . called Melita." This is usually understood to be Malta, although in 1987 the historical geographer Warnecke made a case for a tongue of land on the island of Cephallenia in the Ionian Sea (Details and criticism in Rapske, pp. 37–43). The two initial verses of this chapter have the 'we', but are followed by a story without it, about a poisonous snake from whose bite Paul suffered no harm. The 'we' then resumes. Stories about Paul have, in all these instances, been inserted into a source that did not contain them.

The NT scholar Günther Bornkamm is among those who have even held (p. 104) that the piece of writing into which the insertions were made originally had nothing to do with Paul. This has been rightly challenged by Haenchen (1965, p. 257), who points out that the soldiers, and not only the crew, were already mentioned in this source, which therefore must have been an account of a transport of prisoners, not just a story of maritime adventure. The fact that little about Paul remains once Luke's insertions have been deleted need cause no surprise; for the man was one among the many prisoners, not a guest of honour with a say in what was being done.[18]

vii. A Less Spectacular Beginning

Verdicts on Acts have ranged from dismissing it as a bundle of legends to accepting it as a history whose trustworthiness is unsurpassed.[19] Today conservative commentators still suppose, as does Dunn (1996, pp. xi, 335), that it may well have been written by a companion of Paul. But a few theologians—John Bowden, for instance—are prepared to set it aside as "ideology, party history" (p. 151). Others say that because it shows accurate knowledge of Roman administration it must be accepted as a well-informed account by a meticulous historian. But there is no reason why Luke should not have known a great deal about the Roman Empire, whatever is true of his story. In this connection, Barrett, who by no means wishes to suggest that Luke created this story out of nothing, observes that he himself has read "many detective stories in which legal and police procedures were described with careful accuracy, but in the service of a completely fictitious plot" (1999, p. 525).

What Acts says about the life of Jesus is of course incidental to its account of the early church. Nevertheless, it reproduces (mainly in its missionary speeches) items familiar from the gospels. It alludes to Jesus's baptism, states that he taught, performed many miracles and healings (including exorcisms, 10:38), was betrayed by Judas, indicted by the Jews in Jerusalem (who wanted a murderer released in his stead, 3:14) and tried by Pilate. Acts also follows the gospels in recognizing Jesus as "the Son of man" (7:55f.). I have indicated in Chapter 1 above that a considerable body of Christian literature is extant which is either earlier than the gospels or earlier than the time when they had become generally known, and that it signally fails to confirm any of these items about Jesus's life. Only from the time when the gospels had become available do we find other extant Christian documents beginning to portray him as they do. It would, I think, follow that Christianity did not originate in anything like the way portrayed in the gospels and in Acts, and that criticism of the historical reliability of Acts would have to go well beyond the matters to which I have pointed in the present chapter.

Be that as it may—and I will revert to it in Chapter 3 below—even Acts itself is not able to ascribe to the early churches any knowledge of one item in Jesus's Galilean ministry which, if historical, would have been of great importance to them, namely Jesus's words at Mk. 7:15–19 where, in clear contravention of the Jewish law, all foods are declared clean. (The whole passage is significantly absent from Luke's gospel and is formulated less radically in Matthew's.) Whether a law-free Christian mission was allowable was a major problem for the early churches. Such a mission surely began without prior theological justification, as Paul and Barnabas testify at Acts 15:3f. (cf. above, p. 95), but in time it had to be properly justified. In Acts this is effected in Jerusalem not by appeal to any dominical saying, but by Peter alluding (in Chapter 15) to a vision which had informed him that he was free to eat food which the law designated as unclean— an experience from which he had inferred that association with gentiles is permissible (10:14f., 28f.). Not only Acts but also Paul's letter to the Galatians betray that the Antiochian as well as the Jerusalem church was unaware of any dominical saying which would have settled this issue which convulsed them. It is common to deprecate arguments from 'mere silence', but here we have a clear case of silence concerning something which, had it been known to the parties portrayed, would certainly have affected their behaviour. In sum, Mk. 7:15–19 functions as an equivalent to Peter's vision in Acts. The gentile community behind Mark's gospel (which finds it necessary to explain Jewish customs to its readers) justified freedom from the law by supposing that Jesus himself had endorsed such freedom. The traditions on which Acts drew justified it by ascribing a supernatural experience to Peter.

Altogether, Christian beginnings were surely far less spectacular than Acts suggests. Even in Jerusalem the Christian community will have been unobtrusive and as good as unnoticed. Dibelius made the point, calling the Christians there "a band gathered together in a common belief in Jesus Christ and in the expectation of his coming again . . . , leading a quiet and in the Jewish sense 'pious' existence," sustained only by the "victorious conviction of the believers" (p. 124).

viii. Addendum: Wedderburn on the 'We' Passages

Since I completed this book, A.J.M. Wedderburn's 2002 article on the 'We' Passages in Acts has appeared. It gives a valuable critical review of recent attempts to solve the problem these passages pose, and finally pleads for taking Haenchen's suggestion "somewhat further" by regarding the writer of Acts (who was undeniably at a considerable distance from Paul and from the events described) as a pupil of a pupil of Paul. The immediate pupil of Paul had accompanied him on some of his travels. The author of Acts "felt himself to be writing in the name of this travelling companion" and therefore chose the first person plural for those parts of the narrative where he knew that this man had in fact been present with Paul.

Wedderburn reminds us that there appear to have been a number of post-Pauline 'schools' which interpreted the apostle's ideas in different ways: adventurously and speculatively (as in the letter to the Colossians and Ephesians) or conservatively (as in the Pastoral epistles). He suggests that Acts may also be regarded "as the product of a sort of 'school'-activity"—one which did not write letters in Paul's name, but made a much more indirect connection with him by use of material drawn from the obscure travelling companion.

3

Peter at Rome?
The Literary Evidence

i. Some Notable Silences

Whether Peter was ever in Rome has for centuries been the subject of controversy, the history of which is summarized in Oscar Cullmann's well-known study (pp. 72ff.). Cullmann himself accepts the traditional view but allows that, prior to the second half of the second century, no document asserts his stay and martyrdom there explicitly (p. 113). He notes that "the earliest Christian writings, the letters of Paul, contain no direct or indirect data whatever concerning a stay of Peter in Rome or concerning his death" (p. 79). In Acts, Jesus, after the resurrection, promises "the apostles whom he has chosen" that "you shall be my witnesses (*martures*) . . . to the end of the Earth" (1:2, 8). But Acts' own account limits their activity outside Palestine to temporary absences of Peter and John in Samaria, and leaves wider missionary work to Paul and his associates. If the author had known anything of foreign missions by any of the Twelve, he would gladly have recorded it as fulfilling the promise of 1:8. Instead, they are all dropped from his account in the middle of his book. "Strange to say," observes Cullmann, "Peter vanishes completely from the narrative" (p. 39), and so Acts "constitutes a minus for the traditional view" (p. 82). He also notes, as very striking, "the silence of a Christian writer who lived in Rome,"

namely "Justin Martyr, from whom we possess extensive writings that date from the middle of the second century" (p. 116).
Justin says much of Simon the magician's activities in the city,
but nothing of Peter's polemic against him there, which is the
subject of many later traditions.

A little earlier than Justin, Papias, bishop of Hierapolis in Asia
Minor, mentioned Peter and the first of the two epistles ascribed
to him, but the claim that he linked him with Rome outruns the
evidence. His writings have not survived, but the fourth-century
bishop of Caesarea, Eusebius, notes in his *Ecclesiastical History*
(ii, 15)—I quote the translation by Lawlor and Oulton (p. 48): "It
is said" that Peter "authorized Mark's gospel to be read in the
churches—Clement has given the story . . . and . . . Papias cor-
roborated his testimony." (The reference is to Clement of
Alexandria, who lived half a century later than Papias.) "And [it
is said] that Peter mentions Mark in his former epistle, which
also it is said he composed at Rome itself." Here our two trans-
lators put the first 'it is said' in square brackets, as it is implied,
but not stated, in the Greek. But the second 'it is said' is actually stated, and so there is no suggestion that Papias endorsed
the hearsay that Peter was at Rome, nor that this hearsay originated as early as Papias. D.W. O'Connor observes that, from
what Eusebius here says, it may well have been Clement, not
Papias, who spoke of the tradition that the epistle we know as
1 Peter was written at Rome. O'Connor adds that, in any case,
Papias's interpretations "are often bizarre and reveal either an
overvivid imagination or an uncritical nature" (p. 22).
Nevertheless, as we saw in Chapter 1, extreme conservative
Christian apologists still suppose that he vouchsafes eyewitness
testimony for canonical writings.

ii. 1 and 2 Peter

The author of the first of the two epistles ascribed to Peter in the
NT introduces himself as "Peter, an apostle of Jesus Christ" (1:1).
Nearly everyone takes this to be a claim to be the Galilean fish-
erman who, according to the gospels, accompanied Jesus.
Those who accept this claim as true call the epistle Petrine,

while those who reject it say the letter is pseudonymous. In this sense, the Catholic scholar Raymond E. Brown "inclines towards" regarding the letter as a "post-Peter pseudonymous" document of the 80s (p. 130). M.E. Boring makes a detailed case for dating it at around 90 (pp. 29–34).

While I agree that. the letter was not authored by someone who had been a personal companion of Jesus, I find the term 'pseudonymous' misleading, for it is normally used so as to imply that the writer was acquainted with the canonical gospels, or at least with the traditions underlying them. There is certainly a great deal of literature bearing Peter's name that is pseudonymous in this sense, such as the Gospel of Peter, the Apocalypse of Peter, the Acts of Peter, and numerous others. In the Acts of Peter, for instance, Peter is represented as saying: "God sent his son into the world, and I was with him. And I walked on the water, and myself survive as a witness of it." All these works are productions of the second century or later, but our epistle is not to be classed with them, for it is not based on the gospels or the traditions which went to form them. Kümmel, although he calls it "undoubtedly pseudonymous," nevertheless stresses, in his standard handbook, that it shows "no evidence at all of familiarity with the earthly Jesus," with his "life" or his "teaching" (pp. 423f.). How, then, can we suppose that the author is posing as someone who had been Jesus's companion?

1 Peter shows no contacts at all with the traditions underlying the fourth gospel, and its degree of contact with those which went to form the other three is judged by Boring to be "minimal" (p. 42). Although the gospels will have been written about the same time as this letter, they were still not widely known in Christian circles. What is said of Jesus's Passion in 1 Peter is drawn not from them, but almost verbatim from what is said of the "servant of Yahweh" in Isaiah 53. Hoskyns and Davey, although quite conservative commentators, admit that "the language is so similar that the resemblance cannot be fortuitous" (p. 57). Moreover the epistle assures its readers that governors are sent by the Emperor "to punish those who do wrong and praise those who do right" (2:13f.). He who wrote this surely cannot have believed that the Jesus he worshipped had been

condemned by a Roman governor. The epistle seems to evidence a pre-gospel Christianity in which worshippers had not yet come to believe that their Lord had lived and died in the recent past, in the historical situation specified in the gospels. That the earliest Christians, including the Cephas of Paul's epistles (all written by A.D. 60, well before the gospels) did in fact regard Jesus in a pre-gospel way—as a basically supernatural personage briefly on Earth as a man at some time past in circumstances about which very little was known—is argued in detail in Chapter 1 above. If 1 Peter is appropriately to be called pseudonymous, it must be in the sense that it was written in the name of (and presumably after the lifetime of) this Cephas of the Pauline letters, who was obviously prominent in the church of the 50s, who, however, in my view, like Paul, had no experience of Jesus prior to the resurrection, acquaintance with his ministry being imputed only at a later stage of the developing tradition.

Kümmel goes on to note that the letter is written in "cultivated Greek," with "many rhetorical devices," and with all the OT quotations and allusions deriving from the Septuagint, the Greek version of these scriptures, not from the Hebrew originals. Of course, in the author's missionary situation—he is writing to the "elect" in "Pontus, Galatia, Cappadocia, Asia, and Bithynia" (1:1)—he quotes scripture in Greek. What is significant is that "he betrays no knowledge of the original Hebrew text," "alludes almost unconsciously to Septuagint phraseology," sometimes even "improves the rough grammar and syntax" of the Septuagint when he cites it, and has "numerous allusions to classical and hellenistic culture" (Boring, p. 31). All this shows that his own world of thought is represented by Greek literature.

Those who regard the author as claiming to have been Jesus's companion, and who accept that claim as true, explain these features by supposing that he had the letter written for him by a cultured secretary. Appeal is made to 5:12: "I have written to you through Silvanus"—tendentiously translated, says Boring (pp. 179f.), as "with the help of Silvanus," even though "the phrase to write 'through' someone never refers to the letter's composer or drafter, but to its bearer," as said of this same

Silvanus (Silas) at Acts 15:22f., and often in the church Fathers.

In the present context, where we are concerned to enquire whether I Peter has any connection with Rome, we may note that it concludes with a greeting to the recipients from "her that is in Babylon, elect with you" (5:13). This can be understood as a salutation from the sister church of the Mesopotamian city of Babylon, or its environs. However, as there is no other tradition which knows of missionary work by Peter in that area, it is usual to interpret 'Babylon' symbolically. It commonly stood for 'Rome' in Jewish and Christian circles after Rome had conquered Jerusalem and destroyed its temple in A.D. 70, as Babylon had done 600 years earlier. If that is the meaning here, it constitutes a further argument for dating the epistle "after the 60s and Peter's lifetime" (Brown, p. 130). Certainly, in the NT apocalypse, the book of Revelation written in the 90s, 'Babylon' is a code name for Rome, and figures as the "great city," the "mother of harlots," "drunk with the blood of the martyrs of Jesus" (17:5f.; 18:21–24). Open expression of such hatred of the imperial authorities might have been dangerous; hence this disguise. However, if the author of 1 Peter disguised a reference to Rome, one might expect him to have shared the hatred which, in the apocalypse, made the disguise necessary; whereas in fact his attitude to the authorities is, as we saw, decidedly friendly. Fear God and honour the Emperor is his doctrine (2:17).

J.H. Elliott's careful and detailed study of 1 Peter suggests an alternative reason why the author may have designated his place of writing symbolically as Babylon. The addressees in Asia Minor were clearly exposed to the contempt of their non-Christian neighbours—a contempt which their sectarian exclusiveness had provoked. They were being "reproached for the name of Christ" (4:14), and their unwillingness to keep company with those with whom they had consorted before their conversion to Christianity was resented (4:4). Elliott holds that it is because they were in this sense outsiders in society that the writer refers to them as "of the Diaspora" (1:1), even though many of them were Gentiles.[1] In Jewish usage this term means Jews living outside Palestine; but in 1 Peter it has been appropriated to Christian use to designate Christians at odds with society (p. 46)—just as other epithets (such as 'the elect') which were once exclusive attributes of Israel have been appropriated in this letter, indeed in a way which helps to date it, for such usage indicates a stage when non-Christian Jews as well as pagans had come to be regarded as outside the Christian movement (pp. 48f.). Now Elliott's proposal is that the author may well have claimed to have written the letter in Babylon in order to imply that he, like the recipients, is an outsider viewed with hostility in society; for Babylon is that notorious place where God's people once had sojourned as outsiders (pp. 39, 226f.).

Elliott nevertheless believes that the epistle was written at Rome. But this is not required by his argument; there were many other places in which a Christian writer could feel himself to be an outsider, including, by Elliott's own argument, the area which 1 Peter addresses. Pseudonymous epistles may well have originated in the localities to which they are addressed.

In sum, 'Babylon' at 5:13 may not be used figuratively at all, or if it is figurative, the reference may not be to Rome. Moreover, commentators who regard the letter as pseudonymous—either as falsely claiming authorship by someone who had been a companion of Jesus, or in the alternative sense that I have proposed—must allow that, if Rome is meant, this may be no more than "part of the fictive literary world projected by the pseudonymous style" (Boring, p. 38). This would mean that the author had come to believe, not necessarily for good reasons, that Peter had missionized at Rome, It is, then, not surprising that Cullmann goes no further than to say that "1 Peter probably supposes that at some time Peter was in Rome" (p. 113).

The second of the two epistles ascribed to Peter in the canon can unambiguously be designated pseudonymous. The author purports to be not just 'Peter', but "Simon Peter" (1:1), as in the gospels. Many manuscripts read here "Simeon Peter," the correct Hebrew and Aramaic form of Simon which aims at stamping the writer as the Jewish-Christian apostle. He claims to have been among the witnesses of Jesus's transfiguration (as is recorded of Peter in the gospels), saying:

> We did not follow cunningly devised fables when we made known unto you the power and coming of our Lord Jesus Christ, but were eyewitnesses of his majesty. For he received from God the Father honour and glory when there came such a voice to him from the excellent glory, This is my beloved Son, in whom I am well pleased. And this voice we heard come out of heaven when we were with him in the holy mount. (1:16–18. Cf. Mt. 17:5: And behold out of the cloud a voice saying, this is my beloved Son in whom I am well pleased.)

To claim eyewitness basis for his own doctrines was an obvious way for the author to authenticate them, against the "cunningly devised fables" of the dissidents he is controverting. The arch-conservative apologists of today—such as C.P. Thiede, who will occupy us below—accept the claim as invaluable evidence for the reliability of the scriptures. Yet scholars are almost unanimous in rejecting 2 Peter as a late pseudepigraph, later even than 1 Peter, to which it refers ("this is now, beloved, the second epistle that I write unto you," 3:1). Brown, with most others, puts it considerably later (p. 208). Pheme Perkins thinks it may be "over half a century" later than Paul's letter to the Galatians (p. 125). No other NT book is so poorly represented in the Fathers. Origen is the first to notice it (around A.D. 220), remarking that its authenticity is doubted, although he himself accepted it. A century later Eusebius (iii, 3) discounted it, and recognized only the first of the two epistles ascribed to Peter as "genuine and admitted by the presbyters of old."

Internal evidence also militates against authenticity of 2 Peter. The author incorporates into his letter much of the epistle of Jude, which is itself a late and vituperative attack on dissidents, accepted only reluctantly into the canon (Eusebius still classed it with the disputed books).[2] The author himself points back to Christianity's early days as distant: "the fathers" (the first Christian generation) are already dead (3:4). His designation of Paul as his "beloved brother" (3:15) indicates a time when, as in Acts, Peter and Paul were regarded as having worked harmoniously together, and when the sharp conflicts between the leading Christians of earlier days had been forgotten. The mention in this context of what Paul says "in all his epistles" indicates a time of writing late enough for these letters to have existed as a collection. They are even regarded here as "scripture" (3:16), a term which Christians of the first century had used only for sacred works of the Jews. The author devotes the whole of the second of his three chapters to unsavoury abuse of dissidents, and warns, in his pose as Peter, that such persons will come in the future (2:1–3); but the pose breaks down when he describes them as—in his own second-century situation—having already deviated from the true faith (2:20f.), as reprobates with eyes for nothing but women, and so forth. The most recent detailed discussion (by Peter Müller) finds that, although no one single argument can be said to exclude Petrine authorship, the combined force of several (some of which I have mentioned above) shows the epistle to be a pseudograph and a remarkable combination of Jewish apocalyptic ideas with Hellenistic religious ones. Müller is not impressed by attempts to overturn this verdict by supposing that Peter had the letter drafted by a secretary who was fully conversant with Hellenistic terminology and ideas, or by representing it as a later reworking of an originally Petrine document—against clear evidence of the epistle's overall coherence and unity (pp. 330f.).

This epistle contains no reference of any kind to Rome, but it does allude to Peter's martyrdom: "I know that the striking of my tent will come soon, as the Lord Jesus Christ has revealed to me" (1:14). By the time this was written, the tradition of Peter's martyrdom—already prophesied by the risen Jesus in the chapter appended to the fourth gospel (21:18f.)—was well established. However, "narrative details concerning the circumstances, time and place" long remained "scanty" (Perkins, p. 138).

iii. The Tradition Develops

From the late first century some Christian writers were beginning to suppose that all the apostles had missionized widely. At first, such allegations are imprecise and unspecific. The author of 1 Clement, written about the same time as 1 Peter (the two have affinities[3]), tells that the apostles "preached from district to district and from city to city," and appointed their first converts to be "bishops and deacons of the future believers" (42:4). Justin, while, as we saw, not locating Peter in Rome, nevertheless tells that "from Jerusalem twelve men in number went. out into the world"; and the Shepherd of Hermas, a rambling prophetic work which Hahneman dates at around A.D. 100 (p. 71), speaks of "apostles and teachers who preached to all the world."[4]

Later writers are more concerned to specify localities, and an epistle of around A.D. 170 (quoted by Eusebius, ii, 25) provides the first unambiguous reference to Peter having been in Rome. This is the letter which Dionysius, bishop of Corinth, wrote to the Roman church, in which he calls the churches of both these cities a "planting made by Peter and Paul" who also, "having taught together in Italy, suffered martyrdom about the same time."

There is clearly a good deal of legend here. No earlier writer knows of Peter having been in Corinth. His presence was probably inferred from Paul's mention of a Cephas party or faction there (1 Cor. 1:12). Cullmann notes that the assertion that Peter was one of the joint founders of its church is excluded by I Cor. 3:6 and 4:15, where Paul reminds the Corinthians that he alone is their "father" who had "planted the faith." As for the church at Rome, it had already existed "for many years" (Rom. 15:23) when Paul wrote his letter to it before he had ever visited the place. Nevertheless, Dionysius's view found prompt acceptance. A little later, Irenaeus speaks of the Roman church as having been "founded and constituted by the two very glorious apostles Peter and Paul," and Tertullian specifies their Roman martyrdom. Cullmann (perhaps wryly) notes (p. 117) that the value of this evidence is diminished by Tertullian's adding to it the story that the apostle John was dipped in boiling oil at Rome and yet survived uninjured.

Still later writers credit Peter with twenty-five years in Rome, and make him not the joint but the sole founder of its church.[5] Walter Bauer pointed out that eliminating either him or Paul in this way is only to be expected once the view arose that monarchical episcopacy had already existed in the early church (p. 114). Of the two apostles, Peter was naturally preferred: as a supposedly close companion of Jesus he would have received the true faith, and could therefore strengthen the authority of Rome in its struggle against heretics, particularly against Marcion and his followers, who recognized only Paul as the true apostle. As both Bauer and Karl Heussi (p. 56) observe, making Paul the first in the succession of bishops would have been no adequate protection against these heretics.

Considerably earlier than the epistle of Dionysius are two texts which are claimed as "indirect witnesses" (Cullmann, p. 114) of the martyr death of Peter in Rome. Before looking at these we may briefly consider, as a possible further such witness, a passage of uncertain date in one of the Christian insertions in the Jewish apocalypse known (in its final, Christian form) as the Ascension of Isaiah. The passage prophesies, from the standpoint of Isaiah, that in the world's last days Beliar, the evil prince who has ruled it from the beginning, will descend to Earth from his firmament

> in the form of a man, a lawless king, a slayer of his mother, who himself, even this king, will persecute the plant which the twelve apostles of the Beloved have planted. And one of the twelve shall he delivered into his hand. (4:2f.)

Beliar, in early Christian literature, is a synonym for the archdemon Satan, as at 2 Cor. 6:15 where Paul contrasts Beliar and Christ as parallel to the opposites of darkness and light. The "king" who slew his mother and persecuted the church is clearly the Emperor Nero, who had his mother Agrippina assassinated and "inflicted the most exquisite tortures" on Christians (Tacitus, *Annals*, 15:44). In the Sibylline oracles (a collection of Jewish and Christian oracles written in imitation of the pagan 'Sibylline Books'), Nero, under the name of Beliar, is to lead the armies of the Antichrist. The reference is to 'Nero-redivivus': after his suicide in A.D. 68 the belief arose that he had not died, but had fled to the East and would return at the head of Parthian armies to regain his throne. When years passed without his return, this legend developed into a belief that he had in the meantime died, but would soon come back to life and reassume power.

This Chapter 4 of the Ascension of Isaiah seems to embody a muddled conflation of the living Nero with Nero-redivivus. The living Nero reigned from 54 to 68, but the Nero who, according to this apocalypse, will descend in the form of Beliar will rule, universally worshipped as God, for three and a half years, at the end of which the Lord will come down from the seventh heaven and cast him into hell, whereupon the world will end (4:4–18). If in this whole context it is said that one of the Twelve will fall into Beliar's hands, the one intended must be someone who has survived the reign of the living Nero. O'Connor calls the whole passage "a flowing together of two ideas and a compromise. On the one hand Nero is seen as the Antichrist, and on the other the Devil appears to be the Antichrist. Gradually the second concept gained supremacy" (p. 68).

Any evidential worth of the passage of course depends on when the insertion of which it is a part was added to the Jewish original, and this is uncertain and disputed. Cullmann (p. 112) thinks A.D. 100 most likely, but (as he is aware) Dinkler (p. 216) argues for A.D. 140. O'Connor proposes "a date within the first quarter of the second century, if not earlier," but finds the passage "too vague to serve as a strong argument for the martyrdom of Peter in Rome" (pp. 68, 70). Let us therefore turn to the two texts which are regarded as stronger indirect witnesses, namely the letter of Ignatius of Antioch to the Christians of Rome, and the epistle known as 1 Clement.

iv. Ignatius and 1 Clement

There are seven letters generally accepted as genuinely Ignatian and as written around A.D. 110–18. I am not convinced by recent attempts to dismiss them as forgeries of some fifty years later (Details in my 1999a, pp. 264f.). Christine Trevett's detailed study of 1992 likewise endorses the generally accepted view. If the letters were later forgeries, any testimony they might give about Peter and Rome would of course be worthless.

In the letter to the Christians of Rome, Ignatius, on his way to martyrdom there, states: "I do not give you orders, like Peter and Paul [*ōs Petros kai Paulos*—no verb]. They were apostles. I am a convict" (4:3). Cullmann admits that not a word is said to indicate that the two apostles had been in Rome, and that the sentence could be taken to mean 'I do not command you *as if* I were Peter and Paul' (p. 110), in other words, as a Peter or a Paul, or as any apostle might. Cullmann adds that Ignatius's words in two other epistles (Trallians 3:3 and Ephesians 3:1) could support such an interpretation. The former passage reads: "I did not think myself competent, as a convict, to give you orders, like an apostle." And the latter states: "I do not give you commands, as if I were someone great."

Yet, asks Cullmann, why should Ignatius, in a letter to the Romans, have named Peter and Paul together unless they had both been in Rome? The answer is surely that they were famous enough without that, and indeed are the only two apostles about whom anything much was known in the early church. They are the only persons whom Ignatius anywhere names as apostles. Otherwise he writes only in general terms of "the apostles" and of their "ordinances" (Trallians 7:1). Apostles had come to be regarded as persons of authority, credited with universally binding pronouncements. Merrill points out that letters ascribed to them would naturally have acquired general validity, irrespective of their original addresses (p. 286); and Ignatius may be referring not to the two apostles as much as to their letters. (1 Peter, as well as the Paulines, was then in existence.)

It is, then, inappropriate for Schoedel to speak (p. 176) of Ignatius "selecting" Peter and Paul for mention in his letter to the Romans, and of his doing so because he was "no doubt" aware of "a tradition about their joint presence and their martyrdom in Rome which significantly bolstered the prestige of that city's Christian community." (Schoedel is of course aware that a 'tradition' is not a historical fact.) How little was known of any apostles apart from these two is betrayed by Acts, which gives nothing but the names of nine of the reconstituted post-resurrection Twelve (in which Matthias had replaced the traitor Judas). The remaining three comprise James the son of

Zebedee—of him we learn only that Herod Agrippa I had him killed (12:2)—and his brother John, who is little more than a silent supernumary in stories about Peter, as in the whole of Chapter 3. Clearly, Peter was the only one of the Twelve who figured to any extent in traditions about the early church on which the author of Acts could draw; and even he is abandoned in the middle of the book, leaving further developments to Paul.

Turning now to 1 Clement, this epistle purports to have been written by the church of Rome to the church of Corinth, and is otherwise anonymous. The name of Clement was associated with it (by Clement of Alexandria) from around A.D. 170, and Hagner records (pp. 1, 3) how the Fathers romanced about him in their usual way: Irenaeus makes him a disciple of Peter and Paul, and Tertullian has him consecrated bishop of Rome by Peter himself. Most commentators date this epistle in the 90s. Like 1 Peter, with which, as we saw, it has some parallels, it must have been written before the gospels had become generally known, for, as its 1937 editor Lowther Clarke has said, it shows no knowledge of them and "no trace of any interest in the ministry of Christ or in his miracles, not even in the Passion story," for which, like 1 Peter, it draws on Isaiah 53 (pp. 13, 36). The sayings of Jesus which it quotes (in its Chapters 13 and 46) derive, says Hagner, not from the first three of the canonical gospels, but from "oral tradition"; and it "nowhere convincingly alludes to the Johannine literature" (pp. 273, 287, 332). Yet the author regarded the age of the apostles (among whom he includes Paul, 47:1) as already so much past that at any rate some of the men they appointed to succeed them had died and been succeeded by their own appointees (Chapters 42–44). Hence the epistle can hardly be earlier than A.D. 70–80. The earlier it is put, the more difficult it becomes to explain why, if Peter had been in Rome, this letter from the Roman church is, as we shall see, so vague about him.

Chapter 4 of this epistle lists, in chronological order, OT personages who experienced difficulties or worse as a result of jealousy. The author then adduces examples of similarly caused misfortunes from "our own generation" (5:1). He continues:

(2) By reason of jealousy and envy the greatest and most righteous pillars were persecuted and contended even unto death.

(3) Let us set before our eyes the good apostles;

(4) Peter, who by reason of unrighteous jealousy endured not
one nor two but many labours, and having thus borne his testimony went to his due place of glory.

(5) By reason of jealousy and strife Paul showed the reward of
patient endurance.

(6) After that he had been seven times in bonds, had been driven into exile, had been stoned, had preached in the East and in
the West, he won the noble renown of his faith;

(7) having taught righteousness to the whole world and having
come to the limit of the West, and having borne his testimony
before the rulers, he thus departed from the world and went unto
the holy place, having become a very great example of patient
endurance.

What is said in the first half of verse six probably represents
the author's recollections of 2 Cor. 11:23–33, where Paul reports
that he had often been imprisoned, was once stoned, and had
to flee from Damascus. Commentators who understand the
whole passage as alluding to the Roman execution of Peter and
Paul explain the references to jealousy and strife by supposing
that fellow-Christians—probably Jewish-Christian missionaries
insistent on circumcision—denounced the apostles to the
Romans, or that strife among Christian factions had caused the
government to intervene so as to maintain order. The details,
says O'Connor (pp. 78f.), will not have been edifying, and so
Clement does not give them. It is, however, noteworthy how little is said of Peter (verse 4) in contrast with the much fuller
report concerning Paul in the following verses. Cullmann supposes that this is because "the example of Peter had less to
offer" concerning misfortune due to jealousy (p. 99). Yet jealousy is hardly relevant to much of the passage about Paul—for
instance that he had preached both in the East and in the West,
had gained the noble renown of his faith, and taught righteousness to the whole world. Even his "testimony before the rulers"
is not clearly linked with the jealousy he had to endure; and
Cullmann allows that "grammatically, no doubt, this description

is no longer dependent on the words 'on account of jealousy and strife'" (p. 103). The reason why Clement introduces jealousy at all is that he holds it to be the underlying cause of the recent disorder in the Corinthian church about which his epistle was protesting. It is in support of this protest that he makes cautionary mention of how jealousy had caused misfortune in both ancient and recent times. But the details he gives do not fit this overall schema of causation by jealousy particularly well.

Some commentators have accounted for the thinness of the reference to Peter by supposing that further details were known to the Corinthian recipients of Clement's letter—as if the more substantial information about Paul were not also known in this locality where, as is clear from his epistles, he had more than once missionized. No, we must ask, with Schmiedel (column 4601), why, if Peter had actually died at Rome, so little that is definite should be said of him in a letter of the Roman church which is able to say considerably more about Paul in a passage which gives an account of them both. It is not said that Peter travelled to the West: Uta Ranke-Heinemann finds it significant that the West, and so with it Rome, is assigned only to Paul (p. 222). Nor is Peter said to have given his testimony before rulers. There is, then, no suggestion that he was arraigned by the authorities, as is said of Paul in verse 7. We are not told where Peter endured his labours, only that they were "many," and so presumably spread over a substantial portion of his Christian life. Nor is it said that they resulted in his death. The statement is that "having borne his testimony" (*marturēsas*) "in this way" (*houtō*), viz. by enduring them, he then went to his place of glory. His labours were, then, appropriately rewarded, after his death, by a place in heaven. They need not necessarily have involved more than the kind of imprisonment and beating which he is said in Acts to have suffered as a consequence of "bearing testimony" (5:32) to Jesus's resurrection.

marturēsas is a participle of the verb *martureō*, 'to bear witness'; and the corresponding noun *martus* (it is the noun that is used at Acts 5:32) means 'witness'. Arndt and Gingrich's Lexicon records the following meanings of it: a witness in the legal sense; or, figuratively, "anyone who can or should testify to any-

thing"; or "witnesses who hear a divine message," as Jesus's disciples are to be witnesses (*martures*) of his life, death, and resurrection (Acts 1:8). Later, "in the usage of the persecuted
church, *martus* became 'one who witnessed unto death', a
'martyr'." Thus the word does not always imply martyrdom. Uta
Ranke-Heinemann notes (p. 223) that, in Acts' account of
Stephen's martyrdom, it is not Stephen himself who is called a
martus, but those who are stoning him (7:58f.). In 1 Clement
63:3 there is mention of prudent and blameless men whom the
Roman church sent to Corinth and who "shall be witnesses
(*martures*) between you and us". Furthermore, Ignatius of
Antioch, indicted for his Christianity at the beginning of the second century, eagerly looked forward to his death in the arena
in Rome, yet did not use the word *martyrein*, nor any technical term to designate it. He wrote only of imitating Jesus, of
becoming his true disciple by dying in this way, and of being
ground into the pure bread of Christ by the teeth of the animals. Bowersock observes: "If *martus* had meant martyr at that
time, Ignatius would undoubtedly have availed himself of the
word" (p. 77). Moreover, in the reference to Peter at 1 Clement
5:4, the idea of martyrdom is hard to reconcile with the word
houtō. Martyrdom can occur only once to anybody, but Peter
endured many labours and "in this way" (*houtō*) bore witness
to his convictions. It is inexcusable when C.P. Thiede sup-
presses this word in his English rendering of the passage, and
claims that the Greek implies Peter's martyrdom. He translates
the verse, and comments on it in the words in parentheses, as
follows:

> Peter, who because of unjustified jealousy suffered not one or two
> but many afflictions, and, having giving [sic.] witness (*kai houtō
> marturēsas*—martyrdom literally as a form of witnessing), he went
> to the place of glory which was his due. (p. 186)

This rendition shows how different Thiede is from Cullmann,
who gives a clear and accurate account of the evidence and fully
acknowledges what can be said against his own interpretation
of it. I have found his book invaluable. Thiede is basically a

devotional writer, who concludes his book on Peter with a call to prayer, backed by words from 2 Peter (dated, p. 181, at A.D. 60) which are accepted as words of "Peter himself." Thiede's more recent apologetic interpretations of early Christian material have been justly rejected as arbitrary by Christian scholars (Details in my 1999a book, pp. 5ff.).

O'Connor's treatment of the *houtō* in 1 Clement 5:4 also seems very questionable. He makes it qualify not *marturēsas*, but the going to the place of glory that follows. Instead of understanding the verse as 'having thus borne his witness [by many labours], he went to the place of glory', O'Connor proposes (p. 79): "And thus, bearing his witness [by martyrdom], he went to the place of glory". Going to that place is in this way construed as the result and due reward of his testifying to the faith by accepting execution.

Cullmann cautiously goes no further than to assert that, when the epistle was written, "the word *martyrein* for 'bear witness' is at least already on the way to becoming a technical term for witness by martyrdom" (p. 96). And he allows that, "theoretically," 5:4 can be interpreted to mean that Peter, "in his life, had to suffer manifold trials, that (through preaching) he bore witness, and that then, somewhere at some time, he died" (p. 94). It is certainly noteworthy that the text clearly implies martyrdom in the case of Paul: he "departed from the world" as a result of bearing his testimony before the rulers—this surely implies that he was executed—whereupon he went to the holy place. In what is said of Peter, however, there is no such clear implication that execution intervened between his bearing his many labours and his heavenly reward for doing so.

One may, however, suspect, with Merrill (p. 292), that, although Clement had no knowledge or tradition of the manner or place in which Peter died, he yet thought it eminently proper for him to have died as a martyr. Hence, while not confidently affirming it, he used language which could be taken to intimate it, especially in the context of what precedes and of what immediately follows. Let us look at this context.

The first verse of Chapter 5 introduces this whole account of "those who contended" (in the Greek, the "athletes," *athlētas*) in recent times. There follows, as the first example, the mention of the "pillars of the church" who were "persecuted" and who "contended" (*ēthlēsan*, from the verb *athleō*, to compete in a contest) "unto death." Then at 6:1, after the passage about Peter and Paul, we read:

> Unto these men of holy lives was gathered a vast multitude of elect ones who, suffering by reason of jealousy many indignities and tortures, became a most admirable example among us.

Commentators take this to refer to Nero's persecution of Christians at Rome. Tacitus, writing some twenty years later, likewise calls Nero's Christian victims a vast multitude ("ingens multitudo"); and Clement's statement that the multitude became an example "among us" may well mean 'among the Christian community here at Rome', rather than 'among Christians generally'.

There are, then, clear references to martyrdom in some of Clement's examples of recent misfortunes due to jealousy. Yet these do not all involve martyrdom, for he adds to the instances I have already quoted: "Jealousy has estranged wives from husbands"; and "jealousy and strife have overthrown great cities and rooted up mighty nations" (6:3f.). What all the examples do involve is suffering of some kind, and we should not introduce the idea of martyrdom into those where it is not clearly stated, even if we believe, with Merrill, that Clement himself is giving us a little encouragement to do this in the case of Peter.

What of the "gathering" (6:1) of the vast persecuted multitude unto Peter and Paul? Peter, we recall, after his trials went to the glorious place which was his due, and Paul gave his testimony before the rulers, passed thus from the world and went to the holy place. There follows immediately this statement that a multitude was gathered to them—presumably at the glorious, holy place. The common meeting place, says Schmiedel (column 4599) "is not Rome but heaven," and accordingly the passage says nothing as to the place of death of the two apostles With this, Heussi (p. 23) concurs. Nor is it said that all the Christian examples—the "pillars" (whoever they were), the two apostles and the Neronian victims—all suffered at the same time, any more than did OT personages who were listed chronologically in Chapter 4. The Christian victims indeed suffered in "our generation" (5:1), but this indicates a period which could span between twenty-five and forty years. We recall that, in Chapters 42–44 of the epistle, the lives of the apostles are put at some distance in the past.

Cullmann, however, believes that the words "among us" (6:1), in the sense of among the Christians of Rome, can be extended to what had been said of Peter and Paul because "other really important features" in the words about these two link them with the (Neronian) victims of 6:1 (p. 98). Peter and Paul, he claims, fell victim, like these others, to "non-Christian persecutors as a result of disunity among Christians caused by jealousy" (p. 104). And this must have occurred in Rome; for, first, we know (from 6:1) that jealousy ruled in the Roman church; second, we can infer from Rom. 15:20 that Paul feared difficulties with it because it included both Jewish and Gentile Christians; and, third, we know that he was imprisoned at Rome and at that time "had to expect 'affliction' from other members of the church (Phil. 1:15f.)". Only of the Roman church can all three of these factors be posited (p. 105).

In scrutiny of this widely accepted argument—Brown, for example, finds it persuasive (p. 124n.)—it is relevant to recall that Clement's overall schema of causation by jealousy does not fit his examples particularly well. Cullmann is aware that some commentators take the mention of jealousy as referring only to the life and not to the death of both the apostles (p. 103). Peter, we recall, because of jealousy endured many labours and, *having thus given his testimony*, went to heaven. The words I have italicized can certainly be held to indicate a break between the labours resulting from jealousy and the going to heaven. Moreover, dissension and strife were not especially characteristic of Rome, but were ubiquitous in the early churches. John Fenton has shown that "twenty-four out of the twenty-seven New Testament books are to varying degrees the result of controversy among Christians." Hence "eighty-nine percent of the New Testament is the result of

Christian disagreement," which was sometimes "extremely bit-ter" (p. 106). It is particularly prominent in the epistles. Paul begins his letter to the Galatians by twice cursing Christians who do not accept his own doctrinal niceties. The Anglican minister Graham Shaw calls this "the first recorded anathema in Christian history," not to be trivialized as the work of the dogmatic church of a later century, but firmly embedded in the earliest docu-ments of the first (p. 44). But it was inevitable: theological con-victions are not such as can be demonstrated by experiment or by the exhibition of clear, concrete facts. As to the Roman church being ethnically mixed, this is surely true of all early Christian communities: "No single New Testament document can be labelled as basically Gentile, but for almost every docu-ment it is possible to demonstrate its mixed Jewish-Gentile char-acter" (Marshall, p. 283). Elliott (as we saw in note 1) finds that, throughout Asia Minor all the Christian communities of the late first century were mixed. Finally, Philippians does not claim to have been written from Rome (although it might have been), and it makes no mention of Peter.

Cullmann offers a further argument. He supposes that, if we "must assume with the greatest probability that Clement [at 5:4, considered in the context of 6:1] refers to the martyr death of Peter," then "he at least knew also the place of martyrdom, since it is not customary to hand down narratives of martyrdoms with-out any indication of place. In our passage Clement does not need to mention it, since he can assume that it is known" (p. 96). Lietzmann had already insisted that this place must have been Rome; otherwise the "real place" would have promulgated its claims, or alternatively several would have competed for the honour (pp. 235f.).

Dinkler retorted that Lietzmann "transfers generalizations applicable to the veneration of martyrs in a later age to an early period," and that "it cannot be ruled out that, in the early days, when there was as yet no martyr cult, the fact of martyrdom—with no knowledge of locality—was asserted and passed on as tradition" (p. 204). Schmiedel had already written, some sixty years earlier:

If, let us suppose, Peter had perished while travelling in a distant land, at some obscure place, not as the result of ordinary process of law, but perhaps in some popular tumult, and if also such companions as he may have had perished along with him, then information of his death could reach his fellow-Christians only by report; and if, even at a later date, no Christian church arose at the place where it occurred, no local tradition as to his end had any chance of surviving. Let us only suppose, for example, that Paul had died of the stoning at Lystra (Acts 14:19) or of that with which he was threatened at Iconium (14:5) and either was unaccompanied or was accompanied even in death—what should we, what could Clement have known as to the place of his death? (column 4601)

If we are dealing with stories of martyrdom which are fictions, then the earliest accounts may well be equally imprecise, even tentative. "In the time of Tertullian and Clemens of Alexandria," says Gibbon (in a note to chapter 16 of his *Decline and Fall of the Roman Empire*), "the glory of martyrdom was confined to St. Peter, St. Paul, and St. James. It was gradually bestowed on the rest of the apostles by the more recent Greeks, who prudently selected for their preaching and suffering some remote country beyond the limits of the Roman empire." It is characteristic of the mythological process that originally vague stories are later given an exact setting in time and place—just as personages originally nameless are later supplied with names. (The article 'Names for the Nameless' in Metzger and Coogan's 1993 *Oxford Companion to the Bible* shows how irresistible this tendency has proved to be; and the article 'Magi' in the same handbook gives an almost comical illustration of invention of names and of other specific details.[6]) On the other hand, accounts of martyrdoms which had actually occurred in the second-century churches or later, such as the record of the death of Polycarp (who was burnt at Smyrna around A.D. 155) or of the victims who died at Lyons in A.D. 177, naturally state where the event occurred, thus linking the martyrdom with the place where the martyr was venerated. By this time what we are faced with is a martyr cult.

v. Topographical Support

Topographical support for the Roman tradition about Peter comes only as late as ca. A.D. 200, from the presbyter Gaius. Opposing the Montanist Proclus, who had supported his polemic with the claim that the church of Hierapolis in Asia Minor possessed the graves of Philip and his four prophetess daughters, Gaius retorted that the church of Rome could do even better: "I can show you the trophies (*tropaia*) of the apostles; for if you go to the Vatican Hill or to the Highway to Ostia you will find the trophies of those who have founded this church"—of Peter in the former place and of Paul in the latter.[7] (That the two had jointly founded the Roman church was established doctrine by this time.) Partisan interests are clearly involved here. The Christian East felt the need to prove apostolicity for its doctrines by claiming possession of apostolic burial places. Proclus's argument is that the deceased had contact with the people of Hierapolis, and that what he was teaching was their pure doctrine transmitted to him through intermediaries. If Rome's counter claim of apostolic "trophies" was to have any force, it must likewise have implied that Rome had personal contact with apostles. Philologically, 'trophies' of them could mean their graves, the places where they were martyred, or even merely memorials to them. But possession of memorial monuments would not guarantee the personal contact required by Gaius's argument, and so, presumably, he meant to hint, if not to claim outright, that the trophies mark either their graves or the places where they died. His argument would be strongest if the reference were to tangible graves, rather than to traditional sites of martyrdom authenticated only by fallible human testimony. But if he had been able honestly to claim Roman possession of the graves, he would surely have used the word *taphos* which Proclus had used for his claim. It rather looks as if he had to be content with an ambiguous word which would suggest something more than a memorial monument.

Above all, the late date of Gaius's statement must be kept in mind, together with Cullmann's observations that "in Rome no one took an interest in the graves of the martyrs in the first two centuries"; that "we do not have even the slightest trace of a cult of relics before the martyrdom of Polycarp, and then we are dealing not with Rome but with Smyrna"; and that "even the graves of the Bishops of Rome exist only from the beginning of the third century, and then in the Catacomb of Callistus" (p. 154).

Excavations under the main altar of St. Peter's basilica in Rome have disclosed the remains of a monument which has been taken to be the trophy of Peter to which Gaius referred. Brown cautiously regards it as a "commemorative shrine" which "marks the place where the death and burial were honoured, not necessarily the exact place of burial." The claim that the bones of Peter were also found he regards as "dubious" (p. 97n.). Cullmann (pp. 146–150) gives evidence that the monument may have been built in the second half of the second century (some few decades before Gaius's statement about the trophies) and says that none of the many graves, both pagan and Christian, beneath it are likely to be as early as the first century. (The basilica was built on the site of the one constructed by Constantine, which itself was built on what had been a cemetery.) That Peter's supposed Roman martyrdom should be honoured by a late second-century monument here is not surprising. Nor is it astonishing to find bones in a plot containing graves. Pheme Perkins observes that, in order to claim one of the skeletons as Peter's, scholars have to make a virtue of the absence of first-century markings concerning the apostle by arguing that the danger of persecution required an unmarked grave (pp. 49, 168).

vi. The Mythological Process at Work

The historian Michael Grant finds that the manifold objections which have been made to the traditional view "do not add up to anything like a demonstration that Peter never went to Rome." This is quite true, for it would be impossible to demonstrate such a negative about someone of whom so little is known. It is, however, also true that what tells against the traditional view tends to be very readily brushed aside. Thus Grant supposes that Paul's silences are explicable if Peter went to Rome after Paul had written his letters, or if his epistle to the Romans was addressed only to a section of the Roman community, the section in close contact with him; other Christians may have been there, followers of Peter, who himself may not have led the Roman church, but have gone there as a missionary, as "one elder among others." As for Acts, that its second half "is intended to concentrate on Paul" adequately explains why Peter is simply dropped from its narrative after Chapter 15. The thinness of what is said of Peter in 1 Clement and the total silence of the Roman apologist Justin as to any Roman stay of Peter both suggest to Grant what he has posited apropos of Paul's epistle, namely "the presence of more than one Christian group in Rome." And later exaggerations, such as a twenty-five year sojourn there, do not mean that Peter was not there at all.

But what positive evidence that is acceptably reliable suggests that Peter was in Rome? All that Grant says in this regard is that "there is a large measure of agreement" that he did go there, and probably arrived there "some time between 54 and 58 or possibly as late as 63" (pp. 147–150). His only support for these dates is to list, in a bibliographical note, some works which restate "the Catholic position." Raymond Brown, one of the most reliable of Catholic scholars, is less confident than this would suggest. He of course believes that Peter was martyred in Rome, yet insists that "we have no knowledge at all" of when he came there or of "what he did there before he was martyred."

Brown adds: "Certainly Peter was not the original missionary who brought Christianity to Rome (and therefore not the founder of the church of Rome in that sense). There is no serious proof that he was bishop (or local ecclesiastical officer) of the Roman church—a claim not made until the third century." It is even "likely that the single bishop structure did not come to Rome until ca. 140–150" (pp. 98, 163).

With these reservations Grant obviously agrees. Yet he observes that, if one accepts that Peter was in Rome, one might then consider some of the stories—collected unsurprisingly by C.P. Thiede among others—about with whom and whereabouts he resided there. But the growth of such material is surely adequately explained from the claims and needs of the Roman church.

In all this we can see a good example of the mythological process. In the earliest documents Peter and Paul are in conflict (in Galatians Paul calls him a hypocrite). The next stage was to allege that the activities of the two ran on parallel lines, without conflict, as in Acts, thus reflecting the idyllic unity of the early church. Next we find allegations of active co-operation between them (the joint founding of Christian communities). Finally, Peter is made the sole founder of the Roman church and its first bishop—against the fact that monarchical episcopacy was actually developed only at a later date.

The Roman church has built doctrine on Mary as it has on Peter—with as little justification. But the evidence concerning Mary is another story, some of which I have set out elsewhere, and the whole of which has recently received a good deal of critical attention.[8]

4
Reinterpreting Early Christian Testimony

i. Radical Anglican Theology

a. DON CUPITT AND HUGH DAWES

Evangelicals are determinedly reiterating scriptural doctrines, and Pentecostals are perpetuating the "spiritual gifts" documented in the Pauline letters. But some clergy have come radically to reinterpret the claims made for Jesus in both epistles and gospels, and to question the whole world view which informs these documents. In previous chapters of this book we saw exemplified the mythological process whereby early ideas on one or other specific subjects become, over time, transmuted into very different ones. In this chapter we can see the whole Christian tradition subjected—and quite deliberately—to radical reinterpretation.

That traditional Christian doctrine is no more than provisional is today stressed by Maurice Wiles, Leslie Houlden, and Dennis Nineham—all three are Anglican scholars. Nineham's 1993 book is subtitled *A Study in Religious Change*. It shows how very different the Christianity of the tenth century was even from what counts as strict orthodoxy today; and the author adds that, if we knew as much about the first century as we do about the tenth, there is every reason to think that we should find its Christianity equally foreign to us.

In this chapter I am concerned with clergy, particularly clergy of the established Anglican church, who go much further than these three impressive scholars, and who typify what is now called radical theology. There is, firstly, Don Cupitt, a Life Fellow of Emmanuel College, Cambridge. He launched what has become known as 'the Sea of Faith' movement with a 1984 book of that title based on a BBC television series. He there relates how, as a young Anglican priest, he could not bring himself to tell terminally ill parishioners that their affliction was sent by God as—in the wording of the *Book of Common Prayer*—a "fatherly visitation,"for which they must be thankful and to which they must respond by repenting of their sins. He concluded that the old hypothesis of a transcendent all-good and all-powerful God "cannot solve the problem of evil"; and he came to regard God as "the sum of our values," "the ideal unity of all value", not as an entity outside us. "To speak of God is to speak about the moral and spiritual goals we ought to be aiming at." There is no immortality: brooding over evidence (or lack of it) for life after death "poisons life." In his interpretation, the doctrine of resurrection does not promise another life hereafter, but "tells us to live now a new life that has left fear of death behind." The importance of Christ is that he symbolizes the kind of being we should aim to become, "our own ideal *alter ego*"; and the Kingdom of God is no more than the kind of human society which Cupitt hopes will result from the pursuit of such ideals (pp. 33, 259–272).

In a later (1989) book, Cupitt envisages a future church with a sacramental meal where a bread roll will be broken to the words 'The body of Christ'—taken to mean that "the church now gathered in company is the risen Christ" The formula 'The blood of Christ' will also be spoken as wine is drunk, and will mean that "the church must surrender her distinct identity and must dissolve herself into the common life of humanity" (pp. 170f.). Anthropologists have shown how often a ceremony is kept up and even elaborated for reasons quite different from those which led to its origin, once these latter have been lost from sight. But radical reinterpretations when earlier reasons are extant, as proposed in the case by Cupitt, will inevitably be felt as shocking.

Cupitt's later writings have become increasingly incoherent. "It is hard," he says, "to find the right words for the true God who is not an objective being, not a person, and does not exist as things exist." He concludes, unhelpfully, that "God is such that when nothing is mine and I am nothing, then God is mine" (1991, pp. 74f.). If this seems no more than verbiage, we must recall his suggestion that, for us, there is no reality apart from language. "Many people," he says, "think of the world as being simply there, inertly factual and independent of us." But this is "not so," for "our minds work only in language"; hence "nothing is real and nothing is there until it has been formed and produced in and by language" (1990, p. 194). He is not saying that there is no real world, independent of us, but that it is there *for us* only in so far as we have ideas of it; and for him ideas are no more than words: "Concepts are just words" and "thinking is a *sotto voce* talking to oneself" (p. 157). It is not surprising that a man who holds such views supposes that he is thinking even when he is doing no more than making up sentences. When what is under discussion is not one familiar object, but something more general, such as a class of objects, the class is indeed apt to be represented in the imagination by a word, and then only the associations of the word remain to guide the thinking. But for Cupitt thinking never involves anything more than verbal associations. He is quite explicit about this, saying:

> In order to be a creative . . . you just set two or three words and phrases in place and then lie back and free-associate. Relax. Do nothing. Let your mind wander, diverge. Just let language run, and watch passively to see what it comes up with. When something good crops up, name it out loud so that it gets remembered. Jot it down. That's thinking. (1998, p. 33)

Certainly, readers of Cupitt's books will get the impression that they were written on the basis of 'thinking' of this nature, by setting down what he calls "the torrent of words that runs through me each day" (p. 69). He reiterates that "thoughts are words and they run in trains." When we write a letter "we wait for language to come running, giving us the words we are waiting for. They

just pop up . . . Thinking is a receptive waiting-upon Language"
(p. 51).

That ideas are mere words, even that they invariably depend
on words, has long since been shown to be fallacious. Study of
chimpanzees, and even observation of domestic animals, has
established that mammals other than man form ideas and act on
them, although they have no words. A dog recognizes the same
house as his home and the same cat that belongs in this house
as does his master, for his behaviour towards them is quite different from his behaviour towards other houses and cats. Such
distinctions are obviously based on knowledge that is acquired.
Chimpanzees can rationally adapt means to ends in solving
problems that are of interest to them. It is particularly when animals make mistakes, when they react to something as though it
were something else, that we are able to recognize that their
action is based on notions, albeit in such cases mistaken ones.
I once experienced that two bottles of milk close together on a
doorstep looked so like a seated white cat that the dog with me
gave chase, and desisted only when proximity to the bottles disclosed his error. So long as animals react in the most appropriate way to the events of their environment, we may be misled
by the very perfection of the adaptation to ascribe their actions
to mechanisms that are simpler than ideas, even in instances
where ideas are in fact involved. I have criticized the gross mis-
conceptions underlying common views about the relation
between words, ideas and things elsewhere (most recently in
my 1999b booklet on the origin of language) and have challenged Cupitt's view of language in my 2002 article in the journal *Theology*. Perhaps the chief obstacle to an understanding of
the part played by language in the human thinking process is
the great difficulty of imagining ourselves without it and without any of the ideas which do depend on it.

Another radical Anglican author is Hugh Dawes, who spent
ten years of his ministry as Chaplain to a Cambridge college and
now writes from additional parish experience as vicar of a
Cambridge church. He is "not in the business of recruiting for
heaven" but is glad to work with and for all who live in his
parish, church-goers or not, to help them "fulfill their humanity"

(p. 110). This is not empty talk: so much is clear from the examples he gives of the needy in his own town and his efforts to help them. His concern with the here and now leads him to reinterpret "hallowed formularies" about the hereafter ("even the most hallowed are," he claims, "provisional," p. 3), although he knows that this distresses some of his own congregation. Against such disquiet he cites opinion polls which show that a substantial proportion of Christians share his unbelief in "the historical status" of Jesus's virgin birth and resurrection, and that "almost 31 percent of church-going Anglicans do not believe in life after death"—a doctrine "built upon a separation of humanity from the rest of the animal creation which it is surely going to become impossible in the future to sustain" (pp. 60, 65). He wants to use "the language of resurrection and eternity" in a "non-ultimate way," to indicate that we live on either in offspring who carry our genes or in persons whom we have influenced (p. 66). Again, "wherever light is able to shine through in life, whenever goodness and practical kindness win against uncaring and cruelty, resurrection is at work" (p. 62). The weakness of this kind of reinterpretation of traditional terms is that it is hard to distinguish from the "newspeak" which Dawes himself deplores, where "words mean whatever you want them to" (p. 10).

Dawes is particularly critical of the central Christian doctrine of redemption, which is as mythical for him as it was for Wrede some 100 years earlier. Jesus, he insists, was human, not "a preexistent divine person" who took human flesh "just for a while" and redeemed us with his blood. The idea that the shedding of blood in sacrifice appeases God and atones for sin was natural enough in the environment in which Christianity originated, but today it is "a moral affront," even to many believers (pp. 47–49). Yet the sin of worshippers who are living almost two thousand years later is still held to have brought Christ to the cross, and is even treated as "something to sing about," as in hymns with such words as "it was our sin that brought Him down" (pp. 7f.).

Attempts to attract young people by presenting them with up-to-date packaging (guitar music and other features of the discothèque) of such archaic and unacceptable doctrines are, for

Dawes, completely misguided. As a particularly pernicious corollary of the doctrine of redemption he mentions the idea that our nature is fundamentally depraved, that all goodness must be ascribed to God, any human virtue being "implanted in us from outside as a supernatural corrective for the failings of our natural state," so that "only 'Holy Spirit', the distribution of which or of whom was a church-mediated exercise very firmly 'under God', could enable us to overcome our natures—and even then not all that often" (p. 90). What Dawes is here attacking was for long a very entrenched doctrine. William Temple, later to become Archbishop of Canterbury, wrote in 1934: "All is of God; the only thing of my own which I can contribute to my own redemption is the sin from which I need to be redeemed" (p. 401). This is still squarely in the tradition of Augustine and Calvin; but in 1995 a report by the Doctrine Commission of the General Synod of the Church of England (entitled *The Mystery of Salvation*) offered some compromise, saying: "Of course [!] the inherent goodness of our created nature was marred but not eradicated by the fall" (p. 54).

Liberal theology of the early twentieth century had mounted a protest similar to that of Dawes, but had grossly underestimated the extent to which mankind is capable of evil behaviour—an oversight which prompted a massive reaction from Karl Barth, who declared in the famous second edition of his commentary on Paul's Epistle to the Romans (1921) that "the disgust of men at themselves . . . is the characteristic mark of true religion." Barth held that we cannot understand God with our minds because they, with our whole nature, have been corrupted by the Fall. The only source of God-knowledge is the Bible, which is to be uncritically accepted as revelation. If we ask how our flawed and unreliable minds can nevertheless reliably identify the Bible as revealed truth, Barth replies that only the guidance of our reason by the Holy Spirit can lead us to this insight (see John Kent's summary of Barth's position, pp. 121f.).

For Dawes, Barth bears a good deal of responsibility for the persistence of the view that we can appeal outside or beyond ourselves—to "revelation" as "the giving of truth from above"—

for our knowledge and understanding. He finds this handing over of ultimate authority to allegedly incontrovertible scripture just as tyrannical as "the thought police of Hitler's Germany," which Barth was so concerned to resist (pp. 23–27). Barth, however, found his negative view of human nature confirmed as he witnessed the rise of dictators who suppressed all criticism and sanctioned acts of barbarity. And wholesale endorsement of the 1914 war by theologians he had respected had already shown him that group behaviour even of normal persons can be bad enough. What an individual will with difficulty bring himself to do or to plead for when he is alone and acting under his own responsibility, and where he must expect to bear the blame if his crime or error is exposed, he will do more easily when surrounded by others doing or applauding the same deed. His conscience is supported by what appears to be the general opinion of what is right and permissible. In this way patriotic or protest movements can become fearsome forces, and those activated by them may feel strong enough to make demands unthinkable to them if they had to justify them as individuals.

Dawes is not blind to what he calls "the frightening capacity in human beings for cruelty, destruction and hurt" (p. 43). We who have lived through the past fifty years cannot readily make the mistake made by the pre-1914 liberal theologians. But he does rightly point to examples of morally impressive behaviour by ordinary people which is quite unrelated to any theological commitments and which can be conspicuous in persons altogether lacking them. On this basis he deplores the church's obsession with sin and depravity: "You cannot take part in any main service in the Church of England without having to confess your sin, and Anglican clergy with their daily prayers can find themselves doing this three times a day" (p. 45). I would add that one powerful strand of Christian tradition has represented not only humankind but the whole natural world as 'fallen', even lost, so that knowledge of God was not to be had from it, but rather from what is unnatural, miraculous. Hence Tertullian's famous dictum that he believed in Christianity *because* it is absurd ("Credo quia absurdum est"). The Apocalypse of Peter, for long a popular writing eventually classed as apocryphal, even held that the Earth, as well as man, is to come under the final judgement!

Dawes's arguments seem weakest when he gives his version of what some NT passages originally meant. He is less open to criticism apropos of the original drift of the OT, saying, for instance, that the early chapters of Genesis "seek to tell us, in myths, why things are the way they are: why snakes lack legs; why people speak different languages; and, in the myth of the Fall, why there is sin . . . and why life appears so laborious and painful and ends only in death" (p. 43). These are "early attempts to catch the dilemma of our existential apprehension of ourselves" (p. 38). This sounds better than calling them 'Just-so stories', but really means the same, and is acceptable, although we may query whether their authors really regarded them as no more than mythical. But his suggestion as to what the gospel resurrection narratives originally meant carries less conviction. He thinks that by these stories—which include appearances of the risen one, the empty tomb and "later additions of earthquakes, angels, the dead rising and walking, the flabbergasted guards, the grave clothes neatly folded and the rest"—the first Christians were "struggling to express . . . their faith conviction that, in the case of Jesus at least, evil has not enjoyed the final word," that his death "has not undone his life," and that "his way of living . . . remains valid and true" (pp. 57f.). If it is already questionable to argue that the modern Christian may plausibly interpret the narratives to mean no more than this, it is even less convincing to impute to the first Christians a conviction which they then expressed in such a totally misleading fashion. Dawes's dilemma is clear enough. As a scholar he sees that it is impossible to accept the narratives as records of actual historical events; yet as a Christian he has to represent them as meaning something of significance. He is seeking a more plausible-sounding version of a traditional Christian philosophy of history which held that love will decisively triumph over evil and that in some unclarified sense it has already done so by virtue of Christ's death and resurrection.

It is not difficult to show that resorting to symbolic meaning in order not to admit error is really a little ridiculous. The equivalent in science, notes Richard Dawkins, would be, if the double helix model of DNA were one day to be disproved, for scientists then, instead of accepting that they had simply got it wrong, to come up with something like:

> Of course we don't literally believe factually in the double helix any more . . . It was a story that was right for its own time, but we've moved on. Today the double helix has a new meaning for us. The compatibility of guanine with cytosine, the glove-like fit of adenine with thymine, and especially the intimate mutual twining of the left spiral around the right, all speak to us of loving, caring, nurturing relationships. (pp. 183f.)

Dawes has to face the objection that his "open Christianity" is no longer really Christian at all. He replies that even today's defenders of first- or fourth-century formulations of faith do not interpret their wording in the same way as was done in the past. Change, then, has to be admitted, and the inspiration of the changes he proposes "remains Jesus, together with everything that has flowed from him down the intervening centuries" (p. 112). It is, however, obvious that one might share his views on resurrection (as merely "a way of speaking about the significance of life here and now") and on immortality (as "the handing on of what we represent") without any commitment to Jesus. This is certainly not the case with the less radical reinterpretations of scriptural and patristic statements which he adduces in order to justify his own. He knows too that there are "unattractive elements" in the NT portraits of Jesus—"Jesus the fanatic, Jesus the extremist, Jesus the one who could apparently dismiss and disregard the love and concern of his family" (p. 52). So in spite of the claim to embrace "everything" that has "flowed from him," Dawes admits to selectivity in acceptance of the recorded teachings, but charges the orthodox with being equally selective: they may, for instance, insist on the hard line views on divorce which Jesus states in Mark's gospel, but "the same anxiety over holding to what are alleged to be the authoritative pronouncements of this pre-existent divine being is not seen to anything like the same extent when the subject under consideration is wealth" (p. 73).

That "it is easier for a camel to go through a needle's eye than for a rich man to enter into the kingdom of God" (Mt. 19:24 and its parallels in Mark and Luke) is indeed one of the 'hard sayings' with which commentators have, for centuries, found it difficult to come to terms. In the late second century, Clement of Alexandria, perhaps anxious to reassure wealthy Christians in his city, ruled that, in the gospels, 'riches' means 'desire for riches', so that it is only people who are obsessed with the idea of wealth who will not be saved. Later, Augustine interpreted 'riches' to mean 'pride', so that the rich must dispose not of their wealth, but of this and of other sins (Details in Boniface Ramsey, pp. 35f.). I am not suggesting that the Fathers (any more than the clergy of today) were indifferent to the gross inequalities which characterized human life, then as now; and Ramsey is probably right to say that "the problem of poverty and wealth was the most important specific social issue that the early Church faced" (p. 195). But the sacred texts did not help them to face it sensibly.

b. ANTHONY FREEMAN

Hugh Dawes is still in office, but Anthony Freeman's short 1993 book led to his removal from his clergy training post. He was given a further year in which to consider his position, and when he did not then recant, he was removed from his Anglican parish. Steve Bruce's survey of modern British religion styles him as "the first priest this century to be dismissed for religious dissent" (1995, p. 19).

Freeman himself tells how, after more than twenty years in which he accepted a watered-down Christianity, he suddenly realized at a 'Sea of Faith' conference that it is not necessary to bring the supernatural into his religion at all (1993, p. 11). He fears that, while Christians will denounce him for this, secular humanists will ridicule him for not abandoning religion completely (p. 83). He does squarely face the question as to whether he ought to resign his orders, and quotes the church's own statement that it is "called upon to proclaim afresh in each generation the faith uniquely revealed in the holy Scriptures and set forth in the Catholic creeds." His view is that proclaiming the message afresh allows "re-presenting and re-interpreting" the words, with no "essence or inner core" immune from the process, for the creeds themselves are anything but timeless rulings: their words "were argued and fought over with great fierceness and not a little politics" (pp. 73–76).

This is true enough and is not any more in dispute. Maurice Wiles has shown how, over centuries, the process was repeated whereby each doctrine about the nature of Jesus raised a further question about his nature, and that, of the possible answers, only one was finally tolerated, others being vilified. Wiles concludes that, for the church, the overall result is "a well thought out but over-defined concept of orthodoxy" and "a penchant for mutual vilification and the multiplication of division, together with a built-in resistance to change in the face of new circumstance" (1994, p. 73). However, whether these historical developments suffice to justify the infinitely more drastic revisions of the new radical theology is—as we saw with Dawes—another matter. Wiles does not accept that they do, yet is far from dismissive and, in his review of Freeman's book in the 1994 volume of *Theology*, he expresses the hope that "his voice will continue to be heard . . . both for the clarity of its challenge and for the positive spirituality of its intention."

Freeman's reinterpretations result, then, in "a non-supernatural version of Christianity." God is (as for the 1984 Cupitt) "the sum of all my ideals and values in life" (p. 25)—a "flexible" God, since even an individual's values change over time (p. 28). If only we could accept that "we have only this life to enjoy," we might then be "more positive in our appreciation of it." He is thoroughly repelled (p. 67) by the church's burial prayer in which the minister gives the Deity "hearty thanks" for delivering the deceased "from the miseries of this sinful world." Like Dawes, while not underestimating human capacity for evil, he deplores a doctrine which makes us incapable of anything worthwhile "of ourselves," and which represents eternal damnation as our well-deserved fate, from which only the grace of God will allow some of us to escape. He points to organizations such as Oxfam, Amnesty International, and Greenpeace which do unselfish humanitarian work with no formal religious basis (p. 50).

As for Jesus, Freeman holds that the Fathers and their successors created "a Christ who fulfilled their needs"; so let us do the same and "create our own Jesus"—with the difference that we at least do so "openly and knowingly" (p. 37). Like them, we shall need to be selective of NT material to make of him "a reasonable and usable ikon" (p. 39). But on this basis, he can become "an example, a symbol, a focus for our efforts" (p. 41). In a later book Freeman points out contradictions and discrepancies in the reports of the life of Jesus in different gospels, and infers that the evangelists themselves were writing "creatively" (1999, pp. 82, 84), each one giving his own Jesus story. He explains this by noting (what is quite true) that in NT times so-called Christian 'prophets' spoke what they represented as 'words of the Lord' (cf. above, p. 40)—words they claimed to have received as messages from the risen Jesus. They did not, he says, distinguish sharply, as we moderns do, between the earthly and the post-resurrection lives of their Lord, but believed that "Jesus spoke through his body the Church just as surely as through his individual earthly body." Hence Paul "would quite happily write and tell his churches what 'the Lord' had told him to say about this or that problem that had arisen" (pp. 53f.). Similarly, the evangelists and their audiences "believed that their writing was being done under the inspiration of the risen Lord himself, and that their words were his words" (p. 75). The Lord's Prayer, for instance, as given in Matthew, was probably "composed by the early Church." Matthew "really did believe that when two or three are gathered together in Jesus's name, the Lord was there with them"; and so for him "it really would have been the Lord's Prayer that he was composing" (pp. 52f.). In this way, the evangelists have produced not one objective story of Jesus, but four different ones, and we should follow their lead: "It is for each of us to make our own" (p. 101).

As a further example of 'creative writing' Freeman instances the parable of the Good Samaritan, represented only in Luke and probably never spoken by Jesus (1999, p. 74). It is nevertheless a true story "because its moral message is true" (p. 77).

People's lives "can be transformed by a good story," and Christian faith works for those who are able to see in their own lives "that transforming Christ-like pattern" whereby "love conquers fear, good overcomes evil" and "life is not being rendered meaningless by death." That is "the treasure and the truth of the gospels" (pp. 100f.).

Freeman recognizes that his "Christian humanism"—a Christianity that does not demand an acceptance of the supernatural—entails a revised understanding of liturgical practices. It will no longer be possible to suppose that the bread of the communion service is changed into Jesus's body. Rather is it (as with Cupitt) "the worshippers sharing the bread who are confirmed as the body of Christ" in that they thereby "affirm their fellowship in following the ideals focussed for them in Jesus" (1993, p. 56). But how far can traditional liturgies be retained if their words are so drastically reinterpreted? Freeman allows that there are dangers in saying one thing and meaning another: the habit may spill over into other walks of life where "people expect you to say what you mean and to mean what you say" (1993, p. 6). He finds that he can best "use familiar ancient texts where one is hardly conscious of the words at all." "People love to sing old hymns whose words, if they read and studied them, they would agree to be the most appalling nonsense." (Quite true.) By ritually chanting words hallowed by long use, Christians are "bound together" in fellowship. To this extent, the creed, "when set to music and sung as an act of allegiance to a tradition . . . can be a powerful force for good" (p. 53).

Like many other ministers, Freeman is not impressed by recent attempts to reword the liturgy in language that is more modern. Some people will naturally feel that this "makes us seem too 'matey' with the Almighty" (1999, p. 50). Clearly, the faith, whether old or even updated, needs the support of the solemn emotional associations of archaisms if it is to appeal. Adrian Hastings notes perceptively that the old Prayer Book of 1662 still comes across well in cathedrals, and that this is because they tend to be "frequented by people who are not regular worshippers" (1991, p. 665), whose commitment to the actual doctrines is likely to be correspondingly small. Freeman's experience—that maximum effectiveness is linked with minimum reflection on what is being liturgically said (or sung)—is in line with this.

In a recent article in the bi-monthly magazine of the Sea of Faith Network, Freeman appeals to what he calls "the concept of 'emergence'" as the basis of his Christian humanism. He does not here discuss the history of the concept, but we may note that it goes back to J.S. Mill. Mill observed that, in the case of mechanical phenomena (particularly the communication of motion) we can usually predict what will happen when two causes are jointly operative if we know what effects each of them would in isolation produce, whereas with chemical phenomena this is not the case. I quote from the ninth edition of *A System of Logic* (1875):

> The chemical combination of two substances produces . . . a third substance with properties entirely different from those of either of the two substances separately, or of both of them taken together. Not a trace of the properties of hydrogen or of oxygen is observable in those of their compound, water . . . In the science of chemistry . . . we are not, at least in the present state of our knowledge, able to foresee what result will follow from any new combination until we have tried the specific experiment. (Book III, Chapter 6)

For this apparent generation of new and unpredictable properties Lloyd Morgan, in the 1920s, adopted the term 'emergence' and made it the basis of his doctrine of "emergent evolution," from which it could readily be suggested that the evolution of man represented the emergence of something totally new, not to be found in animal life and not to be accounted for by reference to the ordinary organic laws.

Freeman repeats the example of the combination of oxygen and hydrogen to form a substance with properties that are "emergent" in that, although genuinely new, they were "not added from outside" (2001, p. 12). To relate this to his Christian humanism, he argues that we know God only through Christ, and "on a Christ-centred account, God is not a supernatural agent, external to humanity, but an emergent property of human life itself." The mind of any human being arises by emergence from the complex physiology of his or her body (especially from the brain and nervous system); and "just as the mind or soul is not an added ingredient to the human body, but an integral emergent property of it, so Christ's divinity is not an added ingredient to his human person, but an integral emergent property of it." "His divinity arises from his total humanity, body-and-mind" (pp. 11, 13).

I find it surprising that Freeman, who has studied chemistry, can adduce as relevant Mill's example of the combination of oxygen and hydrogen. Mill was careful to say that we are not, "in the present state of our knowledge," able to know, prior to trial, what will result from such chemical combinations. Since his day it has been realized that the apparent lack of relationship between the properties of chemical compounds and those of their constituent elements was a consequence of our ignorance of the causes of both sets of properties. These causes are now known to lie in the structure (in terms of neutrons, protons and, in particular, the distribution of electrons) of the relevant elements. Once this structure is understood, what will result from combining the elements can frequently be predicted. As early as 1921, on another page of the very number of *Nature* (October 13) which recorded Lloyd Morgan's idea of emergent evolution; (later given more fully in his book of 1923), we can read of "one theoretical prediction," that of "the salt-like character of lithium hydride" having been "confirmed by experiment."

Chemical analogies do not, then, provide any basis from which we can regard as mysterious the emergence of mind from body in man, or can posit the emergence of divinity from body plus mind in Jesus. In any case, how can Freeman be sure that Jesus differed significantly from other men, since he "doubts the possibility" of ever accurately distinguishing what is historically accurate from what is historically dubious in our principal source of relevant information, the gospels (1999, p. 2)? And if Jesus does not differ significantly from other men, how can it be said that we know God only through him?

Greater numerically than outspoken radicals such as Freeman are clergy who, as he puts it, "just keep quiet," silenced by "an obscure combination of fear and loyalty" (1993, p.79). He is aware how easy it is to "preach sermons which are outwardly orthodox, but which thinly veil unbelief." There is really nothing 'obscure' about this—rather is there genuine pathos in that such behaviour illustrates the predicament of men whose mental powers have gone on developing after their career has crystallized. There they are, glued to their professional appointment, with a nice house, and a wife and children to support. So what are they to do? Women, as yet newcomers to the Anglican priesthood, may well experience some form of the problem later. Even doubt, rather than downright unbelief, will engender unhappiness enough, as we may learn from Anthony Kenny's experience that, as a trainee for the Catholic priesthood, he already "began to realize what misery could lie in a life devoted to the spread of doctrines in which one only half-believed" (p. 73).

To 'just keep quiet' is surely as common among teachers in university theology departments as among clergy, as emerges from criticisms of colleagues by professors of theology who refuse to keep quiet. The case of Gerd Lüdemann, Professor of New Testament studies in Göttingen, who has outspokenly repudiated traditional Christian doctrines, may serve to show that this issue has a much wider than merely Anglican context. He notes that, while professors and lecturers in the theological faculty of his university are obligated to teach "in agreement with the principles of the Evangelical Lutheran church," "hardly one of them shares the eschatological presuppositions of the church's tradition, and very few expect, for example, the return of Christ in judgment" (1999, pp. xvi, xix). Many Christian intellectuals, he adds, have abandoned the original meaning of Jesus's resurrection, yet "think it important to maintain the confession of the resurrection, regardless of what may be understood by it" (p. 3). Naturally, he finds the outcry of such persons against his own frankness very much less than frank.

While, then, outspoken radicals may be few in number, they evidence widespread malaise with traditional Christian doctrine.

c. RICHARD HOLLOWAY AND MARK OAKLEY

Richard Holloway, until recently bishop of Edinburgh, has turned against the orthodox views he defended thirty years ago. He now stresses that the sacred texts are "human creations," with a history about which "a great deal" is known (2001, p. 26)—knowledge which, he implies, does not inspire confidence in them. He knows that many scholars regard the fourth gospel as "an imaginative construction" (p. 144), and he does not distance himself from this estimate. He himself draws attention to clearly unhistorical elements in Matthew's gospel (pp. 108, 145). Perhaps he has more confidence in Mark, as the earliest extant gospel; yet it is full of miracles, and he does not dissent from "most interpreters," who regard Jesus's healings as psychosomatic phenomena and allocate his other miracles to "the worldview of his time" (pp. 129, 131f.).

Holloway now speaks for those who, in the light of these developments, cannot accept the scriptures as historically accurate, but who are nevertheless "haunted by some of the values of Christianity and would like to be associated with it in a way that did not violate their moral and intellectual integrity" (pp. 53f.). There are very many people both within and outside the churches who fall into this category, and so what he has to say will be of broad interest.

Holloway has reached the conclusion that "theology is really another aspect of psychology, another way of describing human experience and its struggles with itself" (p. 112). Hence the sacred texts are best understood as "human creations that express the depth and struggles of our own nature" (p. 68). The story of the lost Garden of Eden can be taken as "a metaphor that expresses the human experience of discontent and failure" rather than as "a factual description of an aboriginal catastrophe" (p. 238). The forty years of wandering in the wilderness with its temptations and complaints is "an apt symbol of the human struggle for peace and wholeness" (p. 77). Using this approach to the texts, "heaven becomes an image of longing, hell an image of dread" (p. 238); and the apocalyptic strand in Christianity—"a hunting ground for cranks in every generation"—can now be sensibly used only as "a metaphor or symbol for the unquenchable human longing for a better society" (pp 153f.). Holloway is obviously beholden to Bultmann's principle that, to interpret scripture aright, we must give it the relevance to ourselves which it often appears to lack. Unfortunately, treating any given text in this way leads different exegetes to different (and equally arbitrary) results. According to Bultmann's *Jesus Christ and Mythology* (p. 31), the apocalyptic strand, typified in Jesus's statements that the end of the world is imminent, does not express a longing for social reform, but means that, since none of us knows what the future will bring, we are "to be open to God's future which is really imminent for every one of us."

Holloway dismisses the doctrine of the incarnation—that in order to "reconcile the world to himself" God sent his only son "to an unknown family in a nowhere town" to be virgin born— as no more than a "beautiful story" which, as "myth, metaphor or poetry can be interpreted in several meaningful ways," but which, taken literally, is both "far-fetched" and "morally arbitrary." We are dealing here as much with the atonement as with the incarnation, as the reference to "reconciling" God with man, "alienated by sin," betrays. It has often enough been asked: if Jesus was sacrificed by God to redeem all those who believe in him, why, to an all-powerful deity, was such a sacrifice necessary, and if so why was it not made thousands of years earlier and in less obscure circumstances? Holloway asks, concentrating on the incarnation: why should "the salvation of the world depend upon its hearing about this event and coming to acknowledge the divine status of the child born in such remote anonymity"? (pp. 174f.). He even suggests that the evangelists may have meant such elements in their narratives as no more than "metaphors" (p. 37), and their texts as "highly coded documents" (p. 158), from which lessons, moral or other, can be drawn. In any case they are "good poetry" (p. 18), and much religious language is likewise "a kind of poetry that can illuminate our own existence" (p. 54).

Although Holloway stresses that people should ask "what action this or that belief commits them to," rather than whether it is based on precedents defensible as historical facts, he nevertheless speaks with confidence about what Jesus did and taught (pp. 164, 193, etc.); and when he thus identifies "the way of Jesus," which is to be followed and imitated (pp. 18, 156), he plainly supposes himself to be dealing not merely with a story line in some kind of poetry, but with historical events. Jesus, then, was a preacher, "certainly executed as a messianic pretender" (p. 189) under Pilate. Accordingly, the 'poetry' of the gospels can be no more than an overlay. His estimate of Jesus as a "creative subversive" (p. 187), a reformer who did his best under difficult circumstances, will appeal to the audience Holloway envisages for his book, to the many who wish to retain some allegiance to Christianity without accepting all the claims made in the texts. But it is a position which he affirms quite uncritically. For instance, he must know that the words from the cross given at Lk. 23:34 ("Father forgive them, for they know not what they do") occur only in this one gospel and are absent even from some important manuscripts of it. They are one of three sayings in Luke's crucifixion narrative which replace the single bleak saying from the cross in Mark ("My God, why hast thou forsaken me?") with statements less gaunt and despairing. Yet Holloway adduces these words—without mentioning their defective manuscript attestation or the editorial manipulation of Mark—as evidence that Jesus, "the great prophet of pity" (p. 198), taught forgiveness (p. 223). The saying in Mark is itself a quotation from Psalm 22 and one illustration of the fact that much in the gospels' passion narratives was constructed by musing on the OT, particularly on the Psalms.

Holloway stresses the importance of behaviour, calling Christian belief "an action indicator" (p. 134). Mark Oakley somewhat similarly allows that "in the end . . . all of us who journey the Christian way are unable to prove any of our beliefs except, perhaps, by the way we translate them into the lives we live" (p. xviii). This suggestion that moral action on the basis of religious beliefs goes some way towards vindicating them echoes the 'pragmatism' advocated by William James and others early in the twentieth century. In the opening chapter of his *The Varieties of Religious Experience* (1902) James specifies "moral helpfulness" as one of the criteria for testing the value of "spiritual" states, although in his final conclusions (Chapter 20) he allows that this "merely subjective utility" does not in itself prove even what he specifies as the common nucleus of differing creeds to be true. It is surely obvious that, if I live morally because I believe such living to be required by a deity, this testifies to the strength, not to the truth of my belief.

Oakley is Parish Priest of a London church and Deputy Priest in Ordinary to the Queen. His book, issued in 2001 by a Christian press, was immediately reprinted. Again like Holloway, he speaks of scripture as poetry, but is nevertheless much more ready to accept its claims as historically founded. Thus, he affirms, without argument, that "in the person of Jesus Christ we discover God in human form" (p. 25). He knows that biblical texts "are not always consistent" and—as he puts it, making a virtue of necessity—are "gloriously varied in their outlook" (p. 21). What shook his initial faith was, however, not biblical contradictions, but confrontation, as a member of the chaplaincy team in a London hospital, with suffering which seemed incompatible with belief in an all-powerful and beneficent deity. His book undertakes to assure worried doubters that their reservations about such traditional doctrines are perfectly justified, and are no barrier to true faith, which is "not a proud self-consistent philosophy" but a "collage" pieced together from "the Christian traditions and texts, the myriad experiences of human living, imagination, silence and prayer." God's truth, "often nestles in . . . painful contradiction," making rational criteria such as verification and falsification irrelevant (pp. xvii, 13).

Oakley, then, allows, even stresses, that we cannot draw a monolithic coherent doctrine from the inconsistencies of scripture. But he relies on scripture when it suits him, saying, for instance, that we "know" from the Acts of the Apostles that "God reveals himself in the vitality of Holy Spirit" (p. 11). This knowledge that the faith has such a non-rational basis is his justification for disdaining "fanciful logical thinking" about doctrinal perplexities, and eschewing a "crude literalistic mode" of interpreting doctrine (pp. 27, 35). Today's Church must free itself from "the curse of literalism" and become "a poetic Church," poetry being "the language of paradox, polyvalence and ambiguity" (pp. 42–44). Ambiguity is what he stresses most, and here his debt to modern literary criticism is obvious. "The machinations of ambiguity," says William Empson at the beginning of his influential *Seven Types of Ambiguity* (1930), "are among the very roots of poetry."

I have noted elsewhere how very questionable this popular view of poetry is. Most words are apt to excite in the hearer's mind a variety of thoughts and memories if time is allowed for their revival, and a word or phrase does not have any more associations when it occurs in verse rather than in prose. It may be that, when we come across the word 'golden' in a poem, we shall not expect to find the precious element referred to, as we should if we found the word in a jeweller's catalogue. But this difference can only be due to the fact that, when reading poetry, we adapt ourselves to its conventions, insofar as they are known to us. The associations are in our minds, and may or may not be evoked; Admittedly, in poetry and literature, where the author's purpose is not to elucidate the properties of the universe, the range of suggestiveness can be greater than in chemistry or physics. But we may profitably distinguish between those associations likely to be common between poet and readers—such there must be, otherwise there would be no common language—and those which are peculiar to one reader, and may well result only from protracted reflexion. Empson is typical of the modern critic who, by a process reminiscent of that of psychoanalysts, explores such of his own associations and then says that they are in the poem. He picks out a number of words from, for instance, a Shakespeare sonnet or a speech of Macbeth, searches—sometimes by resort to his dictionary—for alternative meanings, and pretends that these are somehow present in the listener's mind when the words are spoken, so that the poetical effect is produced, or at least enhanced, by "a sort of ambiguity in not knowing which of them to hold most clearly in mind."

This theory makes it easy for the critic to find beauties in almost any kind of verse which, for whatever reason, he wishes to admire. It does not account for poetry as a phenomenon universally present at all stages of civilization, and enjoyed by many who know nothing of this kind of verbal analysis, and who would probably be incapable of it. It tells rather of an artificial cult of recent origin, born in the peculiar conditions of modern society, where a special class of persons has been formed for the professional study of poetry—persons who know that the more uncertain the meaning of a poem is held to be, the greater the scope they, as critics, have in interpreting it.

Similar reasoning enables Oakley to extend this method to theology, to suggest that all kinds of subleties and hidden meanings can be extracted from words associated with belief in God. He is convinced that "there is a whole world of unexplored words, images and ambiguities revolving around belief in God that might yet resonate" (p. 100). His "poetic church" will "confidently use its human imagination for the sake of sacred discovery. . . . Its theology should be inventive" (p. 42) and will certainly not be definitive, but will comprise manifold and even discordant interpretations—presumably as "gloriously varied in their outlook" as he considers the texts of the Bible itself to be.

What does not seem to be understood by many critics is that, although a word may have many meanings, it need not be ambiguous at all, for its meaning may be determined by its context—not only by the immediate context, but by the whole subject matter or argument. But with writing such as Oakley's the context is of little help, as it commonly consists of words which are themselves quite unclear in their meaning. It is not from use of technical terms that this kind of writing is obscure. The words and phrases are familiar enough, and their very familiarity may lead the unwary reader to suppose that they are being used meaningfully. Oakley declares that "Christian faith brings with it a necessary colour and depth, releasing existence into life" (p. 100). The relation between existence and life is unambiguous in statements such as 'life exists on Mars'; and what is meant by releasing something or someone into something else is equally unambiguous when we speak of releasing gases into the atmosphere or poison into the blood stream or a criminal into the community. In such cases, the overall context limits the meaning of words which, in themselves, have numerous meanings.

But when traditional religious propositions are being replaced by imprecise phrases, there is no such clear limiting context which enables us to understand the release by Christian faith of existence into life, nor what Oakley means by the "colour and depth" which are "necessary" to life. Perhaps no more is meant than that Christian belief is what is today termed 'a feel-good factor'. But the apologist finds the ambiguity of the more pretentious wording advantageous.

Oakley's anti-rational standpoint is summarized when he says that "God's revelation of himself is too expansive and penetrating to be propositional." It surely follows that we cannot expect Oakley to specify in propositions what he believes. He will give us instead "the tension of the symbol, the multilayers of the myth and the openness of the poetic"—it is with these that God must be approached "because [sic.] God is both knowable and unknowable" (pp. 38f.). Liturgy must accordingly not be "prosaic" or "didactic," but "inspirited. . . . by a poetic assurance that there is not just one meaning to discover in the sacramental quest through life" (p. 45). How far removed all this is from the pronouncement of the First Vatican Council (1870) which anathematized "him who shall say that it may at times come to pass, in the progress of science, that the doctrines set forth by the Church must be taken in another sense than that in which the Church has ever received and yet receives them"!

d. JONATHAN BLAKE

My final example of recent radical theology from a priest (in this case originally an Anglican, but now an independent minister) is Jonathan Blake's provocatively entitled *For God's Sake Don't Go to Church*, which finds much in the Bible to be simply ridiculous if it is understood as literally true: "It is a world where women get pregnant without sex, where men float on clouds and angels pop round to visit; where dead people climb out of their coffins and water changes to wine; it's a world where snakes talk, the lame walk, and money for your tax turns up inside a fish!" (p. 65). I would add to this that, if we were suddenly confronted with beliefs of this kind from some unfamiliar source, perhaps some other civilization, we should have little hesitation in rejecting them. But we have grown up with the Bible, it forms part of our tradition, and this familiarity inhibits a critical response, even in those who withhold full assent. Blake himself hints at this when he speaks of the "loyalty we all show to what is ours" (p. 96).

Blake describes the traditional doctrine of redemption in language which one might expect to find in journals of militant atheism:

> We are dirty sinners. Jesus is squeaky clean. On the cross Jesus was able by magic to take our dirtiness away and his dying and rising was like a big washing machine bringing us all up whiter than white. All we have to do now is to wear the Jesus badge on our hearts and we're heaven bound. And guess who gives out the badges? The church! (p. 62)

This, he adds, is "the greatest con trick in history."

For Blake, "the brightest and most perfect parts of the Bible are those which speak about love" (p. 70). Much of it speaks of hatred and worse, and must be discarded. Much of what remains cannot be accepted literally, but must—I would add, if from Blake's premises anything is to be left of Christianity—be understood as a kind of poetry (p. 57). Jesus's resurrection is "a poetic symbol of that evolutionary spirit that will not be crushed, of a love and hope that can face and survive anything and everything" (p. 21). His second coming is about whether we live our lives in such a way that we could face a surprise visit from "a good and holy conscience" without fear or shame (p. 85). Heaven is not a real place; we need poetry about it "to help us express the bonds of love which forever tie us to those we love, even beyond death" (pp. 79f.).

These examples show that the principle guiding Blake's reinterpretation of scripture is the same as that which informs Richard Holloway's recent book, namely that religious language is "a way of talking about us, our experience, our lives and our situations" (p. 55). "All spiritual writing is a record not primarily about God, but about ourselves and how we understand our world and our lives" (p. 70). And each of us is something of a special case, with his or her own set of problems (p. 163), which cannot be solved by following any simple set of rules: "There aren't easy right and wrong pathways . . . Nearly every decision is unique and every set of factors different" (p. 81). Religion must adapt to these facts by relinquishing all stereotyping of beliefs and practices. If this is achieved, then "religio-speak can unlock the hidden treasures and darkest secrets of our lives" and "give us the ability to discover and talk about hitherto unreached areas within ourselves" (p. 51).

Whatever we may think of this (from someone who at the same time urges us to "resist any vague or fudgy talk," p. 48), it clearly meets the needs of many; for in the four years since the author relinquished his post as an Anglican vicar and set up as a priest independent of any denomination, his ministry has attracted thousands. He has "not yet encountered a person who had no use for love, who didn't respond when loved, who wasn't damaged through being denied love" (p. 169). His baptisms, marriage ceremonies and funerals are structured accordingly. At his funerals, for instance, "the text has no importance of its own, other than to serve those attending," and "the prayers and the readings must meet and love the mourners in their need" (p. 167). This emphasis on love is perhaps the defining characteristic of today's radical theology. Earlier theology was never able to reconcile the notion that God and Jesus are loving and caring with the idea that, at the final judgment, they will adjudicate with implacable severity. In radical theology, this latter conception of them has simply been dropped.

It will be clear from my quotations that this emphasis on love goes, for Blake as for others whose views are given in this chapter, with strong advocacy of individualism in religious thinking and behaviour, resulting in what its critics call the privatization of religion. This is a likely consequence of any radical break with hallowed traditions, as was evidenced at the Reformation when Catholic orthodoxy was replaced by a multiplicity of Protestant sects. But it is further encouraged today by the popularity of outlooks which stress the rights of the individual and the importance of his or her self-fulfilment rather than duties to larger bodies such as society. For Blake, however, individualism is completely subordinated to love, so that he has no sympathy with self-assertion that is selfish. He has worked extensively among the poor and deprived, and deplores the often negative attitude of ecclesiastical respectability towards them. At the same time, he has had bitter experiences of groups, religious or other, where pettiness and worse is often endemic, so that "you end up with a kindergarten of adults" (p. 31). The complaint has often been made. Werther, the hero of Goethe's novel, and in many instances the spokesman of its young author's psychological insights, could see mankind as comprising only "old children and young children, and nothing more." The individual is dependent on society; yet groups, says Blake, "have an identity, boundaries, a culture and a pattern of life" and are intolerant of deviance (p. 34). This is as pronounced in religious bodies as in others; hence most vicars "opt for an easy life" by "feeding" their people "what they want to hear," thus avoiding "complaints to the bishop" or "mutiny in the pews" (p. 58). Any awkward questions are met "conveniently with an appeal to faith and belief" (p. 43)—as if faith were something that provides a valid criterion for distinguishing between true and false propositions.

It is hard to be critical of a man who tells us: "Visiting the sick and lonely is a quiet part of my work, and at times the most harrowing part is to help and support people, particularly children, preparing to die, and at the last to watch with them to the end" (p. 174). That Blake's book is recommended, among other new titles, by SPCK bookshops is a measure of the profound change in much religious thinking that has become evident in recent decades. Even so, a minister who rejects church-going is surely unique, although many religious persons who were not altogether outside Christianity have done so, with Kant and Kierkegaard as two very well-known examples. The thesis of Kant's *Religion within the Bounds of Mere Reason* (1793), reiterated at its end, is that "everything mankind fancies they can do over and above good conduct in order to make themselves acceptable to God is mere false worship," so that all "outward ceremonial worship" is superfluous and may well encourage the "superstition" that it in some way justifies people in God's sight. If this is less than enthusiastic, Kierkegaard was openly hostile to church attendance. From the standpoint of a faith which posited an exclusively personal relationship between God and the believer, he thought that the church endangered Christianity's survival (see John Kent's discussion of his views, pp. 69–71). But such ideas found little favour with theologians and none at all with ministers.

ii. Responses to Radical Theology

What do its critics make of the new radical theology? Liberation theology and feminist theology are the dominant controversial theologies of today, and these seem more worried about power than about the truth of scripture. However, Cupitt, with his more than twenty books and his Cambridge Fellowship, is prominent enough to have elicited considerable comment. He is not easily pinned down, for he confesses (in his Foreword to Scott Cowdell's 1988 critical account of his views) to having "gone through some odd gyrations and transformations," so that, by the time criticisms reach him, he has "moved on." David Edwards, writing in 1989 as a Cathedral Provost, found many of Cupitt's strictures on historical Christianity entirely justified and sympathized with the experience as a hospital Chaplain which, as I have noted, filled him with revulsion towards Christian teaching concerning sickness. Yet Edwards is avowedly angry with him: "He sounds a bit like a member of the royal household who arranges ceremonies at Buckingham Palace while being a fervent republican." How can he "manage in good conscience to officiate at worship addressed to a God not thought to be real with phrases which he thinks are insults to human dignity and intelligence"? (p. 73). To this Cupitt replied curtly (p. 286 of Edwards' book, which includes responses from the radicals it criticizes): "Since the Church can only be changed from within, I shall stay and serve her as best I can."

The upshot of Edwards's criticisms is that today's Christians are not as uniformly hidebound as Cupitt suggests: he has given "too little emphasis to the fact that the painful lessons have been learnt by millions of modern Christians, including almost all of his fellow theologians." Accordingly, Edwards's own position is at some distance from the dogmatic past; and he concludes this appraisal of Cupitt with: "The final truth on most of the subjects he handles can probably never be said" (pp. 95f.).

Cupitt's assessment of Jesus has naturally provoked dissent. Dean S.R. White complains that his "reduction of Jesus to an ethical exemplar" exposes Christianity's founder to the danger that some other figure on which ethical aspirations could be focussed might easily come to replace him; and "a religion which could even envisage the possibility of dispensing with its founder—to say nothing of its 'Lord'—is in danger of committing suicide" (p. 155). In an early (1977) book, based on a BBC television series, and written in collaboration with its producer, Cupitt could still defend himself against this criticism, because he there held that Jesus's "message is final: nothing more can be said in language," and so he "is rightly called the absolute in time, the one who shows the way to the perfect world" (p. 92). Whether there is in fact a Jesuine "message" which can readily be distinguished from unattractive and other elements in which it is embedded in the gospels, let alone whether it is "final," is surely questionable. Cowdell notes the "devotional tone" of these words of Cupitt, and finds they constitute "quite a high christology" (p. 22). Yet, he adds: "One cannot help but conclude that Jesus and the Christ remain something of a surd in Cupitt's arithmetic" (p. 68).

An atheist's verdict on radical theology is given by Michael Goulder, who resigned his Anglican orders in 1981. He calls it "the grin without the Cheshire cat," the unappealing ghost of theology's former self, although an honest attempt to save something from the wreck. He makes most of his comments as criticisms of his friend and former Birmingham colleague John Hick, whose theology, he says, has "no original sin, no election of Israel as God's people, no incarnation, no resurrection, no providence, etc." But the comments apply *a fortiori* to the even more radical views I have been discussing. (Hick, for all his scepticism, retains the soul and eternal life.)

Adrian Hastings fears what any persistance of the new theology will do to the church. In his 1990 book he describes himself as "a Protestant Catholic" and allows that "all theology is provisional, whether its authors recognize this or not" (p. 4). But in his 1991 history of the English church he warns that no church can survive indefinitely without a modicum of internal coherence, based on what its believers think and on what contemporary society can accept as credible or at least useful. He continues:

> By the 1970s the central tradition of English academic theology, particularly Anglican theology as taught at Oxford and Cambridge, was hardly any longer fulfilling these needs. . . . The theology of Gore, Temple, Ramsey or Farrer was, most certainly, one the Church could live and thrive with. The same cannot be said for that of Nineham, Hick or Cupitt. (pp. 662f.)

If these are the reservations of a Catholic, those of the Orthodox Church are given by Andrew Walker, writing also as Director of the C.S. Lewis Centre which studies the relationship between religion and modernity. He calls radical theology "the third schism"—the first two being the severance from the Eastern Church and the Protestant-Catholic divide. He cannot see with what right the third schismatics can claim to be still within Christianity. How absurd it would be, he notes, for a Communist to tell his comrades that he no longer accepted the tenets of Marxist-Leninism but would nevertheless stay within the Party (p. 208).

Within Anglicanism the radicals are commonly written off as such an insignificantly small group that they can be safely ignored, although I have suggested (above, p. 156) that they are symptomatic of a malaise that goes well beyond themselves. Admittedly, there are factions within the church which are much more powerful and conspicuous than the radicals. In an article of 1993, Richard Holloway, who was then still bishop of Edinburgh, having noted (p. 176) that there is an estimated minimum of 16,000 versions of Christianity in the world today, with additional ones still coming into existence, went on to refer disdainfully to two major factions, namely "the Anglo-Papal absurdists within Anglicanism"—who "claim both loyalty to the Holy See and membership of a church that defined itself historically by separating from Rome"[1]—and their "obverse," namely those Evangelicals who "arrogantly dismiss" other Christian styles. Holloway himself, as we saw, now openly advocates a very radical theology. The Evangelicals from whom he distanced himself are likely to share Calvinistic-Barthian views fiercely hostile to radicalism, like those of the Anglican scholar Edward Norman, who reminded us in 1991 that Jesus spoke of sin and called us to repentance; his religion "was fashioned to vouchsafe salvation to those not worthy of it" because of man's "inherent bias to evil." Norman finds it to be "a real problem for religion in contemporary society that there is no *corps* of religious officials consistently giving off an agreed statement of Christian teaching." Instead, each minister "constructs some understanding of Christianity for himself," and "the result is a religion of private enterprise" (p. 48). In an earlier (1976) survey of the post-1960 church, he deplored this instability. "The slightest breeze" can blow radical theology onto some new tack (p. 435); and what it offers is, he says, scarcely distinguishable from the secular moralism of the intelligentsia, so that the church has dropped its hostility to secular humanism. He allows that true religion is individualistic and private in that it pertains to the condition, and the relation to eternity, of the soul, but not in the sense that it consists of different doctrines for different persons; for "Christ remains unchanging in a world of . . . mutating values," and is not to be identified with "the passing enthusiasms of men" (1979, pp. 76–80).

These positions are reiterated in Norman's *An Anglican Catechism*, published with a commendatory Foreword by David Hope, Archbishop of York. "Christ's little ones" are to be safeguarded from the aberrations of "private option" by an authoritative church (2001, pp. 77, 152). Mankind is inherently corrupt, but this corruption can be overcome, not, however, "by the achievement of moral rectitude, but by right *belief*" (pp. 33, 65, 85; Norman's italics). This, as we saw (above, p. 26), is Pauline doctrine, and for Norman "Christian doctrines are unchanging" (p. 79).

iii. From Dogma to Incoherence

The radicals of today are confronting their church with a more acute form of problems it has had to face since the mid-nineteenth century. Then as now it was often a conviction of the supreme importance of love that prompted critical views. In the 1850s the Anglican Divine F.D. Maurice, who had no sympathy with contemporary developments in biblical criticism, and was conservative enough to defend subscription to the thirty-nine articles of the Church of England as a condition of university study, was nevertheless led, purely by his moral consciousness, to distance himself from the church's teaching on hell—with the result that in 1853 he was dismissed from his Chair of Theology at King's College in London (Thompson, pp. 123, 136).

About the same time, J.W. Colenso, who became missionary bishop of Natal, found himself too compassionate to teach such terrifying orthodoxy to children (White 1962, p. 403); and in his *Epistle to the Romans Explained from a Missionary Point of View* (1861) he held the atonement to be an entirely objective event which redeemed heathens who had not even heard of Christ. For him, the function of the missionary was to tell them this story of Christ's love, not frighten them into Christianity with the doctrine that, unless they accepted it, they would be eternally tormented.

A year earlier (1860) there had appeared the symposium *Essays and Reviews*, by seven scholars, six of them in Holy Orders, where the doctrine of eternal punishment is equally emphatically rejected, and with it the Calvinistic tenet of total human depravity. The book gave further offence by regarding OT prophecies as elucidated by events of the period when they were spoken, not by the life of Jesus, and valuable only as preaching of righteousness. The authors of this symposium were called, parodying Aeschylus, 'Seven Against Christ' (Septem Contra Christum), and pamphlets against them bore such titles as 'Infidelity in High Places', 'Danger From Within', 'What Is It that a Clergyman of the Church of England is Required to Believe?' It was feared that, if such scepticism were allowed an inch, it would soon take a mile. Thus Connop Thirlwall, the most intellectual bishop of his day, wrote: "After the principles laid down in this book have been carried to their logical result, that which is left will be something to which the name of Christianity cannot be applied without a straining and abuse of language." Our churches would be turned into "lecture-rooms for the inculcation of ethical common places."[2] Thirlwall was not pleading for total biblical inerrancy, but he realized, as does Edward Norman today, that you cannot have real Christianity without a Christology which makes Jesus into something more than an ethical teacher or an ethical example.

Two of the seven essayists were prosecuted for heresy, but the sentence against them was overturned in 1864 by Lord Westbury in a higher court. Westbury accordingly "went down in history as the judge who had 'dismissed hell with costs'" (Ellis, p. 189). The entry on him in the *Dictionary of National Biography* (under his original name of Richard Bethell) tells that someone suggested, as an appropriate epitaph, that by this judgement he "took away from orthodox members of the Church of England their last hope of everlasting damnation." The irreversible legal decision meant that a clergyman not only need not believe in the accepted creed, but also need not fear to disown at any rate some of it. Evelyn Waugh recorded what he took to be the consequences when, in his novel *Decline and Fall* (1928), he noted the existence of "a species of person called 'a modern Churchman' who draws the full salary of a beneficed clergyman and need not commit himself to any religious belief."

Even many non-radical clergy seem today more concerned with social and ethical issues than with salvational ones. A 1985 report entitled *Faith in the City* (commissioned by the then Archbishop of Canterbury, Robert Runcie) clearly recognized that people who are unable to cook their food because they do not have money for the repair of a defective cooker will not form a responsive audience to preaching about the boundless love of God. Paul Badham, speaking up for the traditional faith, protests that the whole of this report is permeated with "a sense that the insights of the Bible and the Christian tradition are no longer of any real help to people grappling with the problems of life in Urban Priority Areas" (p. 30). In a series of lectures broadcast by the BBC in 1978 and published in 1979, Edward Norman, then Dean of a Cambridge College and Lecturer in history there, had already protested against widespread clerical "reinterpretation of religious values as political values," symptomatic, as he saw it, of "a real loss of confidence in the traditional claims of Christianity" (pp. 4, 12). For him, what religion "ought to provide is a sense of the ultimate worthlessness of human expectations of a better life on earth," thus reflecting "Christ's own sense of the worthlessness of human values" (pp. 19f., 82).

The problem today, however, is that, for many clergy, much of what has been accepted as 'insightful' in the Bible (Badham) and as pertaining to "the uniqueness of the Christian revelation" (Norman, p. 75) is not only unhelpful and irrelevant, but even an embarrassment, and its implementation in the past even worse. The exclusiveness of such passages as Acts 4:12—"in none other" than Jesus Christ "is there salvation," and "no other name wherein we must be saved"—is no longer sustainable (*pace* the Evangelical Alliance[3]), and its contrast with the tolerance displayed by the pagan religions it displaced is felt as shameful. Surveying the situation from the time when, in the fourth century, Christianity had achieved political power, Ramsay MacMullen observes: "While in the non-Christian thought-world there was virtually no testing of the merits of my god against yours, in Christianity such testing went on continually, continually defining approved worship against its opposite. The wrong was to be swept away by every means." There was to be "no truce with error. Christians might point with envy to the *concordia* that prevailed among non-Christians, just as non-Christians pointed with amazement at the murderous intolerance within the now dominant religion." But for this latter, anything but the strictest orthodoxy was diabolical, and "there could be no compromise with the Devil" (1997, pp. 11f., 14). The ecclesiastical historian W.H.C. Frend, reviewing MacMullen's book in *Theology* (vol. 103, pp. 295f.), comments, I think sadly: "Orthodox Christianity was never a tolerant religion."

The OT has fared even worse than the NT at the hands of historical criticism, which—as Edward Norman noted (1979, p. 82)—has "stripped the experience of the Jewish people of its unique attributes" and caused it to be seen not as "the special dispensation of God," but as that of "a tribal people formalizing in ritual and taboo the events which accompanied and legitimized their seizure of territory from others."

A truly remarkable factor is the part played by a Christian publishing house (SCM) in disseminating the radically critical ideas I have discussed in this chapter. John Bowden, its former Managing Director, himself an Anglican priest, has recently declared that "the Bible can no longer be used as a history book," and that it is time to abandon the OT narrative, the gospel narrative, the Acts of the Apostles and the *Church History* of Eusebius as a basic framework for our understanding of Christianity, since it is all "ideology, party history, which does not fall within the canons of what is acceptable history for us." The dissemination of such critical literature by SCM, and also by SPCK, underlines the contrast between the dominant theological temper of the mainstream churches of today and that of the early twentieth century. The latter is illustrated by Guy Thorne's religious best-selling novel *When It Was Dark* (1903), in which faked but seemingly incontrovertible evidence that the resurrection of Christ never happened is suddenly thrust upon modern Britain and results in society's immediate moral collapse until the fraud is exposed. In this interval, criminal assaults on women increase by some two hundred per cent, and life in Southern Ireland continues normally only because the Vatican both denies the authenticity of the alleged evidence and also forbids Catholics even to discuss it. Alan Wilkinson's survey of the Anglican church at the time of the 1914 war tells (pp. 234f.) that this immensely popular novel was acclaimed by the then Bishop of London in a sermon in Westminster Abbey. The Bishop of Exeter also praised it, and in 1970 Field Marshal Lord Montgomery said—in a radio talk, published in the 'Listener'—that it had been a major influence on his young life. It seems, then, that many in Edwardian England could find it credible that Christianity, and acceptance of the literal truth of the gospels, were the sole factors holding civilization together. Claud Cockburn observes, in his survey of the bestsellers of the time, that the dominance of such notions "seems suddenly to remove the Edwardians to a remote and almost alien world" (p. 36).

Although we have indeed moved on, the present situation is not one of which to be proud. Clergy who have repudiated the old dogmatic religious certainties show commendable courage and social commitment, but are exposed to the danger of replacing the old formulas with what is arbitrary or even too vague to be meaningful. Don Cupitt, for instance, believes—or believed in 1984—that the gospel portraits of Jesus present us with "a challenge to religious creativity," which is to be encouraged, for "the more diverse religious thought becomes the better," and "the work of creative religious personalities is continually to enrich, to enlarge and sometimes to purge the available stock of religious symbols and idioms so that faith in God shall continue to be possible" (1984, pp. 112, 247). 'Creativity'—the new word for 'originality'—is easy if no relation to reality is required. It was long ago said that there is such a thing as original nonsense. If biblical and other early texts constitute the reality with which theology should come to terms, then exegesis of them in radical theology is so remote from their plain meaning, and in some cases from any intelligible meaning, as to be significantly different from the kind of reworking, reinterpretation and development of tradition that is documented in the previous chapters of this book.

Yet near-meaningless formulas have become ubiquitous. Steve Bruce, surveying the overall British religious scene, sees "an increasingly secular people gradually losing faith in the specific teachings of the Christian tradition, but retaining a fondness for vague religious affirmations" (1995, p. 51). Such vagueness is equally common in writers who still affirm the traditional doctrines. The French Jesuit Teilhard de Chardin, who died in 1955, is but an extreme example of the kind of modern orthodox writer who is so imprecise that no one can tell exactly what he is affirming.[4] On the Protestant side at this time, much theology was influenced by Karl Barth's "dialectic"—a word with a certain flavour of subtlety from its association with Plato, Hegel, Marx, and Engels. In time such words, which many use and few understand, become so degraded that misuse of them is no longer possible.[5] For Barth, 'dialectic' meant juxtaposing oppo-site statements in a supposedly meaningful way. Thus he intro-duced his discussion of Chapter 9 of the epistle to the Romans with:

> God confronts all human disturbance with an unconditional com-mand 'Halt', and all human rest with an equally unconditional com-mand 'Advance'. God [is] the 'Yes' in our 'No' and the 'No' in our 'Yes', the First and the Last, and, consequently, the Unknown. (1933, p. 331)

The word 'consequently' at the end of this passage illustrates the way in which Barth validates arbitrary inferences. On an earlier page of this immensely influential book he represents Jesus's resurrection as extra-historical history, saying that there is "no direct and causal connexion between the historical 'facts' of the resurrection," such as the empty tomb, "and the resurrection itself," which is "not a historical event which may be placed side by side with other events," but rather "the 'non-historical' hap-pening by which all other events are bounded" (pp. 203f.). The quotation marks round the words 'facts' and 'non-historical' aim at protecting them from being construed merely in their usual sense; and the purpose of all this dialectic is of course to with-draw the Easter narratives of the NT from the scrutiny of the his-torian, while continuing to affirm what in his Church Dogmatics Barth calls "the concrete objectivity of the history" attested in them (1956, p. 351). He allows that "it is clearly impossible" to extract from these fragmentary and contradictory narratives "a nucleus of genuine history," even that the story of the empty tomb might be a legend. But this would be of no account, since it "demands our assent even as a legend" (1960, pp. 452f.).

Barth is still very much a force to be reckoned with. The recent symposium on him edited by John Webster introduces him as "the most important Protestant theologian since Schleiermacher," and calls his work "central to modern Western theology" (pp. xi, 1). We saw (above, p. 146) the importance he ascribes to the miraculous activity of the Holy Spirit, through which alone human beings, in spite of their flawed minds in their fallen condition, can recover a vital connection with God by recognizing the NT as revelation. George Hunsinger's contribution to Webster's symposium brings out, with almost comical emphasis, how much Barth stakes on the Spirit, saying that in his theology its saving work is "trinitarian in ground, Christocentric in focus, miraculous in operation, communal in content, eschatological in form, diversified in application, and universal in scope" (p. 179).

We no longer have an ecclesiastical organization able to impose assent to its ideas on the whole population. Instead there is intellectual anarchy in which the conflict of ideas and principles is often replaced by rival forms of make-believe. Freedom of ideas and of expression is degraded into licence to talk at random and make phrases. The resulting fantastic 'explanations' may persist because of their tranquillizing value and the absence of ready means of disproof. In the concrete branches of science, words and phrases are kept in constant touch with real things, so that nonsense is excluded or easily detected. But in theology—as also in literary criticism, and indeed in the humanities generally—what is propounded all too often has no contact with reality except to be verbally repeated in various combinations.[6]

5

Conclusion:
Poetry and Piety

To ascertain the extent to which today's theologians still regard the Bible as fundamentally trustworthy, one cannot do better than to consult Routledge's 1995 *Companion Encyclopedia of Theology*. It aims, according to its editors Peter Byrne and Leslie Houlden, to "provide as comprehensive a guide as possible to the present state of Christian theology in its Western academic manifestations and in the setting of the modern world" (p. ix). Its chapter on 'The New Testament in Theology' is said by Houlden (p. 6) to deal with "issues still scarcely absorbed in much of the theological and ecclesiastical establishment," and is written by Heikki Räisänen, who has been Professor of New Testament Exegesis at the University of Helsinki since 1975. What he says must give pause to those who accept early Christian testimony as fundamentally reliable.

Räisänen points to "the wide diversity of beliefs within the New Testament itself," on both historical and theological matters. He notes that the history of the early Church, as it can be inferred from the canonical epistles, is quite incompatible with the version of that history given in Acts, which legitimates Jewish-Gentile table-fellowship (a central issue) by assigning to Peter, James, and the church in Jerusalem exactly the opposite roles to those which, according to the epistles, they in fact played.[1] As for serious theological contradictions, some NT passages represent Jesus's death as an indispensable part of God's plan for human salvation, others as "the typical fate of a prophet, brought about by men's iniquity, but not invested with soteriological significance." Again, either Jesus existed as God's son from all eternity before coming to Earth as a man—the doctrine of, for instance, the fourth gospel—or, as in passages elsewhere in the canon, he was a man who achieved divine sonship only when God raised him from the dead.

Another theological problem to which Räisänen draws attention is that large segments of the NT conflict with much of "the (supposed) Old Testament 'revelation'." Thus Paul, struggling to justify abandoning the concrete demands of the Torah—even though he at the same time wants to uphold some continuity with it—at times relegates this divine gift to Israel to the status of "a demonic trap, designed to mislead (cf. Gal. 4:1–3; 8–11)."

One can but agree with Räisänen that, where such contradictions are involved, talk of 'revelation', 'inspiration' or 'word of God' is not sustainable. And apart from contradictions, some of the teaching ascribed to Jesus is, he says, simply unrealistic: for example what is said about prayer in the Sermon on the Mount (Mt. 7:7–11): whatever you ask will be given to you.

Räisänen next observes that preachers still want to use the Bible as a guide to the way life should be lived today. But today's most pressing needs are for peace and justice, and these are ill-served by the spirit of enmity obtruded in substantial portions of the Bible: "Whether it pleases us or not, in Scripture itself suspicion, even hatred of the 'others' is one conspicuous theme, running from the Old Testament narratives and Psalms all the way through to the book of Revelation." Indeed, the very notion of the absoluteness of Christ has "contributed to the annihilation of those who disagreed, trusting to their own traditions." And it is no way out of all this to "demythologize" offensive or erroneous scriptural notions by reinterpreting the relevant texts "to the point of complete vagueness."

These, then, are the views not of some maverick radical, but of one of today's most distinguished NT scholars; and what he says is accepted by very many biblical scholars, if not by theological systematizers intent on constructing a uniform body of doctrine. In another symposium, published in 2000 by a Christian press, Leslie Houlden intimates that these latter need to take cognizance of "a common perception" of NT scholars that "the New Testament writers constitute a choir of voices, harmonious indeed in their devotion and witness to Jesus, but cacophonous on almost everything else," including on "how they perceive him, what they think he stood for, . . . what really mattered about him, and how one should proceed in the light of him" (pp. 33f.). In the 1995 symposium already quoted Räisänen justly observes that, if only the critical points made by common sense and careful exegesis of both Testaments were taken seriously, the religious quest would be liberated from false expectations concerning the Bible, and any pressure to agree with this or that, or indeed with any biblical strand, would be removed. Nor in his view is any return to a "non-biblical authoritarian theology" feasible. What can still be done is no more than to use the words of the NT—words such as kingdom of God, resurrection, redemption, even Christ or God—as "evocative and challenging symbols." He mentions Johannes Weiss's 1892 book on Jesus's preaching of the kingdom of God as an early impressive example of such "symbolic" theology. As proclaimed by Jesus the kingdom is a supramundane future reality; as interpreted by Ritschl it was "a community of morally acting people," and Weiss found the Ritschelian notion "theologically helpful."

Räisänen believes that in this way theology could become "a sort of poetry." He mentions John Hick's 1975 suggestion that the conception of Jesus as God incarnate living a human life can be regarded as "a mythological or poetic way of expressing his significance for us." The resulting theology will not be definitive, but always open to revision, with the NT seen as "a discussion in the style of the Talmud: open-ended, introducing endless debates."

Räisänen is perfectly open and forthcoming about this major break with what was taught as Christian truth for hundreds of years, and is the very last person who could be accused of any kind of dishonesty. Yet the issue of honesty is not infrequently raised in the face of such a break which has increasingly come to be felt as necessary if Christianity is to survive in a form that can command plausible assent. The issue is addressed, for instance, in J.H. McKenna's recent article in a theological periodical, where he notes that some modern reinterpretations of traditional doctrines—he instances new understandings of the resurrection—are "connected to these old formulations in name only, that is only by using the same term." He finds that the revisions are likely to disguise a fundamental incredulity towards the originals, and to serve as a psychological shield against the upsetting experience that beliefs which have probably been adhered to since childhood through catechism have become incredible.

McKenna is aware that novel interpretations are defended by claiming that the traditional doctrine was itself never static, so that development is to be expected. But this, he says, should not be allowed to obscure the fact that most modern developments "represent significant departures from centuries of prior understanding of Christianity."

McKenna's final suggestion is in line with the proposal of Hick and Räisänen that theology can become what he calls "a form of aesthetics," where Christianity and the texts "become as art and the theologians . . . as aesthetes in the interpretation of these artifacts." This would allow for as great a variety in the interpretation of the religious texts as is familiar in criticisms of literary classics.

Against this, it is to be noted that there are such things as nonsensical novelties, and that these include fanciful interpretations of literary works—interpretations which are impressive only as displays of ingenuity. Literary critics who write in this way do so because they feel they need to do more than repeat the sounder observations of predecessors; and sensible originality about established classics becomes progressively more difficult. It is perhaps not a good idea to encourage the same sort of thing in theology. But the most striking feature of all these proposals which reduce theology to poetry of a kind is the modesty, even triviality of their claims, compared with those made for theology in previous centuries. Nevertheless, as we saw, advocacy of 'poetic theology' is now quite widespread. Matthew Arnold indeed believed that "most of what now passes with us for religion" would be altogether "replaced by poetry," to which "we shall have to turn to interpret life for us, to console us, to sustain us" (*Essays in Criticism*, 1838, ii, 2). But for the generality of mankind religion has shown little sign of disappearing, and poetry has become considerably less important than it was in Arnold's time.

The issue of honesty has to be faced by preachers as well as by scholars, and some disquiet has been voiced by both in a series of articles in the monthly *Expository Times* initiated by its editor C.S. Rodd, who allows that "there must be many of us who fudge the issues." The sermon, he adds, is part of the liturgy, and is now commonly based on readings from the *Revised Common Lectionary*, where many passages in both Testaments which cause offence have been eliminated. The Psalms, for instance, have been carefully selected, and "even some of those included have had offending verses deleted." He nevertheless finds that "all this is entirely right. Worship should be Christian."

Such writing makes it clear that the gap between the pew and the scholar's study is unlikely to be bridged. The liturgical context of preaching is in any case (as Rodd himself stresses) an emotional rather than an intellectual one. The number of distinct emotional states, apart from differences in degree of the relevant emotion, is small, whereas the number of distinct ideas is indefinitely large. Many persons therefore may share the same emotion, even though they may be incapable of sharing the same idea. This accounts for the ease with which an orator or preacher may stir an audience to anger or enthusiasm, and for the immense difficulty of imparting, even to an attentive and selected audience, any precise idea. One can only conclude that the general niveau of discussion is unlikely to improve.

Strong emotions, including fear and the hatred which so often goes with it, have influenced the discussion unhelpfully in the past and continue to do so. The arguments, extending over centuries, as to which propositions about baptism and eucharist were to bring death to their proponents,[2] were obviously underlain by fears about salvation; and the 'creationists' of today fear that, by allowing man's descent from some other primate, and so abandoning the biblical doctrine that he was created in God's image, we shall give him licence to behave in an 'animal' way— the behaviour of animals being supposedly uniformly deplorable, whereas in fact even a dog can be as courageous, as affectionate, and as self-sacrificing as any human. Darwin's ideas were long opposed, from fear of what were taken to be their moral implications,[3] but many Christian groups have now accepted evolution. In a message to the Pontifical Academy of Sciences of 22nd October 1996, Pope John Paul II declared that "new knowledge has led to the recognition of the theory of evolution as more than a hypothesis."

Admittedly, pleasant as well as unpleasant emotions are religiously important. David Martin, who is both a sociologist and an Anglican minister, has summarized the matter nicely, saying: "Faith is good for neighbourliness, peace of mind, children's homes and social ambulance work, bad for peace in the Balkans, the Middle East, India and parts of Africa." He adds: "The only reason it is not bad for peace in North America and Western Europe, apart from Northern Ireland, is that the tide of faith is much lower in the West than elsewhere" (p. 13). That this is so is certainly to some extent due to the impact of the kind of work on the NT and on early Christianity generally that is documented in the present book,[4] even though it would be wrong to suppose that many persons have undertaken the long continued testing of ideas against relevant evidence that has informed this work over some 200 years—testing which is really the only way to determine the validity and the precise extent of application of any principles, religious or other. The usual practice is rather for principles to be formed on the basis of such experience as is furnished by luck or curiosity and retained by memory. Any slight confirmation of the expectancies thus aroused is then readily accepted, while contrary indications are easily dismissed.

Nevertheless, the critical work of the past 200 years has meant that a moderately critical attitude to the Bible has become part of—by no means all of—modern Christianity, as also of modern Judaism. It is a matter of grave concern that there has been no similar development in Islam. Räisänen thinks it fair to ask "whether Muslims might not, and should not, some day be able to adopt a more historical attitude to their Book and whether this might not be beneficial for them—and for the world" (1997, p. 193). Beneficial for the world it certainly would be; but Muslims are surely aware, from the example of Christianity, that it would not benefit what has been taught for centuries as religious truth. Just as the collapse of the Soviet Union has taught Chinese leaders that open discussion brings disintegration, so Muslim authorities know that Christian scholarship has not been overall an aid to devotion.

6

Epilogue

Some Recent New
Testament Scholarship

i. Burton Mack

I have not so far mentioned the important work of Burton L.
Mack (for many years Professor of Early Christianity at the
Claremont School of Theology), largely because I discussed it in
some detail in *The Jesus Legend*. Since then, Mack has published
The Christian Myth (2001), where he again stresses the sheer
variety of religious movements, each one with its own conception of Jesus, which critical scrutiny of the NT and of other early
Christian literature has distinguished. There is, firstly, Q (on
which see above, pp. 43ff.). In *The Jesus Legend*, I gave the arguments which have led scholars to identify Q as a document (not
an oral tradition), probably from Galilee, and written in Greek
before the Jewish War with Rome. It consists largely of teachings
ascribed to Jesus, and betrays no knowledge of the passion story
as given in the gospels, nor of the resurrection. (In this latter
respect it resembles the Gospel of Thomas, an early apocryphal
work.) It does not treat Jesus's death as salvific, and knows
nothing of other Pauline ideas such as a mission to Gentiles or
Christianity as a new world-wide religion.

Other early material portrays Jesus differently again. The
Gospel of Thomas makes him a gnostic spirit, while in the miracle stories incorporated into Mark's gospel he is an exorcist and

healer. Mark himself portrays him as the son of God who appeared as Messiah, was crucified, and will return as Son of man. For Paul he was a martyred Messiah and cosmic Lord, and in the epistle to the Hebrews he appears as a cosmic high priest, presiding over his own death as a sacrifice for sins. Other NT books give yet different portraits, and Mack is insistent that these various figures are to a large extent incompatible and "cannot be accounted for as the embellishments of the memories of a single historical person" (pp. 35f.). Nor can the whole of Christianity be traced to a single event—the so-called 'Easter event', so often taken as a kind of theological counterpart to the Big Bang; for the Passion and the resurrection do not figure in all the documents.

For Mack, even what he distinguishes as the earliest layer of the Q teachings material, which, he finds, has close parallels with the sayings of Graeco-Roman Cynics which were popular at the time, is not to be uncritically accepted as the authentic voice of the historical Jesus (p. 19). Drawing on his premiss that religion is essentially "a social construct" (p. 68), and noting that private clubs and associations were endemic in the Hellenistic world (pp. 105f.), he argues that there were groups, critical of the established order of society, who imagined Jesus as similar to a Cynic teacher:

> The Jesus they remembered may be credited with starting a school tradition. . . . This is the closest we will ever get to the historical Jesus. . . . There is no indication of a grand design to start a new religion, either on the part of the teacher as remembered, or on the part of the school that remembered him. (p. 56)

Mack does not suppose that these people were *influenced* by Graeco-Roman Cynics, but that they resembled them in adopting postures that were significantly different from the official truths and virtues of their day. He is well aware that the relevant material is not identical with what is found in Graeco-Roman Cynicism. Popular Cynicism was oriented towards the individual, encouraging him to idiosyncratic behaviour, voluntary poverty, rejection of family ties and of all manner of pretension and hypocrisy. But in the early Jesus material a Cynic ethic is already "changing into an ethic held to be standard for some social formation" (p. 46)—into a set of community rules and instructions. Thus, encouraging individuals to take a critical attitude to accepted social values yields to "language more appropriate for groups defining their borders" (p. 54).

John S. Kloppenborg Verbin discusses Mack's views sympathetically, noting that the Cynic hypothesis "underscores the possibility that at Q's earliest layer the early Jesus movement adopted postures that were significantly deviant and socially experimental" (p. 442). He is well aware that the "muscular opposition" which this view has met with has been motivated in good part by theological rather than by historiographic interests, in that "a cynic-like Jesus cannot be seen to be in plausible continuity with the exalted Lord of later christological confessions" (pp. 420, 440).

Mack argues, as I have done, that the gospel of Mark, followed by those of Matthew and Luke, are late first-century attempts to merge the type of *christos* traditions of a cosmic saviour who redeemed us by his death (known from the Pauline and some other epistles) with traditions about Jesus's ethical and other teachings represented notably in Q and in early material resembling it. He finds that the two types of material fit together very poorly: "No one has been able to say why Jesus's 'teachings', however construed, motivated the Romans to kill him" (p. 33). The merger, he says, was effected "by using the wisdom tale of the innocent righteous one" as the basis for the passion narrative.[1] Mark also "took advantage of the Roman destruction of Jerusalem to imagine that Jesus had come for the purpose of confronting and reforming the religious institutions of the Jews. Christians could then see themselves as the rightful heirs of the religious legacy of Israel's illustrious history" (p. 52).

Mack is of course aware that Paul had not placed the earthly life of Jesus in a historical setting; but for him this is not, as it is for me, something which makes it near-impossible to link the Jesus portrayed in all the early epistles, Pauline and other, with the teacher of Q and of similar teachings traditions. He supposes that Paul "purposefully" omitted any historical setting because he wished to make only God and Jesus himself motivate Jesus's behaviour (p. 143). On this view, Paul, and the other relevant epistle authors, presumably knew of the historical situation, but deliberately kept silence about it.

Kloppenborg Verbin has protested that Mack's model of separate acts of mythmaking by numerous and very different groups "leaves virtually no room for talk of unity and continuity at all" (p. 363). But the different movements of mythmaking do at least all give the name 'Jesus' to their founder; and Mack is aware that this has to be accounted for (p. 205; see my discussion of the name 'Jesus' on pp. 10ff. above).

In spite of all the evidence that there were many groups from the beginning, creating disparate traditions and responding to other groups differently, the older picture of Christian origins according to the gospel story is still, to Mack's chagrin, the way most contemporary Christians and scholars think about Christian beginnings. "It is," he says, "as if the accumulation of critical information within the discipline of New Testament studies cannot compete with the gospel's mystique. . . . It is as if everyone secretly hopes that the core of the gospel's account will eventually be shown to be true" (p. 60). The reason for this is that what is essential to the continuance of Christian faith is not some unremarkable figure unearthed as underlying the gospel story, but this story itself (p. 38). What is required is a Jesus with theological relevance for today, and this must needs be the Jesus of the gospels. And so, although incident after incident in them is set aside as unhistorical, the claims they make for Jesus continue to be accepted—a perversity, as Gregory Dawes has recently noted (cf. note 4 on p. 214 below).

ii. Rowan Williams

Dr. Williams, who was Archbishop of Wales and has now become Archbishop of Canterbury, is in this respect typical. For this reason, and because of the high office—the effective headship of the Anglican church, whose ostensible head is the monarch—to which he has now been appointed, his views merit attention.

The Nicene creed stipulates that the Son, "for us men and our salvation, came down from heaven, and was incarnate by the Holy Ghost of the Virgin Mary, and was made man." For Williams, this does not mean that somebody living in heaven moved to live on Earth: "the writers of the creed" (they are in fact unknown) "knew they were using a metaphor" and merely wanted to say that "the whole life of Jesus is God's gift to us," so that "it is as if God *had* left heaven to be with us" (Italics original, as throughout in my quotations from Williams).[2] It surely follows that the passage in the fourth gospel, where the earthly Jesus goes so far as to remind the Father of the glory they had enjoyed together "before the world was" (Jn. 17:5), is to be set aside, as are also numerous passages in the epistles which occupied us in Chapter 1 above.

Having thus interpreted 'he came down from heaven' as no more than "vividly mythological language," Williams allows himself what he calls "equal flexibility" in his understanding of 'incarnate by the Holy Ghost of the Virgin Mary'; for he is aware that only Matthew and Luke, and no other canonical writers, use this "language" apropos of Jesus's birth (and do so, we may add, in narratives that are mutually exclusive, as well as each being full of its own difficulties[3]). He does not dispute that these two evangelists did believe that "they were recording real events," but he holds that it was their "theological views" which prompted their conviction that Jesus was actually virgin born. They felt that "not even the physical initiative of a human father can be thought of as complementing or accompanying the divine act that brings Jesus into being." And so "we can see too clearly for comfort what *job* the story is meant to do"—and also "the means by which it might have been built up"; for Isaac, Samson, and Samuel too had "stories told of their miraculous conception and birth by Jews of the New Testament period." In sum, Jesus might have been virgin born, but "there may have been an oddity or mystery about his birth that sparked off legend and speculation."

Williams does not, however, wish to leave his readers with a negative impression on this matter. He writes:

> In the history of the Jews, God's sanctifying power, God's Spirit, has been for centuries pressing this people towards a complete openness, receptivity, vulnerability, which will 'clear a space' for renewing grace to flow freely.

It is far from clear what process is here designated, yet he confidently affirms that "Luke's gospel brings this theme to a dramatic climax" in that "a daughter of Israel finally realizes Israel's destiny by putting herself utterly at God's disposal. . . . The Holy Spirit 'overshadows' Mary so that the child she brings forth is an embodiment of creative holiness, the Word made flesh."

All this adds up to a very qualified defence of the virgin birth; and Williams likewise admits to some frailty in the evidence for the resurrection, saying that the only "early testimony" is Paul's list of persons to whom the risen one had appeared, and that there are "difficulties" with this list.[4] (It does not, for instance, correlate at all well with the appearances specified in the gospels, and it is a mere list, with no indication of the time, place or circumstances in which the appearances occurred.) What the gospels contribute is "a monumentally confused jumble of incompatible stories," the conflict between which has yet to be "satisfactorily sorted out," and all of which "bear the mark of extremely sophisticated literary editing." For instance, the 'amazement' of the disciples when they are confronted with the risen one is "as much literary convention as the 'amazement' of the crowds who witness Jesus's miracles." Thus what these "Easter texts" present are "imaginative approaches"—in the form of stories, "narratives"—to "the question of what it meant and means to say that Jesus, who was deserted and executed, is alive with God and also present to his followers."

"Narratives," particularly when admitted to be a jumble of incompatibles, are not necessarily records of actual occurrences. Yet Williams does not seriously doubt the factual value of these particular stories. He devotes a surprising amount of attention to the most obviously mythical of them, namely that of John 21, a

chapter very widely regarded as a clumsy appendix to the
gospel from a later hand; for it follows what is obviously a
solemn conclusion at the end of Chapter 20, and is also the only
chapter in which there is any mention of the two sons of
Zebedee (a fact which does not suggest authorship of the whole
gospel by one of them, particularly when we find that the very
incidents in which Zebedee's son John figures in the other three
gospels are missing in the fourth). Moreover, Nathanael, who
has not been heard of since his call to discipleship in Chapter 1,
and who is not mentioned at all in the other three gospels, suddenly reappears here in Chapter 21. Even more striking is that
the disciples are here represented as having returned to Galilee
to "go fishing"—as if, following Jesus's death, they had given up
all the hopes they had placed in him; whereas in fact, in Chapter
20, he, already risen, had obviously dispelled their despair by
coming through locked doors into their midst in Jerusalem,
instructing them to go out as missionaries, and giving them the
Holy Ghost so that, in this work, they can forgive sins or withhold such forgiveness.

Williams himself calls this Chapter 21 a "Galilean 'fantasia',"
fragmentary and isolated from the rest of this gospel, where the
disciples have not even been represented as fishermen who had
been called from their nets. His exegesis of the chapter is based
on the following extraordinary psychological premiss:

> God is the agency that gives us back our memories, because God
> is the 'presence' to which all reality is present.

From this he infers that "to be with God is to be (potentially)
present to, aware of, all of one's self and one's past," including
elements of which one has come to be ashamed. But when God
is revealed to us in the person of Jesus, we are not over-
whelmed by these shameful memories; for Jesus, although vic-
timized by man, never condemns those who victimize him: "His
life is defined as embodying an unconditional and universal
acceptance." "He will not 'cast out' any."

Before we see how Williams applies all this to John 21, we
may note that he presumably has in mind Jn. 6:37: "him that

cometh to me"—surely an important qualification!—"I will in no wise cast out." In this same gospel Jesus rejects the Jews as "of your father, the devil" (8:44) and equates 'sin' with refusal to accept him as God's ambassador (8:21–34). In Mk. 11:15 and parallels he is expressly said to "cast out them that sold and them that bought in the temple."

If, however, it is God who enables us to recall our memories, and if Jesus is the victim who never condemns, then the application to John 21 is, so Williams argues, as follows: the situation at the beginning of that chapter is to be understood as implying that the disciples have not merely abandoned the hopes they had placed in Jesus, but have even completely forgotten all about him. They act "as if they had never known him." Only when, in verse 7, they recognize the person confronting them as "the Lord" do their memories of him return, and "it is no longer as if he had never been." These returning memories must include awareness that they had betrayed and failed him. But he then calls them to his service ("feed my sheep"), thus demonstrating that he had forgiven them. Hence, "if God's presence is Jesus's presence, the past"—with its memories of failures and worse—"can be borne." And the experience of these disciples can be generalized as applicable to all. "To be present to myself before the risen Jesus is to be present to God, and to know that the presence signifies mercy, acceptance and hope." In sum: "To know the full scope and the full cost of our untruthfulness and not to be crippled, paralysed, by it is what is given by the risen Christ: memory restored in hope."

So much, then, can pious meditation, coupled with an arbitrary premiss about God and the nature of memory, extract from this "Galilean 'fantasia'." Williams claims to be trying "to keep the devotional and the critical together in one interpretive process." But what he in fact does is to illustrate the gulf between the two. As a scholar he knows that "we cannot reach back behind the preached Christ to a simple, neutral 'Jesus of history'." He presumably also knows that worship of such a simple, neutral figure would be quite inappropriate. And so, as a preacher, he settles for the preached Christ, and unhesitatingly affirms that "Jesus of Nazareth is the face of God turned towards us in history." Indeed, "if Jesus is translucent to God in all he does and is, if he is empty so as to pour out the riches of God, if he is the well-spring of life and grace"—and Williams shows no sign of reluctance to accept these conditional propositions— then "he *is* God" and "not simply a man witnessing a vision or transmitting a word from the Lord."[5]

iii. Edward Norman

Altogether one may say, as a generalization, that while in the past few decades, and on both sides of the Atlantic, much of the Christian scholarship in the universities has moved in a markedly critical direction, the churches and their scholars have taken the opposite course, and have been concerned to reaffirm traditional dogma. If the University Professor Burton Mack illustrates the one development, the other is unambiguously represented by Edward Norman, whom we have already met as a staunch traditionalist, and who is now Chancellor of York Minster. They are both well aware that the Bible does not represent different faiths as equally valid. "The Christian myth," says Mack, "calls for conversion and obedience. . . . There is no place under the canopy projected by it for all the peoples of the world who are not Christian." Talk of, for instance, a "Judeo-Christian tradition," intended as a post-holocaust *rapprochement* between Jews and Christians, is merely "an overlaying of myth upon myth"; for "only by reading the Christian Bible with sentimental naiveté and overlooking two thousand years of persecution can a Judeo-Christian tradition even be imagined" (pp. 190f.). Norman agrees that Christian doctrines call for obedience, but for him they are no myths, but revelation; and (in his two most recent books, of 2001 and 2002) he even queries the appropriateness of ordinary reasoning in discussion of them, saying that "secular modes of intellectual enquiry" are "sometimes inappropriate when applied to data which derives from Revealed Truth" (2002, p. 62). Such modes "cannot be used to reinterpret Christian teachings except in extremely disciplined conditions" (p. 20); and these teachings show that, "however noble and helpful other religious traditions may be, it is the death of Jesus which alone activates redemption," for "no one comes to the Father except through the dispensation of Christ" (2001, p. 60; cf. Jn. 14:6). For Norman, "the biblical and therefore Christian understanding of humanity, and of divine judgement, makes it clear that the greater part of the human population of the world has always been destined for ultimate extinction" (2002, p. 82). Not that we are to take literally the NT "symbolism" of hell, couched in "cosmic models of reality which are no longer credible." But the substance of this teaching—"a judgement in which there will be a decisive act of divine discrimination"—is unaltered (2001, pp. 58f.). Norman is no fundamentalist and finds evangelicals frequently unhelpful: "Their characteristic insistence on attributing divine causation to trivial daily incidents detracts from their authority" (2002, p. 68). The Bible he accepts is the Bible as interpreted by the church. He allows that quite possibly "miraculous explanations were wrongly attributed by common piety to events in the Bible which were not in themselves mysterious" (pp. 69f.). Even in the accounts of Jesus's ministry, the truth taught sometimes "becomes expressed in the images of a folk miracle—the wedding at Cana for example" (Jn. 2:1–11). But "the Incarnation, the Resurrection, and the ascension" are truly miraculous and are not to be set aside or interpreted symbolically (2001, pp. 41f.).

Norman's quarrel with the predominantly liberal Christianity of Western Europe is that it quite wrongly represents Christ as concerned with human welfare rather than with sin and corruption (2002, p. 3). True Christianity is not a mere "check-list of common decencies" (p. 12), but requires belief in doctrines and submission to God; and these should come before welfare, obsession with which has led many Christians to deplore so much in Christianity's history—the Crusades (fancy being ashamed of the Crusades!), the church's support of slavery, the subordination of women, and so forth. Such "guilty moralism" and shame-facedness on the part even of church dignitaries is "in extraordinary contrast to the assertive view of their past currently broadcast by leaders of, for example, Islam and Judaism" (pp. 8f.). And "in principle" such assertiveness is quite proper:

"The peoples of Northern Ireland and of the Islamic lands are correct: the service of God, as understood, has a priority over mere human need" (p. 58).

iv. The Shifting Balance

It is only to be expected that, in the face of critical work exemplified by writers reviewed in this volume, many Christians, both lay and clerical, should feel driven to question much in the traditional faith, and to accept the authority of the Bible only in a highly qualified sense, while others are driven equally strongly to reaffirm the old doctrines. Additional to both groups are the many who, though not in themselves particularly religious, do not wish positively to distance themselves from religion. The then religion correspondent of *The Times* noted there (on 12th December, 1985) that, although less than three percent of the English population regularly attend the services of the Church of England, opinion polls nevertheless show that "'C of E' remains what the majority of English people call themselves if asked. It is an attitude which ranks the church among the public utilities, like gas or electricity, or occasionally among the emergency services, like the police or the fire brigade." These very numerous persons feel quite at ease with those religious writers and teachers who are ready to make all sorts of concessions—and as we saw in Chapter 4, the Church of England has come to condone a substantial measure of unbelief in its ministers—but do not find the uncompromising dogmatism exemplified in Edward Norman at all attractive. Norman himself is very well aware of this, but finds comfort in the reflection that, in spite of the decline of dogmatic Christianity in the West, Providence has matters firmly in hand. The revival of the Eastern church after the collapse of the Soviet Union, and the enthusiastic reception of the faith in the emergent nations of the Southern hemisphere, are "shifting the balance of Christianity as the Providential scheme unfolds" (p. 153).

Notes

Chapter 1
A Revolution in Christology

1. As a signal example I mention the Catholic Truth Society's pamphlet *Did Jesus Exist?* (1986), by John Redford, which caricatures my views and then refutes the caricature. (I respond to Redford in Chapters 2 and 3 of Wells 1996.) But the Catholic Truth Society is "not in the business of being objective"—so one of its spokesmen told Eileen Barker (as she records, p. 205n.) as justification for rejecting her pamphlet on the Unification Church.

2. Wedderburn writes, in an article where he is particularly concerned to contest any indebtedness of earliest Christianity to the mysteries, that the hero of Apuleius's account "undergoes a 'voluntary death' and learns therein that the goddess to whom he is committing himself has in her hands the keys of the underworld and the power to save, just as his earlier vision of her . . . promised that he would see her shining in the underworld" (1987, p. 59). Wedderburn also notes that "generally initiates in the mysteries looked for salvation through their initiation in one or more of the following ways: (1) it assured them of the favour of their deity who had power to protect them in this world and beyond the grave; (2) sometimes the initiation may have taken the form of a proleptic experience of triumphing over death through the beneficent power and protection of the deity; (3) sometimes they may have been shown in their rites

that one of the deities in their cult had mastered death or had been brought safely through death to a blessed existence beyond the grave" (p. 56). He denies that this third factor is evidenced in Paul's ideas of salvation, since, in the mysteries, "the victory over death is usually dependent upon another deity, the mother or sister or spouse or lover of the dying one". But in Paul it is also 'another deity', namely the father of the dying one, who raises him, as Rom. 8:11 (to which Wedderburn himself refers) says.

3. Paul uses the name 'Cephas' in four chapters of 1 Corinthians and in the first two chapters of Galatians. He mentions 'Peter' as an alternative name for this same person only at Gal. 2:7–8 (although some mss have replaced 'Cephas' with 'Peter' in some of the other passages). It is certainly strange that two different names are used within this single sentence for one person, and in my 1999a book I noted (p. 53) John O'Neill's 1972 suggestion that 'Peter' is here a post-Pauline gloss, introduced so as to substantiate the view (based on interpretation of Mt. 16:18) that Peter, not James, was the leader of the Jerusalem church. The German NT scholar Ernst Barnikol pruned the text even further. As they stand, verses 6–9 read, in literal translation:

(6) Those who were of repute added nothing to me,

(7) but on the contrary, seeing that I have been entrusted with the gospel *of the uncircumcision, just as Peter with that of the circumcision,*

(8) *for the [one] operating in Peter to an apostleship of the circumcision operated also in me to the Gentiles,*

(9) and knowing the grace given to me, James, Cephas and John who were reputed to be pillars, extended to me and Barnabas the right hand of fellowship, so that we [go] to the Gentiles, they to the circumcision.

The words I have italicized are present in all the extant mss, but these are considerably later than the original, and if the italicized passage is excised, Paul never mentions Peter anywhere.

Barnikol gives three principal reasons for regarding the italicized words as later additions to Paul's text. First, 'operating in Peter' and 'operating in me' is expressed in the Greek here by the relevant verb followed by the noun or pronoun in the dative case, without intervening preposition, and this usage with this verb is non-Pauline. Second, the references to two contrasting gospels, with two contrasting but equally valid apostleships, cannot be original, since in the previous chapter Paul has insisted, in the strongest possible terms, that there is only one gospel (1:6–9). If these references are removed, there remains an acceptable text in which the three "pillars" of the Jerusalem church recognize that Paul has been "entrusted with the gospel," and where they have "added" no conditions or restrictions to his preaching it to Gentiles.

Barnikol's third reason for amending the text in this way is his weightiest. In Europe, he says, the text had been expanded to its present form by the time of Irenaeus, who appeals to it (*Adv. Haer.* iii, 13) as refuting the views of the heretic Marcion. But in the Bible of the North African church, the original text survived at least until the time of Tertullian; for he wrote five books to refute Marcion's claim that only Paul was a genuine apostle, yet he never once appeals to Gal. 2:7–8 which, as it stands in our mss (and as cited by Irenaeus), completely undermines Marcion's position, in that here Paul is represented as granting to Peter a status equal to that which he claimed for himself. Tertullian's failure to adduce verses 7–8 is very striking, as he does refer to verses 1–5, and more than once to the second half of verse 9 (where Paul's mission to Gentiles is welcomed), and then to what follows in verse 10, etc. The necessary inference, says Barnikol, is that in his Bible verses 7–8 must have lacked their present references to Peter, which were interpolated some time in the late second century for the very purpose of discrediting Marcion's one-sided championship of Paul. They express the "classic anti-Marcionite church dogma of the harmonious parallel work of both apostles" (pp. 296, 298).

In the gospels it is the name Cephas that is rare, while 'Peter' and 'Simon Peter' occur repeatedly. Cephas is mentioned only at Jn. 1:42, where Jesus tells Simon "You shall be called Cephas," and the evangelist adds "which means Peter." (The Greek *petros* is equivalent to the Aramaic *kepha*.) In the other three gospels, where there is no mention of Cephas, Jesus names Simon as Peter.

To judge from Paul's references, Cephas must have been a significant figure in the Jerusalem church. For me, the important point is: even if Paul did occasionally call him Peter, there is nothing in Paul's writings to support the view that he had the career and the personal connection with Jesus alleged of Simon Peter in the gospels. Gal. 2:11ff. shows that the accord between Paul and the others did not last, that Cephas was threatening what mattered most to Paul, who here condemns his behaviour in the strongest terms. Anxious as he here is to resist Cephas's pretensions, he would surely have alluded to one or other of the discreditable incidents in the career of the Simon Peter of the gospels, if he had in mind this person, who was rebuked by Jesus as "Satan," fell asleep in Gethsemane, and went on to deny his master in cowardly fashion.

4. On this, see Wells 1999a, pp. 126f. and references in note 7 there, particularly to Vielhauer and Guenther. Briefly, in the gospels Jesus does not appear to twelve, since Judas had defected and (according to Acts) was replaced by Matthias only after the appearances had ceased with the ascension. Moreover the way Paul introduces (1 Cor. 15:3) the list of persons to whom appearances had been made suggests that he is here quoting from a pre-existing creed. If 'the twelve' in this creed had been an important group, he would surely have mentioned them elsewhere, and would not, as he does, have named the leaders of the Jerusalem church as Cephas, James, and John. This "almost complete absence" of any kind of twelve from Paul's letters has been called "one of the most disconcerting elements in these letters when they are compared to the Acts of the Apostles" (Bernheim, p. 195), which (as I show in Chapter 2 of this book) not altogether successfully tries to represent twelve who had been companions of Jesus's ministry as a body of great importance in the early church. Some commentators have suggested that the community which formulated the creed from which Paul on the one occasion quoted knew the twelve not as companions of the earthly Jesus, but as a group of enthusiasts who, having heard of the appearance to Cephas, interpreted it as presaging a general resurrection of the dead. In this exalted state of mind the group will have become convinced that Jesus had appeared also to them, but, as the hope of a general resurrection was not fulfilled, it will quickly have disbanded, and so was not again mentioned in any NT epistle (Pauline or other).

5. Doherty, pp. 286–290. In this important book, the whole of this chapter on these second-century apologists repays careful study. But I find Doherty's conclusion too radical, namely that all these apologists could offer pagans a Logos religion with no mention of Jesus only because they regarded "the Gospel story and its central character" as a myth on a level with pagan religious myths, "a fictional symbolical tale like those of the Greeks" (p. 283). Tatian, to whom he here appeals, in fact contrasts (Chapter 21) pagan myths, as "nonsense," with the Christian story that God has been born in the form of man.

6. That the supreme God "should take human shape and suffer earthly humiliation is naturally incomprehensible to the pagans. But both Origen and the Apologists try to meet this by treating Jesus less as an historical personality than as a Hellenistic 'second God', the timeless Logos which was God's agent in creating and governing the cosmos. The human qualities and human sufferings of Jesus play singularly little part in the propaganda of this period; they were felt as an embarrassment in the face of pagan criticism" (Dodds, pp. 118f.).

7. A little later, Eusebius (contradicting what he has just quoted Papias himself as saying) says that Papias "actually heard" two of the presbyters. But this is only half-heartedly alleged, for he adds: "At least he mentions them frequently by name and gives their traditions in his writings."

8. Cf. R.G. Heard, pp. 12–16: "The Prologue to John dates from the fifth or sixth centuries and its material is of no historical value." It "appears to stand at the end of a long chain of invention and misunderstanding." That it existed in the second century "cannot be reconciled" with the silence of Irenaeus and of all third- and fourth-century writers.

9. In his most recent book, Lüdemann (on whom see p. 156 above), after discussing in detail the relevant NT texts, concludes that "Jesus did not rise from the dead" and that, in consequence, "if we take historical knowledge and ourselves seriously, we can no longer be Christians" (2002, p. 166). He adduces "depth psychology" to explain (unconvincingly for me) how belief in Jesus's resurrection arose in disciples who, he assumes, had known him personally, and in Paul, who had not. But any weakness here does not impair Lüdemann's account of the texts and the conclusion he draws from it.

10. Maurice Wiles observes that "the Council of Jerusalem (or the author of the Book of Acts, if he is the real originator of the phrase) has a lot to answer for when it employed the words 'It is the decision of the Holy Spirit, and our decision. . . .' (Acts 15:28). For if that is intended as a reason why the Gentile churches should accept the decision of the council, it smacks more of authoritarian manipulation than of acceptable religious reasoning" and "is even more dangerous as paving the way for claims about the inerrancy of councils" (1994, p. 162).

Chapter 2
The Acts of the Apostles:
A Historical Record?

1. The earliest known manuscript of Luke's gospel (papyrus 75, dated A.D. 175–225) already has the title 'Gospel according to Luke'; but it is widely held that the titles of all four canonical gospels were added by second-century guesswork. Conzelmann (1987, p. 3) notes that the title of Acts is "hardly original" and that "even in the Hellenistic period a title is superfluous for a Greek book." Possibly the title was added when the two books Luke-Acts were separated in the sequence of canonical texts. If the title were original, the book would not have been called "Lucae de apostolis testificatio" by Irenaeus, nor "commentarius Lucae" by Tertullian (Vielhauer, p. 399).

2. Martin Dibelius held that, in antiquity, a dedication made a manuscript ready as a literary work for the book market, that it could not come on to the market without bearing its author's name, and that any other name for the author of Luke-Acts than the one we know from church tradition is unlikely. According to this argument, in antiquity no anonymous work could include a dedication. Haenchen has however pointed out (1965, pp. 231, 233) that in fact there are such works. He instances the epistle to Diognetus (a letter of the second or third century written by an unknown Christian to an otherwise unknown inquirer), the four books on rhetoric *Rhetorica ad Herennium* of the first century B.C., and, even within the NT itself, the epistle to the Hebrews.

3. Paul mentions a "fellow worker" named Luke in Philemon 24. Colossians 4:14 conveys greetings from "Luke the beloved physician" and 2 Tim. 4:11 represents Paul as saying "only Luke is with me." Barrett has observed wryly that, of these two references, "the former is in an epistle of doubtful authenticity, the latter in one almost certainly pseudonymous" (1994, p. 30n.3).

4. Cadbury 1920. His findings are summarized by de Zwaan, pp. 38f.

5. Schmiedel, column 43. This article, like others by Schmiedel in the same *Encyclopaedia Biblica*, is replete with insights which even today are in many quarters only grudgingly accepted. Haenchen has noted, apropos of equally valuable pioneer work by Eduard Zeller: "It is amazing how much that is important is to be found in the older literature, although it has been duly forgotten and has had to be rediscovered" (1965, p. 230n.).

6. Details in Haenchen, 1971, pp. 336ff. I followed him on this in Wells 1982, pp. 153ff. Cf. also pp. 106f. above on Paul's visits to Jerusalem.

7. On Paul and Corinth, see Bornkamm, Chapter 8. Acts mentions only his first visit (18:1–17). 1 Corinthians, written later in Ephesus, shows that the Corinthian church had by then split into factions. Paul sent Timothy there to deal with the trouble, but his visit was not a success. When a further letter also proved ineffectual Paul went in person, but was rebuffed, and his whole authority was put in question. After returning to Ephesus he sent Titus with a further letter to the rebel church, and himself went into Macedonia to meet Titus, who was by then on his way back with news that the trouble had been settled. Paul then made his third and final visit to Corinth, to which there is only a brief and vague allusion in Acts (cf. above, p. 106). He apparently spent a peaceful winter there before returning to Jerusalem via Macedonia.

8. Lk. 19:41–44; 21:20, 24. Details in my 1982 book, pp. 113–17, and a briefer account in Wells 1999a, pp. 26ff.

9. Mk. 14:28 ("After I am raised up I will go before you into Galilee") is omitted in Luke's gospel. And Mark 16:7 ("Go, tell his disciples and Peter, He goeth before you into Galilee, there shall ye see him, as he said unto you") is reworded by Luke so as to delete the instruction to go to Galilee, and to make the words into a mere reminder that "while he was still in Galilee" he had foretold his crucifixion and resurrection (Lk. 24:6–7).

10. The various and not altogether consistent facets of Luke's depiction of the Jews are discussed by Wilson, 1995, pp. 64–71.

11. "The form of this world is passing away" (1 Cor. 7:31). "The end of all things is at hand" (1 Peter 4:7). "Children, it is the last hour" (1 Jn. 2:18). "Behold, I come quickly" (Rev. 22:12).

12. Lk. 10:9, 11 "The kingdom of God is come nigh"; 21:32 "This generation shall not pass away till all things be accomplished." There are other similar passages. Wilson has shown that this gospel alternates between affirming and denying the proximity of the *parousia* and its attendant circumstances. He attributes this clash to the evangelist's concern to combat two extremes which the delay of the *parousia* had already provoked, namely scepticism as to whether it would ever occur at all, and a fervent renewal of apocalypticism, with false Messiahs coming forward (1973, pp. 67ff.).

13. A typical passage is Jn. 5:24f.: "He that heareth my word . . . hath eternal life and cometh not into judgement, but hath passed out of

death into life. . . . The hour cometh, and now is, when the dead shall hear the voice of the Son of God, and they that hear shall live." At 3:18–19 we learn that the "judgement" is not something of the future, yet to come, but is accomplished now by belief or disbelief in the name of Jesus. Hence believers are already saved and unbelievers already condemned.

14. 'Jésus annonçait le royaume, et c'est l'Église qui est venue" (p. 155).

15. Mark's Jesus had said (8:34): "If any man would come after me, let him deny himself and take up his cross and follow me." Luke reworded this as "take up his cross daily and follow me" (9:23), thus replacing a reference to martyrdom with one suggesting the frustrations to which Christians were exposed in daily living.

16. Paul had trouble with Roman authorities at Philippi (Acts 16:20ff.) probably because he was taken for a Jewish missionary, propaganda on behalf of Judaism being forbidden among citizens of a Roman colony (Haenchen 1971, p. 496n.5). Acts does in fact make pagans at Philippi describe Paul and his associates as "Jews" who "advocate customs which it is not lawful for us Romans to accept." Although this is represented as a pretext, covering their real reason for hostility (the financial interests of a pagan cult), it was probably the real reason.

17. In the narrative concerning the prophets who came from Jerusalem to Antioch, some Western witnesses of 11:28 read: "And there was much rejoicing; and when we were gathered together, one of them named Agabus spoke . . ." Epp (p. 99) allows that "this variant does not have the strongest 'Western' attestation." It was presumably absent from the Western text of Irenaeus, for he first has Luke accompanying Paul in the 'we' passage of 16:10, and would surely not have overlooked an earlier 'we' at 11.28. The 'we' there shows that the scribe imagined the author to be present in Antioch and introduced the 'we' because he identified him with the "Lucius" of Cyrene, said at 13:1 to be at Antioch (cf. Conzelmann 1987, p. 90; Haenchen 1971, p. 374n.7).

18. Porter's article surveys all the 'we' passages and the protracted discussion to which they have given rise. His own conclusion is that "the author of Acts has utilized a continuous, independent source probably discovered in the course of his investigation. The source was thought to have merit for the narrative, although it does not necessarily carry the weight of an eyewitness" (p. 573).

19. Dunn (1996, pp. xxiii–xxvi) gives a useful survey of recent literature in which both extremes are represented.

Chapter 3
Peter at Rome? The Literary Evidence

1. Older commentators (from Origen to the nineteenth century), inferring from Gal. 2:7 that the apostle Peter missionized Jews, and believing 1 Peter to have been written by him, naturally assumed that the work was addressed to Jews. Now that it is widely regarded as written about the year 90 by an unknown author, there is greater awareness of indications within the letter itself of a gentile, or mainly gentile, address—as when it is implied that the addressees were idolaters before their conversion (4:1–4). Elliott notes that these former pagans may well have included some "whose contact with Christianity was mediated through an earlier association with the synagogue as proselytes to Judaism" (p. 66), as there were certainly Jews enough in the area to which the epistle is addressed, some of whom will also have converted to Christianity. Such recruits would explain "the knowledge and persuasive force of the Old Testament which 1 Peter assumes". "Sociologically and historically viewed," says Elliott, "the assumption of exclusively Gentile-Christian or, for that matter, exclusively Jewish-Christian communities throughout Asia Minor in the time of 1 Peter is preposterous" (pp. 45f.).

2. On the relation between Jude and 2 Peter and on the date and distasteful character of both, see Sidebottom's commentary.

3. Parallels between 1 Clement and 1 Peter are listed and discussed by Hagner, who does not think they are all fortuitous or attributable to a common tradition, but that Clement used 1 Peter (p. 246)—although he notes that some scholars think that the evidence for literary dependence can be employed in either direction. The two works are quite close in time: Elliott puts 1 Clement "shortly after" 1 Peter (pp. 87, 281).

4. Justin, *Apol.* I, 39:3; Shepherd, *Sim.* 9:25, 2.

5. The development of the tradition through Irenaeus and Tertullian to Eusebius is documented by Hennecke, 1965, pp. 47–50. He also gives (p. 49) an impressive list of books and articles which have disputed, "from many different sides," the tradition of a stay by Peter in Rome.

6. "In western Christianity the Magi are assumed to have been three in number since [at Mt. 2:11] three gifts are mentioned; eastern tradition gives their number as twelve. They travelled by camel, as is

normal practice in desert regions even today. Their names
(Balthasar, Melchior, and Caspar in the west) are supplied [even]
later. The fact that they are wealthy and converse with King Herod
leads to their identification as three kings."

7. Details in Eusebius, *Ecclesiastical History*, ii, 25, 7 and iii, 31, 3–4.

8. Chapter 3 of my 1989 book gives a full critical account of the
(mutually exclusive) birth and infancy narratives of Matthew and
Luke. The other two gospels make no mention of the circumstances of Jesus's birth, but record only his adult ministry and his
Passion. Räisänen's 1989 study shows that, in Mark, Mary typifies
the whole generation of Jesus's contemporaries who fail to understand his true significance, whereas Luke treats her as one who has
true faith in him, as "a prototype of the Christian" (p. 198), behav-
ing as a Christian should. For Matthew she has no such paradig-
matic function. Matthew's interest is not in her person, but in her
office, her function as the virgin chosen by God to bring the
Messiah into the world (p. 75). In the fourth gospel she puts in only
two appearances: at the wedding feast at Cana in Chapter 2—neither this occasion nor the stupendous miracle Jesus works at it is
noticed in the other three gospels—and at the crucifixion scene,
where, in marked contrast to the passion narrative of the other
gospels, the fourth evangelist has her standing at the foot of the
cross, together with "the beloved disciple." (In the other gospels,
no disciple receives this appellation, and all of them flee at Jesus's
arrest.) Räisänen rebuts various attempts (typical of modern literary
criticism) to force arbitrary meanings on the few relevant texts of
this fourth gospel, which, he finds, is concerned to show that
Jesus's messianic behaviour is prompted only by God, not by any
human agency, not even that of his mother.

Elsewhere in the NT, Mary is mentioned only at Acts 1:14,
where the author wishes to give the impression that Jesus's family
belonged to the earliest church from the first; but as he had no real
information about them, he was not able to work them into any
further narrative.

Prior to the gospels, Paul had said that Jesus was "born of a
woman"—a phrase used in Jewish literature to mean 'human
being'—and his purpose was to affirm that this supernatural personage had indeed so far lowered himself as to assume human
form (cf. above, p. 5). Paul shows no knowledge of the circumstances of his birth, and of his parentage says only that he was
descended from David. The whole of the NT evidence for this

ancestry is flimsy (cf. my 1982 book, pp. 174ff.). The "woman adorned with the sun" in Rev. 12 is not Mary, but a symbol of the persecuted Christian community, the true Israel. The earliest non-canonical writer to name Mary, and to represent her as the virgin mother of Jesus, is Ignatius of Antioch (ca. 110 A.D.).

In sum, "not only Paul and Mark, but Hebrews, James, Jude, the latest Gospel John, and apparently all Christian preaching before the appearance of Matthew in the last quarter of the first century, seem to have ignored the notion of a virginal conception" (Parrinder, p. 117). Catholics are required to believe not only that Mary conceived Jesus without sexual intercourse, but also that she was born free from the stain of original sin, that she remained a virgin for the whole of her married life, and that "when the course of her earthly life was completed," she was taken up "body and soul" into heaven. Lüdemann, discussing these doctrines, says that "they heighten the significance of Mary almost without limit" (1998, p. 17).

Chapter 4.
Reinterpreting Early Christian Testimony

1. It is pertinent to observe that, if, as Bishop Holloway wished, we are to take seriously the circumstances under which his church 'defined itself historically by separating from Rome', we might find some inconsistency in the way this church has long looked askance at divorce, even though it owes its existence to willingness to grant its founder, Henry VIII, the divorce and remarriage he could not obtain from Rome.

2. This and further details concerning *Essays and Reviews* of 1860 are given in my 1997 article.

3. The exclusive doctrine of Acts 4:12 is expressly endorsed in the report on *The Nature of Hell*, published by the Evangelical Alliance (ACUTE Publications) in 2000. It subscribes "to the uniqueness of Jesus Christ and to the supreme authority of the Bible" (p. xiii), scripture being "entirely trustworthy and supremely authoritative on all matters of faith and conduct". Hence those who have "refused Jesus Christ" will be "condemned to hell," and this will involve not merely "separation from God," but also "severe punishment." In his sovereignty, God may condescend to "save some

who have not explicitly professed faith in Jesus Christ," such as people who died never having heard of him, or those with "severe mental disabilities." We are nevertheless "not at liberty to presume that any specific individual will be saved apart from professing faith in Jesus Christ." Church leaders should make all this clear to their congregations, and may also find it necessary to "include mention of hell" when dealing with terminally ill people who are uncommitted or only partially committed to Jesus (pp. 130–33).

This sectarian zeal is only partially redeemed by the—relatively recent—concern of Evangelicals with helping the poor and needy. Not so long ago, they regarded social amelioration solely as a means to evangelization; but now, what Clive Calver, their Director General, in 1995 called "a fresh passion for community involvement and socio-political responsibility" has emerged among them (p. 209). Yet it is hard to understand how they can be so insensitive to what is questionable or worse in scripture. Are we really to urge the rich to "weep and howl" for the "miseries" that are coming to them (James 5:1)? Are we to hate our closest relatives in order to be Jesus's disciple (Lk. 14:26), to refrain from resisting evil, including assault (Mt. 5:39), and to feel perfectly confident that God will always supply food and clothing (Mt. 6:25–33)? If these injunctions need not be taken literally, then the same must surely be true of the threats of hell-fire in Matthew and elsewhere.

4. Teilhard undertook to console the "nine out of ten practising Christians" who feel that the time spent on earning a living is "time taken away from prayer and adoration," the ideal life being "for those who have the leisure to pray or preach all day long." The many unfortunates who are debarred from this should reflect that

> By virtue of the Creation and still more of the Incarnation, *nothing* here below *is profane* for those who know how to see. On the contrary, everything is sacred to the men who can distinguish that portion of chosen being which is subject to Christ's drawing power in the process of consummation. (p. 38)

It would be more helpful if he would explain how one can recognize that part of 'being' which is 'chosen', and then go on to distinguish which portion of this is subject to Christ's drawing power, and finally when exactly this drawing power is to be recognized as 'in the process of consummation'. Unless all this is explained, one cannot even consider the arguments because they are not intelligible.

Teilhard writes of the 'soul' as if everyone knew what this is, and as if he were entitled, as an expert, to make unsupported assertions about it. He also shares a vice of many political ideologists, namely to represent, by means of brief labels, various 'heresies' as hostile forces with pernicious effects. Thus he writes, in a note at the head of Part 1: "The least admixture of what may be called Pelagianism would suffice to ruin immediately the beauties of the divine milieu in the eyes of the 'seer'." Communist literature is full of this sort of thing. Y.M. Steklov's 1928 *History of the First International* describes French internationalists as "still under the spell of an outworn utopism, and in especial still influenced by the relics of Proudhonism." The sentence perfectly illustrates the tendency to substitute nicknames for rather ill-defined sets of abstract propositions, and then, without reference to the propositions themselves, to treat these names as maladies which afflict different individuals more or less severely at different times. Steklov's index specifies Anarchism, Bakuninism, Blanquism, Economism, Possibilism, and the like.

5. In Plato the dialectical method consists in a series of questions and answers by means of which propositions are analysed. (The verb *dialegomai* means 'converse', and *dialektikē technē* is the art of debate.) This analysis often consisted in the statement of a proposition, its rejection, and the substitution of some kind of modification or compromise.

Hegel stereotyped this into the sequence of thesis, antithesis, and synthesis, but also made it into far more than just a method of discussion; for he supposed that the universe is rational, meaning that the course of events in the history of the world follows the same sequence as a rational discussion. Hence we may trace between successive historical events a relation which can be denoted by the terms thesis, antithesis, and synthesis: first one form of social organization, of philosophy, of art, etc. appears, and is then replaced by something opposed or contradictory, and ultimately a compromise is reached. Thus does the universe proceed dialectically.

This, whether true or not, is at least intelligible. But Hegel then asserted that thesis and antithesis, because they are reconciled by a synthesis, are not in fact opposed. Since they may be harmonized, they cannot be really different. Since they ultimately coalesce, they must be of the same nature. Thus opposites are after all identical.

Engels tried to make some sense of this last proposition by claiming that dialectics means paying attention to the transition, the metamorphosis. In the Introduction to his *Anti-Dühring* he opposes the "dialectical" view of things, which takes into account their perpetual flux and change, to the "metaphysical" method, which analyses the world into stable permanent entities. In fact, however, description must involve both. Motion and change are not to be disregarded, but they cannot be described without reference to some determinate entities.

Engels further illustrates his conception of dialectics by claiming, in the same book, that practically the whole of what exists develops in accordance with what he calls the law of negation of the negation. He plainly believes that, in what he offers as numerous examples of this development, he is using the word 'negation' in one and the same sense throughout—otherwise there can be no pretence that all the different phenomena illustrate the working of the same law. What he is in fact doing is taking a number of totally unrelated sequences and calling them by the same name. (For detailed justification I refer readers to pp. 205–214 of Wells 1959.)

6. Detailed analysis of such abuse of language in literary, religious, and philosophical writing is given in Ronald Englefield's 1990 book, where what is required for statements involving general and abstract ideas to be meaningful is also clearly indicated.

Chapter 5
Conclusion: Poetry and Piety

1. Räisänen refers to Philip Esler's book, which gives (p. 107) the following summary of what Esler calls the way Luke "re-writes" the history of early Christianity relating to Jewish-Gentile table-fellowship: "Was not Paul known as the pioneer, if not the initiator, of the great task of bringing the message of salvation to the Gentiles, while Peter was the evangelizer of the Jews (Gal. 2: 1–10)? Then Luke makes Peter begin the mission to the Gentiles (Acts 10:1–11, 18). Had not Peter come to Antioch and, at the instigation of James, broken off table-fellowship with the Gentile Christians there (Gal. 2: 11–14)? Not at all, says Luke: it was other Christians with Pharisaical links who caused the trouble in Antioch (Acts 15:1, 5), for Peter had seen Jewish-Gentile commensality as commanded by

God as early as the conversion of Cornelius and this attitude had been endorsed by the Jerusalem church on that occasion and was subsequently re-affirmed by that church, under firm direction by James during an authoritative council (Acts 11:1–18; 15:6–26). Had there not been a tremendous showdown between Paul and Peter over the table-fellowship in Antioch, with Paul failing to carry the day on that issue? By no means, Luke tells us, there never was any dispute between Peter and Paul on this or any other issue." To speak, as Esler does, of Luke "re-writing" the history suggests that he knew the earlier accounts and knowingly deviated from them. I have argued in Chapter 2 above that it is much more likely that he had to construct his own version from relatively sparse material, which he interpreted so that it accorded with what was for him the proper dignity of the early church.

2. The well-known case of Thomas Cranmer, Archbishop of Canterbury from 1533, may serve as an example. The third (1997) edition of *The Oxford Dictionary of the Christian Church* records that the Church of England owes to him "the masterly English style of the liturgy in use almost universally for some 400 years." But he was burnt at the stake in Oxford in 1556 by Catholic Christians, "officially," says Maurice Wiles, "for erroneous teaching about the nature of Christ's presence in the eucharistic elements," and had himself earlier "been responsible for condemning to death some who held more extreme Protestant views than his own on that same issue (1999, pp. 84f.).

3. Natural selection, which Darwin posited as the mechanism of evolution, was widely interpreted as a martial theory of survival, of battle with and destruction of enemies (although survival may in fact in some circumstances be favoured by co-operation, not by conflict). It was further supposed that Darwinism implied the moral virtuousness of such a deathly struggle, that the 'fittest' rightly eliminate the disadvantaged. Against this misconception S.J. Gould has insisted (in his book of 2001) that the 'is' of nature, whatever this 'is' may be, should not be allowed to determine the 'ought' of man's moral behaviour. Admittedly, moral maxims will be of little use if they conflict with factual truths. A maxim (moral or other) will be valid only if it is related to a natural law, viz. to a statement in general terms from which we may infer what will happen in certain definable circumstances. Thus it is a natural law that ether takes fire when brought close to a naked flame, and it is a maxim to keep it in glass-stoppered bottles away from fire. If one's inten-

tion were to cause an explosion, the maxim would be reversed, but
the law remains the same. Hence you cannot tell someone what he
or she should do unless you know what he is aiming at, or what
you want him to aim at. If this is not known, one can tell him only
the consequences of different possible actions. Thus science
informs us impartially how events and actions are related, and pre-
cept follows only when we know what event is desired. Gould is
quite right to stress that what is to be desired is not to be inferred
from what actually happens in any randomly observed set of circumstances. If what we desire is protection from injury and
exploitation, we see that there must be certain general rules of
behaviour within our community, whether or not such rules obtain
in non-human communities.

4. Different but equally relevant documentation is given by Gregory
    W. Dawes in his book of 2001 which came to my notice only when
    I had completed the present book. Dawes begins by asking: if what
    is represented as *history* in the Bible can no longer be taken as a
    reliable account of the past, why should the Bible's *religious* claims
    be taken any more seriously? (p 37) He concludes his survey of dif-
    ferent answers that have been given to this question by allowing
    the "sceptical" answer to be "inescapable" (pp. 368f.).

Epilogue
Some Recent New Testament Scholarship

1. I have not covered this aspect of pre-Christian Jewish Wisdom lit-
    erature in this present book. Briefly, in the wisdom tale the right-
    eous man—no particular person is meant—will be persecuted but
    vindicated post mortem. In the Wisdom of Solomon his enemies
    have condemned him to "a shameful death" (2:20), but he then
    confronts them as their judge in heaven, where he is "counted
    among the sons of God." Cognate is the martyrological book 2
    Maccabees, with its belief in the resurrection of the faithful; and 4
    Maccabees adds to this the idea that someone steadfast in the faith
    unto martyrdom can benefit others, because God will regard his
    death as a "ransom" for their lives, as an expiation for their sins
    (6:28f.; 17:21f.). That a martyr's death could function as an atoning
    sacrifice, to be followed by his immortality, was, then, a not unfa-
    miliar idea in the Hellenistic environment of early Christianity.

2. This and other quotations from Williams concerning the incarnation and the virgin birth are from his 'Born of the Virgin Mary', pp. 23–27 of his 1994 book.
3. Details in Chapter 3 of Wells 1989.
4. This and the following quotations from Williams 1982, pp. 1, 3, 13–14, 25–26, 29, 33–36, 42, 83, 96, 107, 116, 117.
5. This and the previous quotation are from Williams's 'Risen Indeed', which comprises pp. 67–71 of Williams 1994.

Bibliography

Anderson, N. 1973. *A Lawyer among the Theologians*. London: Hodder and Stoughton.

Arndt, W.F., and F.W. Gingrich. 1957. *A Greek-English Lexicon of the New Testament and Other Early Christian Literature*. A translation and adaptation of W. Bauer's *Griechisch-Deutsches Wörterbuch zu den Schriften des Neuen Testaments und der übrigen urchristlichen Literatur*. Chicago: University of Chicago Press.

Attridge, H.W. 1989. *A Commentary on the Epistle to the Hebrews*. Hermeneia Series of Commentaries. Philadelphia: Fortress

Badham, P. 1989. Some Secular Trends in the Church of England Today. In *Religion, State, and Society in Modern Britain*, edited by P. Badham. Lampeter: Mellen, 23–33.

Barker, Eileen. 1989. Tolerant Discrimination: Church, State, and the New Religions. In Badham 1989, 185–208.

Barnett, P.W. 1981. The Jewish Sign Prophets, A.D. 40–70. *New Testament Studies* 27, 679–697.

Barnikol, E. 1998. The Non-Pauline Origin of the Parallelism of the Apostles Peter and Paul. Galatians 2:7–8. English translation of the German of 1931. *Journal of Higher Criticism* 5(2), 285–300.

Barr, J. 1977. *Fundamentalism*. London: SCM.

Barrett, C.K. 1968. *A Commentary on the First Epistle to the Corinthians*. London: Black.

———. 1994. *A Critical and Exegetical Commentary on the Acts of the Apostles*, Volume 1. Edinburgh: Clark.

———. 1998. Volume 2 of the above.

———. 1999. The Historicity of Acts. *Journal of Theological Studies* 50, 515–534.

Barth, K. 1933. *The Epistle to the Romans*. English translation of the sixth edition. Oxford: Oxford University Press.

———. 1956 and 1960. *Church Dogmatics*. English translation of Volume 3, Part 2 (1960) and Volume 4, Part 1 (1956). Edinburgh: Clark.

Bauer, W. 1972. *Orthodoxy and Heresy in Earliest Christianity*. English translation from the German of 1934. London: SCM.

Bernheim, P.A. 1997. *James, Brother of Jesus*. English translation. London: SCM.

Blake, J. 1999. *For God's Sake Don't Go to Church*. New Alresford (Hampshire): James.

Boring, M.E. 1999. *1 Peter*. Abingdon New Testament Commentaries. Nashville: Abingdon.

Bornkamm, G. 1975. *Paul*. English translation from the German of 1969. London: Hodder and Stoughton.

Bostock, D.G. 2001. Osiris and the Resurrection of Christ. *Expository Times*, 112, no.8, 265–271.

Bowden, J. 1997. Appendix to his English translation of G. Lüdemann, *The Unholy in Holy Scripture*. London: SCM.

Bowersock, G.W. 1995. *Martyrdom and Rome*. London: SCM.

Brown, R.E. 1983. Rome. In *Antioch and Rome. New Testament Cradles of Catholic Christianity*, by R.E. Brown and J.P. Meier. New York: Paulist, 87–216.

Bruce, S. 1990. *The Rise and Fall of the New Christian Right*. Oxford: Clarendon.

———. 1995. *Religion in Modern Britain*. Oxford: Oxford University Press.

Bultmann, R. 1960. *Jesus Christ and Mythology*. London: SCM.

Cadbury, J.H. 1920. *The Style and Literary Method of Luke*. Harvard Theological Studies 6. Cambridge (Massachusetts): Harvard University Press.

———. 1955. *The Book of Acts in History*. London: Black.

Calver, C. 1995. Afterword. In *Evangelical Faith and Public Zeal*. A symposium edited by J. Wolffe. London: SPCK.

Cockburn, C. 1972. *Bestseller: The Books that Everyone Read 1900–1939*. London: Sidgwick and Jackson.

Collins, J.J. 1998. *Jewish Wisdom in the Hellenistic Age*. Edinburgh: Clark.

Colpe, C. 1961. art. Samaria. In *Die Religion in Geschichte und Gegenwart*. Third edition, edited by K. Galling. Volume 5, columns 1350–55. Tübingen: Mohr.

Conzelmann, H. 1971. *Geschichte des Urchristentums*. Göttingen: Vandenhoeck and Ruprecht.

———. 1987. *A Commentary on the Acts of the Apostles*. English translation. Hermeneia Series of Commentaries. Philadelphia: Fortress.

Couchoud, P.L. 1938. The Historicity of Jesus. *The Hibbert Journal* 37, 193–214.

Cowdell, S. 1988. *Atheist Priest? Don Cupitt and Christianity*. Includes a Foreword by Cupitt. London: SCM.

Cullmann, O. 1962. *Peter: Disciple, Apostle, Martyr*. Second edition, revised. London: SCM.

Cupitt, D. 1977. *Who Was Jesus?* (written with P. Armstrong). London: BBC.

———. 1984. *The Sea of Faith: Christianity in Change*. London: BBC.

———. 1989. *Radicals and the Future of the Church*. London: SCM.

———. 1990. *Creation Out of Nothing*. London: SCM.

———. 1991. The Bible and the God of Israel. In *Using the Bible Today*, edited by D. Cohn-Sherbok. London: Bellow, 71–75.

———. 1998. *The Revelation of Being*. London: SCM.

Dawes, G.W. 2001. *The Historical Jesus Question: The Challenge of History to Religious Authority*. Louisville: Westminster John Knox Press.

Dawes, H. 1992. *Freeing the Faith: A Credible Christianity for Today*. London: SPCK.

Dawkins, R. 1998. *Unweaving the Rainbow: Science, Delusion, and the Appetite for Wonder*. London: Penguin.

De Jonge, M. 1988. *Christology in Context: The Earliest Christian Responses to Jesus*. Philadelphia: Westminster.

Dempster, M.W. et al., eds. 1999. *The Globalization of Pentecostalism*. Oxford: Regnum.

Dibelius, M. 1956. *Studies in the Acts of the Apostles*. English translation, edited by H. Greeven. London: SCM.

Dinkler, E. 1959. Die Petrus-Rom Frage. *Theologische Rundschau: Neue Folge* 25, 189–230.

Dodd, C.H. 1968. *The Interpretation of the Fourth Gospel*. Cambridge: Cambridge University Press.

Dodds, E.R. 1965. Reissued 1990. *Pagan and Christian in an Age of Anxiety*. Cambridge: Cambridge University Press.

Doherty, E. 1999. *The Jesus Puzzle: Did Christianity Begin with a Mythical Christ?* Ottawa: Canadian Humanist Publications.

Downing, F.G. 2000. *Making Sense in (and of) the First Christian Century*. Chapters 6 (Deeper Reflections on the Jewish Cynic Jesus, 122–133) and 7 (Cynics and Christians, 134–147). Sheffield: Academic Press.

Drijvers, H. 1992. Syrian Christianity and Judaism. In *The Jews Among Pagans and Christians in the Roman Empire*, edited by Judith Lieu et al. London: Routledge, 124–146.

Dunn, J.D.G. 1985. *The Evidence for Jesus*. London: SCM.

———. 1996. *The Acts of the Apostles*. Peterborough: Epworth.

Edwards, D.L. 1989. *Tradition and Truth: The Challenge of England's Radical Theologians 1962–1989*. London: Hodder and Stoughton.

Ehrman, B.D. 1999. *Jesus: Apocalyptic Prophet of the New Millennium*. Oxford: Oxford University Press.

———. 2000. *The New Testament: A Historical Introduction to the Early Christian Writings*. Second edition. Oxford: Oxford University Press.

Eisenman, R., and M. Wise. 1992. *The Dead Sea Scrolls Uncovered*. Shaftesbury (Dorset): Element.

Ellegård, A. 1999. *Jesus One Hundred Years Before Christ*. London: Century.

Elliott, J.H. 1982. *A Home for the Homeless: A Sociological Exegesis of 1 Peter, Its Situation and Strategy.* London: SCM.

Ellis, I. 1980. *Seven Against Christ: A Study of 'Essays and Reviews'.* Leiden: Brill.

Englefield, R. 1990. *Critique of Pure Verbiage: Essays on Abuses of Language in Literary, Religious, and Philosophical Writings.* La Salle (Illinois): Open Court.

Epp, E.J. 1966. *The Theological Tendency of Codex Bezae Cantabrigiensis in Acts.* Cambridge: Cambridge University Press.

Esler, P.F. 1987. *Community and Gospel in Luke-Acts.* Cambridge: Cambridge University Press.

Eusebius. 1927. *Ecclesiastical History.* English translation by H.J. Lawlor and J.E. Oulton. London: SPCK.

Evans, C.F. 1990. *Saint Luke.* London: SCM, and Philadelphia: Trinity International.

Fenton, J.C. 1980. Controversy in the New Testament. *Studia Biblica 1978*, Volume 3. Edited by E.A. Livingstone. Sheffield: JSOT, 97–110.

France, R.T. and A.E. McGrath, eds. 1993. *Evangelical Anglicans.* London: SPCK.

Freeman, A. 1993. *God in Us: A Case for Christian Humanism.* London: SCM.

———. 1998. *Gospel Treasure.* London: SPCK.

———. 2001. Christian Humanism. A Gospel to Proclaim. *SOF* (= Sea of Faith), no. 45, 11–13.

Freke, T. and P. Gandy. 1999. *The Jesus Mysteries.* London: Thorsons.

Frend, W.H.C. 1986. *The Rise of Christianity.* London: Darton, Longman, and Todd.

———. 2000. Review of MacMullen 1997. In *Theology* 103, no. 814, 295f.

Furnish, V.P. 1989. The Jesus-Paul Debate. In *Paul and Jesus: Collected Essays*, edited by A.J.M. Wedderburn. Sheffield: Academic Press, 17–50.

Gill, D.W.J. and C. Gempf, eds. 1994. *The Book of Acts in Its Graeco-Roman Setting.* Grand Rapids: Eerdmans, and Carlisle: Paternoster.

Gore, C. 1890. The Holy Spirit and Inspiration. In *Lex Mundi: A Series of Studies in the Religion of the Incarnation*, edited by Gore (1889). Tenth edition. London: Murray, 315–362.

Gould, S.J. 2001. *Rocks of Ages: Science and Religion in the Fullness of Life.* London: Cape.

Goulder, M. 1983. Chapters 1, 3 and 5 in *Why Believe in God?*, by M. Goulder and J. Hick. London: SCM.

Grant, M. 1994. *Saint Peter.* London: Weidenfeld and Nicolson.

Grant R.M. 1990. *Jesus After the Gospels: The Christ of the Second Century.* London: SCM.

Grässer, E. 1965. Der historische Jesus im Hebräerbrief. *Zeitschrift für Neutestamentliche Wissenschaft* 56, 63–91.

Griffiths, J.G. 1970. Edition of Plutarch's *De Iside et Osiride*. Cardiff: University of Wales Press.

Haenchen, E. 1965. Das 'Wir' in der Apostelgeschichte und das Itinerar. In a volume of Haenchen's collected essays entitled *Gott und Mensch*. Tübingen: Mohr, 227–264.

———. 1971. *The Acts of the Apostles: A Commentary*. English translation of the 1965 German edition. Oxford: Blackwell.

———. 1980. *Das Johannesevangelium: Ein Kommentar*. Posthumously edited by U. Busse. Tübingen: Mohr.

Hagner, D.A. 1973. *The Use of the Old and New Testaments in Clement of Rome*. Leiden: Brill.

Hahneman, G.M. 1992. *The Muratorian Fragment and the Development of the Canon*. Oxford: Clarendon.

Hamerton-Kelly, R.G. 1973. *Pre-Existence, Wisdom, and the Son of Man*. Cambridge: Cambridge University Press.

Harnack, A. 1961. *History of Dogma*. Reprint edition of the English translation, Volume 4. New York: Dover.

Hastings, A. 1990. *The Theology of a Protestant Catholic*. London: SCM.

———. 1991. *A History of English Christianity, 1920–1990*. Third edition. London: SCM.

Hayman, P. 1990. Monotheism: A Misused Word in Jewish Studies. *Journal of Jewish Studies* 42, 1–15.

Heard, R.G. 1955. The Old Gospel Prologues. *Journal of Theological Studies* 56, 1–16.

Hennecke, E. 1963 and 1965. *New Testament Apocrypha*. Edited by W. Schneemelcher. English translation edited by R. McL. Wilson. London: Lutterworth. Volume 1, 1963; volume 2, 1965.

Heussi, K. 1936. *War Petrus in Rom?* Gotha: Klotz.

Hinchliff, P. 1964. *J.W. Colenso: Bishop of Natal*. London: Nelson.

Holloway, R. 1993. Evangelicalism: An Outsider's Perspective. In France and McGrath 1993, 174–183.

———. 2001. *Doubts and Loves: What Is Left of Christianity*. Edinburgh: Canongate.

Hooker, Morna D. 1991. Jesus and History. In Linzey and Wexler 1991, 21–31.

Horbury, W. 1998. *Jewish Messianism and the Cult of Christ*. London: SCM.

Hoskyns, E. and F.N. Davey. 1958. *The Riddle of the New Testament*. First published in 1931. London: Faber and Faber.

Houlden, J.L. 1973. *A Commentary on the Johannine Epistles*. London: Black.

———. 1991. Is the New Testament Trustworthy? In Linzey and Wexler 1991, 32–38.

———. 2000. The Humble Role of New Testament Scholarship. In *Theological Liberalism*, a symposium edited by Jeannine Jobling and Ian Markham. London: SPCK, 31–42.

Hunsinger, G. 2000. The Mediator of Communion: Karl Barth's Doctrine of the Holy Spirit. In Webster 2000, 177–194.

Jackson, F.J. Foakes, and K. Lake, eds. 1922. *The Beginnings of Christianity. Part 1: The Acts of the Apostles*, Volume 2. London: Macmillan.

Janssen, Martina. 2000. Apokryphe Jesustraditionen. In Lüdemann 2000, 813–876.

Kenny, A. 1986. *A Path from Rome: An Autobiography.* Oxford: Oxford University Press.

Kent, J.H.S. 1982. *The End of the Line? The Development of Christian Theology in the Last Two Centuries.* London: SCM.

Kloppenborg Verbin, J.S. 2000. *Excavating Q: The History and Setting of the Sayings Gospel.* Fortress Press edition. Edinburgh: Clark.

Koester, H. 1989. From the Kerygma-Gospel to Written Gospels. *New Testament Studies* 35, 361–381.

———. 1990. *Ancient Christian Gospels: Their History and Development.* London: SCM, and Philadelphia: Trinity International.

Krieger, K.S. 1998. Die Zeichenpropheten. In *Von Jesus zum Christus.* Festschrift for P. Hoffmann, edited by R. Hoppet and U. Busse. Berlin: De Gruyter.

Kümmel, W.G. 1975. *Introduction to the New Testament.* English translation of the 1973 German edition. London: SCM.

Lietzmann, H. 1927. *Petrus und Paulus in Rom.* Second edition. Berlin: De Gruyter.

Lieu, Judith. 1986. *The Second and Third Epistles of John. History and Background*, edited by J. Riches. Edinburgh: Clark.

———. 1991. *The Theology of the Johannine Epistles.* Cambridge: Cambridge University Press.

Lindars, B. 1972. *The Gospel of John.* New Century Bible. London: Oliphants.

———. 1991. *The Theology of the Letter to the Hebrews.* Cambridge: Cambridge University Press.

Linzey, A., and P. Wexler, eds. 1991. *Fundamentalism and Tolerance.* London: Bellow

Lloyd Morgan, C. 1923. *Emergent Evolution.* London: Williams and Norgate.

Loisy, A. 1904. *L'évangile et l'église.* Third edition. Paris: Bellevue.

Lowther Clarke, W.K. 1937. *The First Epistle of Clement to the Corinthians.* London: SPCK.

Lüdemann, G. 1998. *Virgin Birth? The Real Story of Mary and Her Son Jesus.* English translation of the German of 1997. London: SCM.

———. 1999. *The Great Deception: And What Jesus Really Said and Did.* English translation of the German of 1998. Amherst (New York): Prometheus.

———. 2000. *Jesus nach 2000 Jahren. Was er Wirklich sagte und tat.* Lüneburg: Zu Klampen.

———. 2001. *Paulus der Gründer des Christentums.* Lüneburg: Zu Klampen.

———. 2002. *Die Auferweckung Jesu von den Toten: Ursprung und Geschichte einer Selbsttäuschung.* Lüneburg: Zu Klampen.

Mack, B.L. 2001. *The Christian Myth: Origin, Logic, and Legacy*. London: Continuum.

MacMullen, R. 1984. *Christianizing the Roman Empire*. New Haven: Yale University Press.

———. 1997. *Christianity and Paganism in the Fourth to Eighth Centuries*. New Haven: Yale University Press.

Macquarrie, J. 1998. *Christology Revisited*. London: SCM.

MacRobert, I. 1989. The New Black-Led Pentecostal Churches in Britain. In Badham 1989, 119–143.

Maddox, R. 1982. *The Purpose of Luke-Acts*. Göttingen: Vandenhoeck and Ruprecht.

Marshall, I.H. 1973. Palestinian and Hellenistic Christianity. *New Testament Studies* 19, 271–287.

Martin, D. 2000. Christianity: Converting and Converted. *Modern Believing* 41(1), 13–22.

McKenna, J.H. 2001. Honesty in Theology. *Heythrop Journal* 42, no. 1, 50–65.

Meier, J.P. 1999. The Present State of the 'Third Quest' for the Historical Jesus. *Biblica* 80, fasc. 4, 459–487.

Merrill, E.T. 1924. *Essays in Early Christian History*. London: Macmillan.

Merx, A. 1909. *Der Messias oder Ta'eb der Sainaritaner*. Giessen: Töpelmann.

Metzger, B.M. 1968. *The Text of the New Testament*. Includes a list of the Greek papyri. Oxford: Clarendon.

Montefiore, H.W. 1964. *The Epistle to the Hebrews*. London: Black.

Montgomery, J.W. 1971. *History and Christianity*. Leicester: Inter-Varsity.

Moody Smith, D. 1984. *Johannine Christianity*. Columbia: University of South Carolina Press.

Mülller, P. 2001. Der 2. Petrusbrief. *Theologische Rundschau* 66, 310–337.

Murray, G. 1950. *Stoic, Christian, and Humanist*. Second edition. London: Allen and Unwin.

Nineham, D.E. 1977. Eyewitness Testimony and the Gospel Tradition. In *Explorations in Theology I*. London: SCM, 24–60.

———. 1993. *Christianity Mediaeval and Modern: A Study in Religious Change*. London: SCM.

Norman, E. 1976. *Church and Society in England, 1770–1970*. Oxford: Clarendon.

———. 1979. *Christianity and the World Order*. BBC Reith Lectures, 1978. Oxford: Clarendon.

———. 1991. *Entering the Darkness: Christianity and Its Modern Substitutes*. London: SPCK.

———. 2001. *An Anglican Catechism*. London: Continuum.

———. 2002. *Seculärisation*. London: Continuum.

Oakley, M. 2001. *The Collage of God*. London: Darton, Longman, and Todd.

O'Connor, D.W. 1969. *Peter in Rome: The Literary, Liturgical, and Archaeological Evidence*. New York: Columbia University.

Parrinder, G. 1992. *Son of Joseph: The Parentage of Jesus*. Edinburgh: Clark.

Perkins, Pheme. 2000. *Peter: Apostle for the Whole Church*. Edinburgh: Clark.

Porter, S.E. 1994. The 'We' Passages. In Gill and Gempf 1994, 545–574.

Price, R.M. 2000. *Deconstructing Jesus*. Amherst (New York): Prometheus.

Räisänen, H. 1987. *Paul and the Law*. Second, revised edition. Tübingen: Mohr.

———. 1989. *Die Mutter Jesu im Neuen Testament*. Helsinki: Suomalainen Tiedeakatemia.

———. 1992. *Jesus, Paul, and Torah: Collected Essays*. Sheffield: Academic Press.

———. 1995. The New Testament in Theology. Chapter 7 of *Companion Encyclopedia of Theology*, edited by P. Byrne and L. Houlden. London: Routledge, 122–141.

———. 1997. *Marcion, Muhammad, and the Mahatma*. London: SCM.

———. 2000. *Beyond New Testament Theology*. Second edition. London: SCM.

Ramsey, B. 1993. *Beginning to Read the Fathers*. London: SCM.

Ranke-Heinemann, Uta. 1994. Petrus in Rom? Chapter 13 of her *Nein und Amen: Anleitung zum Glaubenszweifel*. Munich: Knaur, 217–230.

Rapske, B.M. 1994. Acts, Travel, and Shipwreck. In Gill and Gempf 1994, 1–47.

Ringgren, H. 1947. *Word and Wisdom: Studies in the Hypostatization of Divine Qualities and Functions in the Ancient Near East*. Lund: Ohlssons.

Robbins, V.K. 1978. By Land and Sea: The We-Passages and Ancient Sea Voyages. In Talbert 1978, 215–242.

Rodd, C.S. 2000. In Honesty of Preaching: How Honest Can the Preacher Be? *Expository Times* 111, no. 7, 221–24.

Schmiedel, P.W. 1899. arts. Acts of the Apostles (columns 37–57), and Simon Peter (columns 4559–4627) in *Encyclopaedia Biblica*, edited by T.K. Cheyne and J.S. Black. London: Black.

Schmithals, W. 1997. *The Theology of the First Christians*. English translation from the German of 1994. Louisville (Kentucky): Westminster John Knox.

Schoedel, W.R. 1985. *A Commentary on the Letters of Ignatius of Antioch*. Hermeneia Series of Commentaries. Philadelphia: Fortress.

Schürer, E. 1973. *The History of the Jewish People in the Age of Jesus Christ*. New English edition by G. Vermes et al., Volume 1. Edinburgh: Clark.

Scott, M. 1992. *Sophia and the Johannine Jesus*. Sheffield: Academic Press.

Shaw, G. 1983. *The Cost of Authority: Manipulation and Freedom in the New Testament*. London: SCM.

Sidebottom, E.M. 1967. *James, Jude, and 2 Peter*. New Century Bible Series of Commentaries. London: Nelson.

Simon, M. 1975. The Religionsgeschichtliche Schule Fifty Years Later. *Religious Studies* 11, 135–144.

Stanton, G.N. 1995. *Gospel Truth? New Light on Jesus and the Gospels*. London: Harper Collins.

Strecker, G. 1960. William Wrede: Zur hundertsten Wiederkehr seines Geburtstages. *Zeitschrift für Theologie und Kirche* 57, 66–91.

———. 1996. *The Johannine Letters*. English translation from the German of 1989. Hermeneia series of Commentaries. Minneapolis: Fortress.

Talbert, C.H., editor. 1978. *Perspectives on Luke-Acts*. Edinburgh: Clark.

———. 1997. *Reading Acts: A Literary and Theological Commentary on the Acts of the Apostles*. New York: Crossroads.

Teilhard de Chardin, P. 1960. *Le Milieu Divin: An Essay on the Interior Life*. English translation from the French of 1957. London: Collins.

Temple, W. 1934. *Nature, Man, and God*. London: Macmillan.

Theissen, G. 1983. *Psychologische Aspekte paulinischer Theologie*. Göttingen: Vandenhoeck and Ruprecht.

Thiede, C.P. 1986. *Simon Peter from Galilee to Rome*. Exeter: Paternoster.

Thompson, D.M. 1993. F.D. Maurice: Rebel Conservative. In *Modern Religious Rebels*, edited by S. Mews. London: Epworth, 123–143.

Trevett, Christine. 1992. *A Study of Ignatius of Antioch in Syria and Asia*. Lewiston (New York): Edwin Mellen.

Tuckett, C.M. 1991. On the Stratification of Q. In *Early Christianity, Q, and Jesus*, edited by J.S. Kloppenborg, with L.E. Vaage. *Semeia* 55, 213–222.

———. 1996. *Q and the History of Early Christianity*. Edinburgh: Clark.

Tyson, J.B. 1986. *The Death of Jesus in Luke-Acts*. Columbia: University of South Carolina Press.

VanderKam, J.C. 1994. *The Dead Sea Scrolls Today*. London: SPCK, and Grand Rapids: Eerdmans.

Vielhauer, P. 1975. *Geschichte der urchristlichen Literatur*. Berlin: De Gruyter.

Walaskay, P.W. 1983. *'And So We Came to Rome': The Political Perspective of St. Luke*. Cambridge: Cambridge University Press.

Walker, A. 1986. The Third Schism: The Great Divide in Christianity Today. In *In Search of Christianity*, edited by T. Moss. London: Firethorn, 202–217.

Warnecke, H. 1987. *Die tatsächliche Romfahrt des Apostels Paulus*. Stuttgart: Stuttgarter Bibelstudien.

Webster, J., ed. 2000. *The Cambridge Companion to Karl Barth*. Cambridge: Cambridge University Press.

Wedderburn, A.J.M. 1987. The Soteriology of the Mysteries and the Pauline Baptismal Theology. *Novum Testamentum* 29(1), 53–72.

———. 1999. *Beyond Resurrection*. London: SCM.

———. 2002. The 'We' Passages in Acts. *Zeitschrift für neutestamentliche Wissenschaft* 93, 78–98.

Wells, G.A. 1959. *Herder and After: A Study in the Development of Sociology*. The Hague: Mouton.

———. 1971. *The Jesus of the Early Christians*. London: Pemberton.

———. 1982. Reissued in 1988. *The Historical Evidence for Jesus*. Buffalo: Prometheus.

———. 1986. *Did Jesus Exist?* Second edition, revised. London: Pemberton.

———. 1989. *Who Was Jesus? A Critique of the New Testament Record*. La Salle (Illinois): Open Court.

————. 1991. *Belief and Make-Believe: Critical Reflections on the Sources of Credulity*. La Salle (Illinois): Open Court.

————. 1996. *The Jesus Legend*. Chicago: Open Court.

————. 1997. German Bible Criticism and the Victorian Church. *Journal for the Critical Study of Religion, Ethics, and Society* 2(1), 55–67.

————. 1999a. *The Jesus Myth*. Chicago: Open Court.

————. 1999b. *The Origin of Language*. London: Rationalist Press Association.

————. 2002. Don Cupitt's Religion of Language. *Theology* 105, 201–210.

Wenham, J. 1991. *Redating Matthew, Mark, and Luke*. London: Hodder and Stoughton.

Werner, M. 1941. *Die Entstehung des christlichen Dogmas*. Bern/Leipzig: Paul Haupt.

White, P.O.G. 1962. The Colenso Controversy. *Theology* 65, 402–08.

White, S.R. 1994. *Don Cupitt and the Future of Christian Doctrine*. London: SCM.

Wiles, M. 1994. Orthodoxy and Heresy. In M. Wiles, *A Shared Search*. London: SCM, 63–73.

————. 1999. *Reason to Believe*. London: SCM.

Wilken, R.L. 1984. *The Christians as the Romans Saw Them*. New Haven: Yale University Press.

Wilkinson, A. 1978. Reissued 1996. *The Church of England and the First World War*. London: SCM.

Williams, C.G. 1981. *Tongues of the Spirit: A Study of Pentecostal Glossolalia and Related Phenomena*. Cardiff: University of Wales Press.

Williams, R. 1982. *Resurrection: Interpreting the Easter Gospel*. London: Darton, Longman, and Todd.

————. 1994. *Open to Judgement: Sermons and Addresses*. London: Darton, Longman, and Todd.

Wilson, S.G. 1973. *The Gentiles and the Gentile Mission in Luke-Acts*. Cambridge: Cambridge University Press.

————. 1995. *Related Strangers: Jews and Christians, 70–170 C.E.* Minneapolis: Fortress.

Wrede, W. 1907a. *Paul*. English translation from the German of 1904. London: Green.

————. 1907b. *Vorträge und Studien*. Tübingen: Mohr.

Zeller, D. 1998. Hellenistische Vorgaben für den Glauben an die Auferstehung Jesu? In *Von Jesus zum Christus*. Festschrift for P. Hoffmann, edited by R. Hoppe and U. Busse. Berlin: De Gruyter, 71–91.

Zwaan, J. de. 1922. The Use of the Greek Language in Acts. In Jackson and Lake 1922, 30–65.

Zwiep, A.W. 1997. *The Ascension of the Messiah in Lukan Christology*. Leiden: Brill.

Index of New
Testament References

Matthew

1:21	10
2:11	207
4:24	3
5:28	55
39	210
44–46	55
6:3	56
25–33	210
7:7–11	180
16:18	200
17:5	121
19:24	150
24:37	45
27:4–5	89
28:9–10	39

Mark

1:34	37
3:22	70
6:17ff, 35ff	59
7:34	59
15–19	112f
8:1ff	59
34	206
10:17–22	29
11:15	194
14:28	205
36, 62	14f
66–71	78
16:7	205

Luke

1:3	61
32–33, 67–77	33
6:13–16	87
9:23	206
10:9, 11	205
11:30	45
14:26	210
17:26	45
19:41–44	33, 205
21:20	205
24	33, 205
32	205
22:3	49
30	91
23:34	159
24:6–7	205
47	84
49, 50	82

John

1:5	54
42	201
2:1–11	196
3:18–19	206
5:24–25	205f
6:37	193
7:38–39	101
8:21–34, 44	194
12:31	36
13:18, 27	49

General Index